The Life and Thought of Their Eminences, the Imams
Mūsā ibn Jaʿfar al-Kāẓim, Muhammad ibn Ali al-Jawād,
Ali ibn Muhammad al-Hādi, and Hasan ibn Ali al-Askari

With a bilingual rendition of the Ziārat-e Jāmeʿa Kabīr
(attributed to Imam Hādī ﷺ)

Mehdī Rahīmī and Abdullāh Tāherkhānī

Translated and Annotated
by Blake Archer Williams

Copyright © 2022 by Blake Archer Williams

All rights reserved. No part of this publication may be reproduced, distributed, or transmitted in any form or by any means, including photocopying, recording, or other electronic or mechanical methods, without the prior written permission of the publisher, except in the case of brief quotations embodied in critical reviews and certain other noncommercial uses permitted by copyright law. For permission requests, write to the publisher, addressed "Attention: - Permissions (The Unknown Imams)," at the email address below.

Lantern Publications
info@lanternpublications.com
www.lanternpublications.com

Ordering Information:
Quantity sales. Special discounts are available on quantity purchases by corporations, associations, and others. For details, contact the distributor at the address below.

Shia Books Australia
www.shiabooks.com.au
info@shiabooks.com.au

A catalogue record for this book is available from the National Library of Australia

ISBN- 978-1-922583-21-5

First Edition

In the Name of God,
the Most Compassionate, the Most Merciful

Table of Contents

Imam Mūsā ibn Ja'far al-Kāżim 9
    1. Prelude 9
    2. Birth 10
    3. The Consolidation of Imam Mūsā's Imamate 14
    4. The Imam's Character Traits 18
    5. The Knowledge of the Imam 40
    6. The Imam's Role in the Cultivation of the Muslims 57
    7. The Imam and his Relations with the Authorities 73
    8. A Sampling of the Words of the Imam 85

Imam Muhammad ibn Ali al-Jawād 87
    1. Prelude 87
    2. Birth 92
    3. Imam Jawād's Imamate 96
    4. The Imam and his Relationship with the People 98
    5. The Imam's Marriage 115
    6. The Imam's Companions 124
    7. The Martyrdom of the Imam 130
    8. A Sampling of the Words of the Imam 134

Imam Ali ibn Muhammad al-Hādī 139
    1 Birth 139
    2 The Imam's Character Traits 141
    3 The Imam and his Relations with the Caliphs 184
    4 Imamology in the Words of the Imam 202
    5 The Ziārat-e Jāme'a Kabīra 207
    6 The Imam's Students 233
    7 The Imam's Martyrdom 242
    8 A Sampling of the Words of the Imam 244

Imam Hasan ibn Ali al-Askari 245
    1. Preface 245
    2. Birth 247
    3. The Succession to his Father 251
    4. The Imam's Piety 252
    5. The Imam's Social and Ethical Character Traits 254
    6. The Tale of Lady Narjis 260
    7. The Reign of the Caliphs during the Time of the Imam 270
    8. Guidance 276
    9. From the Letters and Will of Imam Hasan al-Askari 284
    10. Some of the Miracles of Imam Hasan al-Askari 289
    11. Some of the Companions of the Imam 294
    12. Martyrdom 298
    13. A Sampling of the Words of the Imam 302

Prayers of God's Peace and Blessings

In keeping with the Islamic practice of showing respect for the name of God, and sending prayers of God's peace and blessings whenever the name of His blessed Prophet, Lady Fāṭima, and the Twelve Imams is mentioned, as well as for asking God to hasten the reappearance of the Lord of the Age on the Earthly plane, one or more of the following Arabic symbols have been employed throughout the text. They are repeated for their great rewards.

 Used exclusively after the name of God, meaning "the Sublimely Exalted", or, as a prayer, "[May His name be] Sublimely Exalted".

 Used exclusively after the name of the Prophet, meaning "May the peace and blessings of God be unto him and unto [the purified and inerrant members of] his family"

 Used for any of the Twelve Imams or past prophets of God, meaning "May God's peace be unto him".

 Used for two or more of the Twelve Imams or past prophets of God, meaning "May God's peace be unto them".

 Used for Lady Fāṭima, meaning "May God's peace be unto her".

 Used for a plurality of the Fourteen Immaculates, meaning "May God's peace be unto them all collectively".

 Used for the Lord of the Age (the Twelfth Imam), meaning "May God hasten the advent of his noble person".

Names and Dates of the Twelve Imams

No	Konya (Patronymic)	Name	Dates of Birth-Death Islamic	Christian
1	Ab'al-Hasan	Ali b. Abū-Tālib	-23 to 40	600–661
2	Abu Md.	Hasan ibn Ali	3–50	624–670
3	Abu Abdullah	Husain b. Ali	4–61	626–680
4	Abu Md.	Ali b. Husain	38–95	658–712
5	Abu Ja'far	Md. b. Ali	57–114	677–732
6	Abu Abdullah	Ja'far ibn Md.	83–148	702–765
7	Ab'al-Hasan	Musa b. Ja'far	128–183	744–799
8	Ab'al-Hasan	Ali b. Musa	148–203	765–817
9	Abu Ja'far	Md. b. Ali	195–220	810–835
10	Ab'al-Hasan	Ali b. Md.	212–254	827–868
11	Abu Md.	Hasan b. Ali	232–260	846–874
12	Ab'al-Qāsim	Md. b. Hasan	255–Present	868–Present

Acknowledgments

All translations of verses of the Quran are Muhammad Asad's, with the occasional minor change.

Names and Dates of the Abbāsid Caliphs

	Caliph	A. H.	Christian Era Date
1	As-Saffah	131 – 136	25 Jan. 750 – 10 June 754
2	Al-Mansur	136 – 158	10 June 754 – 6 October 775
3	Al-Mahdi	158 – 169	6 October 775 – 24 July 785
4	Al-Hādī	169 – 170	24 July 785 – 14 September 786
5	Harun ar-Rashid	170 – 193	24 July 786 – 24 March 809
6	Al-Amin	193 – 198	24 March 809 – 27 Sept. 813
7	Al-Ma'mun	198 – 218	7 September 813 – 7 August 833
8	Al-Mu'tasim	218 – 227	7 August 833 – 5 January 842
9	Al-Wāthiq	227 – 232	5 January 842 – 10 August 847
10	Al-Mutawakkil	232 – 247	10 August 847 – 11 Dec. 861
11	Al-Muntasir	247 – 248	11 December 861 – 8 June 862
12	Al-Musta'in	248 – 252	8 June 862 – 17 October 866
13	Al-Mu'tazz	252 – 255	17 October 866 – 9 July 869
14	Al-Muhtadī	255 – 256	9 July 869 – 22 June 870
15	Al-Mu'tamid	257 – 279	26 June 870 – 15 October 892

Imam Mūsā ibn Ja'far al-Kāżim

1. Prelude

Two centuries had not yet passed since the dawning of the sun of Islam when the unhappy dusk of oppression and false deification and hypocrisy was already upon us. The city is quiet and seems to be desolate. Any stranger who approaches the city from afar would think that everyone has perished; but this is not the case. In the midst of a dark and damp dungeon in the middle of the city, where Abbāsid henchmen pass the night patrol with drawn swords at the ready, a flame shines brightly, offering some heat and light. In the heart of the dungeon there is a man in a posture of prostration, occupied with devotions to his Lord – devotional laments and supplications whose melody is sweeter than the Psalms of the prophet David, and which mysteriously course through the arteries of society, giving it its lifeblood.

The person who is in a posture of prostration on some rough burlap matting with his forehead down on the dust, who stands alone against the armies of oppression and idolatry and hypocrisy, and who is vested with the responsibility of guarding the eternal tree of authentic Islam – Shī'a Islam – is none other than Imam Mūsā al-Kāżim.

The guardianship of the authentic and vivifying teachings of Islam in those troubled times had been entrusted to him. He was the guiding beacon of the sincere devotees of God ﷻ during the ideologically perilous times of the reign of the hypocrite caliphs of the Abbāsid dynasty. Imam Mūsā al-Kāẓim ﷺ was the safe harbor in which the stranded, marooned and broken ships of the Islamic community could dock and be saved from the lethal storms which threatened the community of faith. The origin of these dangers, i.e., the blood-thirsty Abbāsid tyrants who had taken up their position at the pulpit of the Prophet ﷺ and who falsely laid claim to be the heirs to his teachings, usurping the legitimate and God-given right of the Imams ﷺ, saw Imam Mūsā al-Kāẓim ﷺ as the sole remaining obstacle in the way of their carrying out their evil plans. Thus, they conspired day and night against him, sending spies and ultimately, imprisoning him in their dungeons in order to cut the community off from access to his magnanimous presence. But Imam Mūsā al-Kāẓim ﷺ was like the sun, who cannot be hidden behind a cloud, and he continued to provide heat and light and to give life and succor to the community of the faithful, nullifying the Abbāsids' conspiracies and intrigues against God ﷻ and humanity. But ultimately, the blood-thirsty Abbāsid predators who saw Imam Mūsā al-Kāẓim ﷺ as an obstacle in the path of their attaining to their inhuman objectives, stained their polluted hands with the pure blood of the Imam, plunging an entire world into the grief of the bereaved, thinking that they had thereby attained their goal, oblivious to God's promise to humanity that [61:8] *God ﷻ has willed to spread His light in all its fullness, however hateful this may be to all who deny the truth.*

2. Birth

We are at Abwā, a village between Mecca and Medina. There is a spring here which gushes forth crystal-clear water, and date palms whose statures, it would seem, reach up into the firmaments, and whose shade beckons the weary and heat-struck traveler towards itself. In a corner of this waystation for travelers by caravan, the soul of a great woman whose name is Āmina rests beneath the ground. Āmina is the mother of the Final Prophet ﷺ and Messenger of God ﷺ. On occasion, a true believer from among the community of Muslims takes the toil of the journey upon himself and makes the pilgrimage to her grave in order to be able to pay their respects to a woman who cradled and nursed and cherished and raised a person whose spiritual stature is greater than the whole of creation itself.

On the morning of that day, Āmina had a great and honorable visitant – a man from the pure progeny of her son Muḥammad, the Chosen One (*al-muṣṭafā*), had made pilgrimage to her. The great man was Imam Jaʿfar as-Ṣādiq ﷺ who eagerly awaited the birth of a child whom Almighty God ﷺ had ordained was to be his successor and the successor to the Messenger of God, and to be the leader (*imām*) of the inhabitants of the world. The time of birth was at hand. Imam Jaʿfar as-Ṣādiq ﷺ had travelled to the quiet and tranquil village of Abwā so that the sweet recollection of the birth of the Most Noble Prophet ﷺ might be refreshed in his mind.

The village of Abwā seemed different that morning. The rays of the sun had cast a golden hue on the trunks of the tall date palms, which in turn cast long shadows on the mud roofs of the houses of the village. The pleasant sounds of the camels and herds of sheep who were ready to head out to the plains ahead of their shepherds could be heard, filling the ears with the reverberations of life.

Next to the village, a gentle breeze caressed the surface of a pond from which women drew water, causing ripples to appear in its calm and clear surface. A few doves fly with alacrity over the pond and back again, on occasion making the plunge downward and dipping their breasts into the refreshing water against the heat of the desert.

A little further out, a solitary palm tree had cast the shade of its green parasol on the resting place, and on that morning, a woman was bent over in reverence and respect and was kissing the dust of the grave while gently weeping and whispering confidences under her breath. The following could be discerned from her words which were carried over by the breeze:

"Greetings to you, O Āmina! O revered mother of the Prophet ﷺ of God! May God ﷻ have mercy on you, for your troubles in having closed your eyes to the world so far afield from your birthplace.

"I am Hamīda, your bride. I am pregnant with a child from the seed of your progeny, and given the pain of the birth pangs which I have been enduring since last night, I do believe that I shall give birth to this blessed child this very day in this village and at the side of your grave.

"O great lady who is resting under this earth! My husband has told me that this child of mine shall be the seventh successor of your son, the Great Prophet ﷺ of Islam.

"[I beseech you to] supplicate God, O my Lady, to ensure that my child is born wholesome and in good health!"

Hamīda stood up graciously, shook the dust off the hem of her dress, and laden as she was with child, carefully made her way back to the village.

A short while later, when the sun had reached its zenith and the doves of the village fluttered about in Abwā's blue skies, a cry of joy was heard in the village, and women could be seen rushing happily from the alleys of the village toward the grave by the pond.

Momentarily, two women arrive at speed to the pond with large earthenware pots in order to draw water. If we could have put our ear to the ground to hear what they said, this is what we would have heard:

"They say that after he heard of the birth of his son, Imam Ja'far as-Ṣādiq ؉ said, 'The leader [of the community] after me and the best of God's creatures has been born'".

"I think that they had named him Mūsā[1] even before he was born."

The eye of the imagination takes flight and, soaring over this scene at the pond, fixes on a shepherd in the desert who prods a sheep forward

---

[1] The Anglophone pronunciation of the name is Moses.

with his staff, unaware of the occurrence in the village. For a moment it appeared as though the shepherd was Moses, and the scene was set in the Sinai Desert. Which Pharaoh of the day has this Moses been born to go up against in battle?

That day was the seventh day of the month of Safar, in the hundred and twenty eighth lunar year after the migration of the Most Noble Prophet ﷺ from Mecca to Medina,[2] and the blessed child was named Mūsā [or Moses, in its English pronunciation]. His father Imam Ja'far as-Ṣādiq ؏ was the most preeminent man on the face of the earth at the time, and his mother was the learned and honorable and pure Lady Hamīda. The most famous of the titles of the Seventh Imam is "al-Kāżim" (one who has forbearance) which was given to him on account of his extreme forbearance and restraint. He was [also] called the Godly Devotee (*al-'abd as-sālih*) on account of the longevity of his devotions.

In the 'Iraq he was known as *bāb al-ḥawā'ij* (the door to [the fulfillment of] one's needs) toward [i.e. in attaining proximity to] God, and this was because those who would seek intercessory recourse (*tawassul*)[3] with him would have their needs fulfilled. His patronymic was "Abul-Hasan", meaning the father of Hasan. His most famous progeny was the Eighth Imam, Imam Ali ibn Mūsā ar-Riḍā ؏, as well as another son of his, Ahmad ibn Mūsā, known as Shāh-Cherāq (who is buried in Shīrāz, in south-central Iran), and not least, Her Eminence Lady

---

[2] The migration of the Prophet from Mecca to Medina is the event upon which the beginning of the Islamic calendar and era is pegged. It occurred in the year 622 of the Christian Era.

[3] *Tawassul* is a specific type of intercessory recourse in which someone resorts to or takes recourse in various instruments that have been made available to him by Allah ﷻ (such as the supplications or the spirit of a prophet or saint) as an intermediary means for help in his endeavors to recommend himself to the notice and favor or mercy of God.

Ma'sūma, who is buried in the famous shrine at Qom in north-central Iran.

His Eminence Imam Mūsā Kāżim ﷺ succeeded his father to the office of the imamate (the religio-political and spiritual leadership of the community of faith) after his father attained to martyrdom in the 148th lunar year of the Islamic calendar. He was twenty years old at the time. He too attained to martyrdom at the hands of the Abbāsid caliph Hārūn or-Rashīd at the age of fifty-five, after being at the helm of the imamate for thirty-five years.

3. The Consolidation of Imam Mūsā's Imamate[4]

It was a tradition among our honorable Imams ﷺ to stipulate and name their successors to the office of the imamate (and thus to the functions of the juridical, religious, and political leadership of the community), so as to preclude those who wanted to take political advantage of these leadership transitions from being able to do so; and also in order that their true followers would be in no doubt as to who is to lead their community after the death of their Imam. Thus, this tradition was maintained in the case of Imam Mūsā al-Kāżim ﷺ as well. In addition to clear and undeniable stipulations of his imamate which go back to hadīth[5] reports from the Prophet ﷺ of Islam himself, he was also designated as the successor to his

---

[4] A large split in the community followed the death of Imam Ja'far as-Sādiq's ﷺ eldest son, Ishmael (Ismā'il). A significant number of the Imam's followers erroneously believed Ishmael to have been designated as Imam Ja'far as-Sādiq's ﷺ successor, and this gave rise to a schism in the community of the Shī'a out of which the Ismā'īlīs arose. This is the reason why attention has been paid to this matter in this chapter.

[5] *Hadīth*: A report of a saying or deed of the Prophet or one of the Imāms. The Prophet and the Imāms being embodied revelation, reports of their words and deeds comprise a body of scripture that is complementary to the Quran.

father Imam Jaʿfar as-Sādiq ﷺ on numerous occasions, notwithstanding the oppressive atmosphere under the rule of the Abbāsids.

The importance of these stipulations is obviated when we consider that oppression and the suppression of any form of political opposition had reached such depths during the reign of the caliph al-Mansūr that Imam Jaʿfar as-Sādiq ﷺ felt the need to designate several legatees and successors (*wasīy*; plural, *awsīā*) as decoy measures in order to relieve the pressure which was being brought to bear by the ruling regime against the succession process and against his legitimate successor.

Among these decoys, the names of Mansūr al-Dawānīqī (i.e. the name of the usurping Abbāsid caliph himself), as well as those of the names of the governor of Medina, and the names of Imam Jaʿfar as-Sādiq's ﷺ wife and two of his [other] sons can be seen. The use of this tactic caused confusion both in the Abbāsid government as well as in the ranks of the general public.

But Imam Jaʿfar as-Sādiq ﷺ stipulated Imam Mūsā Kāẓim ﷺ as his successor in secret to his trusted companions. It will suffice our present purposes to point to a few hadīth reports to this effect:

1. Ali ibn Jaʿfar states: "My father Imam Jaʿfar as-Sādiq ﷺ told a group of his trusted companions, 'Accept my stipulation to you concerning [the designation of] my son Mūsā [to my succession], because he is the most preeminent among my sons as well as among all who are in my circle who are to outlive me. He shall be my successor after me, and the *hujjat*[6] (proof) [of God][7] for all His devotees.'"

---

[6] *Hujjat*: the perfect evidence of all truth and the conclusive argument and evidentiary proof against all falsehood on Judgement Day.

[7] *Hujjatullāh*: (36:12} ... *For of all things do We take account in a manifest Imām* (*imāmin mubīn*) (who shall be called to testify and provide evidence on all matters on the Day of Judgment). This is the meaning of the word hujjatullāh or God's proof, which is one of the names given to the Imāms by the Quran: The hujjat is

2. Omar ibn Abān states: "Imam Ja'far as-Sādiq ﷺ mentioned the Imams ﷺ who were to follow in his wake. I mentioned the name [of one of his sons] Ishmael, but he said, 'No. I swear [upon my oath] to Allāh! This matter is out of our hands. It is in the hands of God ﷻ.'"

3. Zurāra, one of the most prominent of Imam Ja'far as-Sādiq's ﷺ companions and students states: "I was in the presence of (literally, 'at the service of') His Eminence [Imam Ja'far as-Sādiq ﷺ]; to his right was seated the master of [i.e. the leader from among] his progeny, His Eminence Mūsā Kāżim ﷺ, and before him was placed the deceased body of his senior son, Ishmael.

He told me, "Zurāra, go and fetch Dāwūd ar-Raqqī, Hamrān and Abū-Basīr."[8]

I complied, and others also came, to where the room was filled with about thirty people. The Imam ﷺ told Dāwūd ar-Raqqī,

"Draw the cloth away from the corpse."

When Dāwūd did so, His Eminence ﷺ said,

"Dāwūd! See whether Ishmael is dead or alive." Dāwūd said,

"He is dead, my lord."

The Imam ﷺ allowed all present to examine the corpse, and every one of them testified that Ishmael had indeed died. The Imam ﷺ then said,

"Bear witness, O God! That I went to such lengths in order to prevent any misunderstandings among the people."

He then ordered Ismael's body be washed and ritually embalmed in preparation for burial, and to be enshrouded. And when this process was completed, the Imam ﷺ told Mufaḍḍal,[9]

---

the perfect embodiment and clear evidence of all truth on Earth and the conclusive argument and evidentiary proof against all falsehood on Judgement Day.

[8] These are the names of three of the Imam's companions.

[9] Another senior companion of the Imam's.

"Open [the shroud at] his face."

Mufaḍḍal did so. The Imam ﷺ then asked him,

"Is he dead or alive?"

Mufaḍḍal said, "He is dead."

The Imam ﷺ yet again allowed all present to examine the corpse, and every one of them testified that Ishmael had indeed died. The Imam ﷺ then said,

"Bear witness, O God! But a group who wish to extinguish the Light of God ﷻ will nevertheless consider Ismael to be an Imam."

At this point, Imam Ja'far as-Sādiq ﷺ pointed to his son Mūsā al-Kāẓim and said, "[61:8] *God ﷻ will perfect His light in all its fullness, however hateful this may be to all who are bent on denying the truth.*"

After Ishmael was buried, Imam Ja'far as-Sādiq ﷺ asked those present, "Who is the person here buried?"

Everyone replied, "Your son Ishmael."

Imam Ja'far as-Sādiq ﷺ said, "Bear witness, O God!" He then took hold of his son Mūsā's hand and said, "He is with *al-ḥaqq* (truth, justice; that which is truly real and ever-lasting, the ultimate reality) and *al-ḥaqq* is with him until the Day of Resurrection."

4. Manṣūr ibn Ḥāzim has reported: "I told Imam Ja'far as-Sādiq ﷺ: 'Would that my father and mother were sacrificed for your cause! The lives [of people] are in danger of death at any moment of night or day. In the event that such an eventuality overcomes you, who will be our Imam?' The Imam ﷺ placed his hand on the right shoulder of his son Abul-Hasan Mūsā ﷺ and said, 'If anything should happen to me, this son of mine will be your Imam.' That noble personage was five years old at that time, and Abdullāh, another of Imam Ja'far as-Sādiq's ﷺ sons, who was later considered by a number of people to be the Imam after his father's death, was present among the gathering with us."

5. Shaykh Mufid – may God's mercy be upon his pure soul – states, "A group of the senior companions of the Sixth Imam ﷺ (the mention of whose names will take up too much time and space) have reported the details of the succession of Imam Mūsā Kāżim ﷺ, as have Ishāq and Ali, two of Imam Mūsā Kāżim's ﷺ brothers, in all of whose virtue and soundness of character there can be no doubt."

With all of these stipulations and assertions, it was evident for the followers (or partisans; *Shī'a*) of Imam Ja'far as-Sādiq ﷺ and those who were close to him that his son Imam Mūsā Kāżim ﷺ is to succeed him as the Imam of the community, and not his other son Ishmael, who predeceased his father, nor yet Ishmael's son who was named Muhammad, nor Imam Ja'far as-Sādiq's other son, Abdullāh. Yet, despite this, after the death of the righteous Imam, a group came to believe in the imamate of Ishmael, or in that of Ismael's son Muhammad, or in the imamate of Imam Ja'far as-Sādiq's ﷺ other son Abdullāh, deviating from the clear path set for them by Imam Ja'far as-Sādiq ﷺ [primarily for political, psychological and personal reasons].

4. The Imam's Character Traits

Imam Mūsā Kāżim's ﷺ unique understanding of God, his spiritual proximity with his Lord, and the luminosity of his essence (which is the exclusive province of the Purified Imams ﷺ), all contribute to his devotional humbleness and intimacy with God ﷻ. He considered devotion to God ﷻ to be exactly that which God ﷻ has characterized in the Noble Quran, namely, that devotion to God ﷻ is the ultimate purpose of creation. After his social obligations, Imam Mūsā Kāżim ﷺ did not consider any other act to have the same weight of priority as that of his ritual devotions and supererogatory acts of supplication and worship. When the Imam ﷺ was imprisoned in the dungeons of the tyrant Hārūn or-Rashīd, he said, "O Lord! How long has been the time wherein I beseeched Thee to afford me the opportunity to devote myself to Your worship; and now you have provided me with this opportunity, for which [blessing] I thank Thee."

Of course, this sentence is also an indication of the intensity of the Imam's ﷺ social preoccupations and responsibilities in the period prior to his imprisonment. When His Eminence the Imam ﷺ was imprisoned in Rabī' Prison, the caliph al-Hārūn would on occasion go to a rooftop from which he had a view of the Imam's ﷺ prison yard and would look inside the prison. He would always see something like a discarded piece of cloth in the corner of the prison.

Once he asked, "Whose robe is that?" To which Rabī' replied, "That is not a robe. That is Mūsā ibn Ja'far ﷺ who spends most of his time in devotional prostration and worship of his Lord." Hārūn said, "Truly, he is the most devout of the men of the House of Hāshim."[10] Rabī', whose curiosity had been aroused, asked: "Then why have you ordered that he be treated harshly in prison?" Hārūn said, "Woe to you! What other choice is there?!"

Once Hārūn sent a beautiful maidservant to Imam Mūsā ﷺ in the hope that if His Eminence ﷺ were to be tempted by this seduction, that Hārūn could then use this in his propaganda to agitate against the Imam. The Imam ﷺ told the man who delivered the girl, "You have pegged your hopes on such gifts and pride yourselves on them; but I have no need for such gifts."

Hārūn grew angry at news of this rebuttal and ordered the maidservant to be taken to the prison and to tell the Imam ﷺ, "We have

---

[10] The House of the Prophet ﷺ.

not placed you here in this prison at your own behest!" [I.e. The choice of your having this maidservant as your companion is not yours to make.]

It was not long before Hārūn's agents, who were tasked with spying on the prison and reporting back to Hārūn, informed him that the maidservant spent most of her time in devotional prostration and worship of the Lord. To which Hārūn retorted, "I swear [upon my oath] to Allāh! Mūsā ibn Ja'far has bewitched the girl!"

He summoned the maidservant and questioned her, but she had nothing but good things to say about the Imam ﷺ. Hārūn ordered his agent to keep the maidservant in his own quarters and not to speak a word of this affair to a soul. The maidservant continued to spend her time in devotional prostration and worship of the Lord, and did so until her death, which occurred a few days before the martyrdom of Imam Mūsā ﷺ.

Imam Mūsā ﷺ often repeated the following supplication: "O Lord! I beseech Thee for peace and tranquility of mind at the time of death and mercy and forgiveness at the time when I am called to account."

His recitation of the Quran was very pleasant and emotive, to the point that whoever heard his recitations would break down and weep uncontrollably. The people of Madīna used to call him *zayn al-mutasajjidīn*, which means "the ornament of those who spend the night hours in devotion to God ﷻ."

Imam Mūsā ﷺ was called "al-Kāẓim" (one who has [a great deal of] forbearance) on account of his extreme forbearance and restraint. He was a paragon of clemency. During the era of the Imam ﷺ, the Abbāsids had instituted severe political suppression and would appropriate people's property and possessions in the name of the public treasury and waste it on profligate spending in pursuit of their own carnal pleasures.

As a result of this pillage of the public treasury, poverty and indigence had reached untold depths. The general populace was uneducated and poor, and did not have the means to educate themselves. Thus, they would fall prey to the false anti-Ālid propaganda[11] of the Abbāsids, as a consequence of which some would verbally attack Imam Mūsā al-Kāẓim ﷺ out of their ignorance. But the great man would sooth his assailants with the greatness of his character and forbearance, and provide them with a lesson in the proper mode of ethical conduct with his equanimity.

There lived in Medina a man from the progeny of the second caliph Omar who harassed the Imam ﷺ, and at times would insult him by hurling imprecations at him. Some of the Imam's ﷺ associates suggested that the man be put to death, but the Imam ﷺ categorically forbade such a crime. Then one day the Imam ﷺ inquired as to the whereabouts of the man's abode, which was on the outskirts of Medina. He saddled a pack animal and headed to the man's home. He found him in his field and entered it still mounted on his ride. The rancorous man yelled, "Don't trample on my crops!" the Imam ﷺ ignored him and continued toward him undeterred. When he reached him, he dismounted and asked him in a cheerful and magnanimous manner, "How much have you spent on this field?"

"A hundred Dinars."

"How much do you hope to profit from it?"

"I cannot foresee the future."

"I asked how much you hoped to gain."

"I hope for a profit of two hundred Dinars."

---

[11] Propaganda aimed at libeling and slandering Imam Ali ﷺ and his progeny.

His Eminence gave him three hundred Dinars and added, "You can keep the crops yourself. God ❀ will grant you that which you hope for."

At that point, the man rose up, kissed His Eminence the Imam's ﷺ forehead, and asked him to forgive him his trespasses against him. The Imam ﷺ smiled and returned.

On the following day, that man was seated in the mosque when the Imam ﷺ made his entry. As soon as the man saw the Imam ﷺ, he said, "God ❀ knows better to whom to entrust His ministry." (This was an acknowledgement of the merit and worthiness of Imam Mūsā al-Kāẓim's ﷺ candidacy for the imamate.)

The man's friends asked him in astonishment, "What's going on? You used to revile him!" But he praised the Imam ﷺ once more, causing his friends to distance themselves from him with hostility. The Imam ﷺ turned to his companions who had earlier suggested that they kill the man and asked, "Which is better then, your intention, or the way in which I brought him onto the [right] path?"

The Imam ﷺ did not look at the material world in terms of a goal in itself; and if he earned some money, he liked to use it in the service of others: to provide peace of mind to an anguished soul, or to feed the hungry, or to clothe the indigent.

Muḥammad ibn ʿAbdullāh al-Bakrī reports: "I was in a very difficult position financially, and I travelled to Medina in order to see if I could borrow some money. But no matter whose door I knocked on, I did not meet with any success, and I became very despondent. I resolved to go to the house of Abul-Ḥasan Mūsā ibn Jaʿfar ﷺ and complain about my lot in life to that great man.

After asking around for his whereabouts, I found him busy tilling a field in one of the villages on the outskirts of Medina. The Imam ﷺ came to me and greeted me and we had a luncheon together. After the meal was consumed, he asked if I had called on him with some business in mind.

I told him my story. The Imam ﷺ arose and went to a room at the side of the field, and when he returned, he had with him three hundred gold Dinars, which he gave me. I thanked him and mounted my ride, having attained my purpose, and returned to Medina."

'Ays ibn Muhammad, whose age had reached ninety, reports: "It was a year in which I had planted melons, cucumbers, and squash. We were approaching the harvest when a plague of locusts destroyed all of my produce, inflicting one hundred and twenty Dinars worth of damage.

Right around this time, His Eminence Imam Kāẓim ﷺ – who, it would seem, looked out for the interests of each and every one of us Shī'a – came to me one morning, greeted me and asked how I was doing. I told him that the locusts had destroyed my whole crop.

He asked, "What is the extent of your loss?"

I said, "With the cost of the camels factored in, it comes to one hundred and twenty Dinars."

The Imam ﷺ gave me one hundred and fifty Dinars. I told him, "Seeing as your presence is so bounteous, please come to my field and offer a prayer."

The Imam ﷺ came and offered a prayer and said, "It is related from the Prophet ﷺ: 'Stick with [= work] what remains of a property which has been damaged."

I watered that same tillage and God ﷻ granted me of His abundance, such that I was able to sell the yield of its produce for ten thousand Dirhams."

Shaqīq al-Balkhī was a famous man known for his piety and attainments to inner spiritual states. He reports: "I started toward Mecca in the year 149 AH with the intention of making the Major Pilgrimage (*hajj*), joining the caravan of the Hajj pilgrims in Qādisīya. While I was looking at the throng of people and their clothing and ornaments, my glance fell upon a handsome youth whose face was luminous and who had donned a [coarse] woolen robe over his attire and who followed the rest of the group at a little distance on his own.

I thought to myself that he must be one of those Sūfīs who will undoubtedly become a burden to the rest of the group for his needs and expenses. I resolved to go to him and reprimand him. I approached him with this intention in mind, but just as I did so, he called me [by my name] and said, "[49:12] *Refrain from suspicion and distrust [of one another] for, behold, suspicion and distrust are sins [in and of themselves]*."

When I heard this verse of the Quran being uttered by that young stranger, I was startled and came to a halt. He in turn let me be, and moved on. I thought to myself "This was not an ordinary occurrence. He called me by my name without knowing me, and unveiled the intention which I held in my heart. He must be one of the righteous servants of God ﷻ. I shall go and join him, ask his forgiveness, and benefit from his presence."

I made haste to join him, but try as I might, I could not find him. He had disappeared from before my eyes; until we reached the town of Wāqasa, at which point my eyes fell upon the youth once more. He was deep in prayer and was performing the ritual devotions, but his devotions were different than those of the rest of us. His limbs trembled, and tears streamed from his blessed eyes. His devotions were made with a [complete] presence of the heart, and with humbleness and humility. It seemed as though he had no thought for the world or the people in it, and that his spirit had journeyed to the Celestial Kingdom.

I sat and waited for his ritual devotions to be completed. I then got up and headed toward him. But before I got to him, he turned around and called to me and said, "[20:82] *God ۝ forgives all sins unto any who repents and attains to faith and does righteous deeds, and thereafter keeps to the right path.*"

After having recited this noble verse of the Quran, he again left me to myself. And once again the certainty came to me that he is one of the select persons in God's creation who has attained to such a high spiritual station because of his servitude to God ۝ to the point where he has knowledge of domains of reality which are beyond the ken of ordinary human perception (*al-ghayb*) and consequently has access to people's hearts and minds.

I came across him for the third time in the land of Manā. He was standing at a well with a pail in hand. Suddenly the pail was released from his grip and fell into the well. The youth raised his hands heavenward and said, "You are the provider of every one of my needs, Lord. You are the provider of my water, my daily sustenance, and my every need."

After this supplication, the water of the well rose up, so that the pail of water came up and was now positioned on the ground! The youth reached for it and grabbed it and began to make his ritual ablutions with the water from it. He then made four cycles of ritual devotions. I again focused my attention on the way in which he made his prayers. His body shivered and trembled, and his eyes were welled up with tears. He was fully focused on his devotions, which he performed with great care. He was immersed in the supplications of his needs to He who is without need.

After the completion of the ritual devotions, I ran toward him this time so as not to lose him. I reached him and offered him my salaams.[12] He returned my salaams warmly. I asked him to be so kind as to grant me the remains of the water in the pail. He said, "God the Sublimely Exalted has placed all of His patent and latent bounties at our disposal, and this is on account of our devotions and good deeds. If you follow in our path of friendship and devotion [to God], you too shall be the beneficiary of God's special graces."

He then gave me the water in the pail as a gift. I drank it, and it tasted as sweet as honey. I swear [upon my oath] to Allāh that in all my life I had never tasted water as clean and sweet as the water from that pail.

Then I no longer saw him until we arrived at Mecca. During a starless night when the sky was dark and black and clouds had covered the firmaments like a canopy, I came across him once again by the well of Zamzam. He was occupied in ritual devotions and prayer this time as well, and in the same fashion, with humbleness and humility, trembling and with tears in his eyes. His face and shirt were wet with the profusion of his tears, and his body shuddered and quivered as he wept.

His devotions lasted until sunrise. When the call of the *mu'addhin*[13] was heard from afar, he made the two cycles of the morning ritual devotions, after which he started the ritual invocations and glorifications of God ﷻ (*tasbīh*). He then entered the position of complete prostration, placing his forehead on the ground, and remained in that position for a long time without moving. He then arose and proceeded to perform the ritual circumambulation (*tawāf*) of the House of God ﷻ (the Ka'ba), performed the *tawāf* ritual devotions, and exited the Ka'ba.

---

[12] Offering salaams in greeting is a form of prayer wherein one asks God ﷻ to give peace and tranquility of mind to the one who is the subject of the supplication.

[13] The prayer crier.

I proceeded to follow behind him when suddenly I saw a large crowd thronging around him, treating him with great reverence and respect. They were like moths hovering around an open flame; they hovered around the light of his presence, following him [wherever he went]. I asked someone next to me who this great personage was. He said, "He is His Eminence [Imam] Mūsā ﷺ, the son of [Imam] Ja'far ﷺ, the Seventh Imam and leader of the Shī'a."

I told myself, "All of these miraculous wonders and marvels cannot emanate from any source other than the Household of Purity and Immaculacy, the Household of the Prophet ﷺ of Islam."

One day His Eminence Imam Mūsā ﷺ, the son of Imam Ja'far ﷺ, was passing by a street of the city of Baghdad. The loud clamor of song and dance music could be heard coming from a large and beautiful house which obviously belonged to a member of the wealthy class who enjoyed partaking in the pleasures of this world. The Imam ﷺ hesitated and paused for a short while, and a servant girl who wanted to bring out the trash opened the front door.

The Imam ﷺ asked her, "Whose house is this?"

She said, "This is Bishr's house."

"Is he a bondsman or a freeman?"

"A freeman, of course."

"Yes, it is evident that he is a freeman, for if he were a bondsman [of God], his situation would be very different than this."

The maidservant returned to the house, wherein Bishr asked her the reason for her tarrying.

She said, "I was talking to Imam Mūsā Kāẓim ﷺ."

Bishr asked, "And what did the master have to say?"

She said, "He asked if the owner of this house was a freeman or a bondsman. I told him that he is a freeman, and the Imam ﷺ said, 'Yes, it is evident that he is a freeman, for if he were a bondsman [of God], his situation would be very different than this.'"

When Bishr heard these words, he suddenly awoke from his sleep of heedlessness, and in his distraught state, left the house barefoot in pursuit of the Imam ﷺ. When he caught up to him, he cast himself onto the Imam's ﷺ feet, repented of his past sins, and ultimately became known as one of the righteous persons of his day. From that day forward, people called him Bishr the Barefoot.

The Abbāsid caliph al-Ma'mūn was asked, "How did you come to be enamored with Imam Riḍā ﷺ?"

He said, "It was on account of my father. Once we were travelling from Baghdad to Madina. The dignitaries of Madina came to greet my father, where my brother and I, together with the commanders of the army, were all present. Whoever came would dismount from his ride at the periphery of the palace and would come to see my father on foot, would kiss his hand and sit on the floor. My father would speak a few words with him, give him a pouch of gold as a gift, after which the dignitary would go through the proper protocols of showing due respect and take his leave. During this process, it was announced that Mūsā ﷺ, the son of Imam Ja'far ﷺ has come to see my father. My father stood up, rearranged his attire, and told the chamberlain, "This guest is very dear to me. Allow him to enter the palace with his mount."

That man entered the palace grounds and came up to the foot of my father's throne mounted on his ride. My father stood up and greeted him and helped him dismount. He took his hand, kissed it, and brought him along and sat him down, after which he sat next to him like a student in awe of his master, and talked with him for a while. My father then bade the Imam ﷺ farewell and ordered me and my brother Amīn and the commanders of the army to escort the Imam ﷺ to the outer gate of the palace. That night I asked my father, "Father! Who was that honorable man who had a gaunt but luminous countenance for whom you stood up and showed such respect and humility?"

He said, "That was Abul-Hasan, [Imam] Mūsā ﷺ, the son of [Imam] Jaʿfar ﷺ."

"So? What is he then?" I asked.

My father replied, "He is the Imam and leader of you and me and of all the people of these lands."

So I asked, "Are you not then the leader of the people?"

He said, "No. The succession [to the Prophet ﷺ] (the caliphate or *khilāfaʿ*) rightly belongs to him and to the House of [the Prophet ﷺ through] Ali ibn Abī-Tālib ﷺ."

I then asked, "If that is the case, then why do you not return his right to him instead of imprisoning and exiling him and his supporters??"

He replied, "[The authority which obtains from the power of] rulership [i.e. politics] does not respect even the bond that exists between father and son. If one day you, who are my son, interfere with my authority to rule and want to take it out of my hands, I would not stop at destroying even you."

People will stop at nothing in their quest for power and their lust for leadership and governance.

All of the above now having been said, we can see that it is clear that the words of the caliph al-Maʾmūn concerning his amity with Imam Riḍā ﷺ was nothing more than his chicanery for deceiving the people, and the people of Iran in particular. Because the people of Iran played a significant role in the overthrow of the erstwhile Abbāsid caliph al-Amīn and in bringing al-Maʾmūn to the throne; and al-Maʾmūn made such speeches in order to win over the hearts and minds of the Iranian people who always had the love of the Ahl al-Bayt ﷺ (the Members of the Household of the Prophet ﷺ) in their hearts; while inwardly, all of the usurping Abbāsid caliphs were die-hard enemies of the Immaculate Imams ﷺ of the Ahl al-Bayt ﷺ.

Imam Kāżim was busy working a field which belonged to him personally. He was sweating profusely because of his hard work, such that sweat trickled down his entire body. One of the Imam's companions who went by the name of Ali ibn Abū-Hamza saw the Imam in this state. He approached the Imam, offered his salaams, and said, "My lord, why do you not delegate this task to someone else?"

The Imam said, "Why should I? People who were better than me always performed such tasks themselves."

"Such as who?" I asked.

"Such as the Most Noble Prophet, and the Commander of the Faithful[14], and all of my forefathers before me [back to those two noblemen]. Working a field is a prophetic tradition, as it is a tradition of their [legitimate] successors and that of the righteous bondsmen of God."

Ma'tab was Imam Ja'far as-Sādiq's bondsman and confidante; after the martyrdom of Imam Ja'far as-Sādiq, he was privileged to spend the rest of his life in the service of Imam Kāżim. It is related from him that he reported:

"His Eminence Mūsā ibn Ja'far was busy at work in his date-palm plantation, pruning date clusters. At this time, I saw one of the workers furtively take a cluster of dates and throw it behind a wall.

I went up to him and confronted him concerning what I had seen. He denied he had done such a thing, but when I brought the cluster of dates to him, his face lost its luster and went pale. I took him to the Imam, showed him the date cluster and said, "I saw this man secretly hide this cluster of dates behind a wall so that he could get to it later."

---

[14] In its Shī'a usage, this title is reserved exclusively for Ali b. Abī-Tālib.

The Imam ﷺ turned to the worker and asked, "Have you been suffering from hunger?"

The man said, "No, my lord."

The Imam ﷺ then asked, "Were you in need of it?"

The man repeated, "No, my lord."

"Then why did you take it?"

The man said, "I was suddenly overcome by the urge to do so; I know I did a bad thing, and I am sorry, and ask for your forgiveness."

The Imam ﷺ said, "The right thing to do would have been for you to have told me [of this desire of yours]. But be on your way, and take this cluster of dates; you can have them. But do not do such a thing again."

The Imam ﷺ then said, "Let him be and do not tell anyone about this incident, so that his reputation remains intact."

Imam Kāẓim had a few Negro slaves who helped him in his upkeep of his field and orchard. They were highly skilled at their tasks, and the Imam ﷺ would at times consult them concerning agricultural matters. Some of the Imam's ﷺ associates reproached him, saying, "O son of the Apostle of God ﷺ. Why do you consult slaves? Surely, this is beneath you!"

The Imam ﷺ replied, "They work in fields and in orchards and have experience [in these matters]. Perhaps Almighty God ﷺ deigns to manifest that which is for the best by way of what they have to say about these things. I consult them concerning that which they have expertise in, not about that which they have no knowledge of. Experience and intelligence have nothing to do with whether one is black or white or with the color of one's skin."

Abdur-Rahmān ibn Ya'qūb was a famous dignitary who was an antagonist of Imam Mūsā Kāżim's ﷺ. He used to lead a teaching circle in which a number of people participated, and in which he used to propound his beliefs, which were contrary to the beliefs of the Imāmī (Twelver) Shī'a. One of his students who attended this circle was called Ja'far al-Ja'farī, who was also his sororal nephew and, contrary to his uncle, was a follower and supporter of Imam Mūsā Kāżim ﷺ and did not accept his uncle's views. Nonetheless, he would always attend and participate in his uncle's teaching circle.

One day, Imam Mūsā Kāżim ﷺ asked him, "Why do you attend the teaching circle of Abdur-Rahmān ibn Ya'qūb? People see you doing this, and this is not a good thing."

Ja'far al-Ja'farī replied, "He is my uncle, and so I go to see him sometimes."

The Imam ﷺ said, "But he says things about God ﷻ which are incorrect, and he holds views that are deviant. You should either keep his company, or stay with us and leave him alone."

Ja'far said, "It is true that his beliefs are distorted, but what possible harm can there come from my attending his classes? It is not as if I share his beliefs or accept them."

The Imam ﷺ said, "One who keeps another's company is not immune from the latter's evil. Have you heard the story of the person who lived during Moses' times?"

"No."

"He was a companion of His Eminence the prophet Moses ﷺ and his father was a follower of Pharaoh. When the tribe of the Israelites – who had accepted Moses' ﷺ prophethood – were passing the river Nile, the good son went to see his wayward and morally corrupted father and drowned together with Pharaoh's legion.

When news of this reached Moses ﷺ, he said, "That man drowned. May God ﷻ have mercy on his soul. He disagreed with his father's creed. But when God's wrath reaches the sinner, anyone who keeps their company will find no escape and will be ensnared [together with them]."

It is reported that Imam Mūsā Kāẓim ﷺ stated: "One day, a man who by all appearances was a benevolent and religious man called upon Imam Ja'far as-Ṣādiq ﷺ and said, "O Abā-Abdullāh[15], why have you distributed your wealth in such a manner? Would you not have had greater security and peace of mind if you had kept it all in one place?"

It seems the Imam ﷺ had invested his wealth in different activities such as trading goods, farming, animal husbandry, and so on, and took a small but fair profit from each activity, most of which he expended on those in need...

Imam Ṣādiq ﷺ responded, "I have divided my wealth so that a greater number of people can avail themselves of its benefits. If a portion of it is lost to pestilence or bad weather or the like, the other portions remain secured; and the sum total [of the profits] will [in any event] end up in the same purse [i.e. the purse out of which the needs of the indigent are seen to]."

A man came to Imam Mūsā Kāẓim ﷺ and stated, "I have become tired and weary of the world and I have no wish from God ﷻ other than that He grant me death."

The Imam ﷺ said, "Instead of asking for death, ask for life so that you will be able to obey and worship God, rather than rebelling against Him. If you live and perform righteous deeds it will be better for you than

---

[15] This is the *kunya* or patronymic of the Imam ﷺ, meaning 'father of Abdullāh'.

if you die, for in that case you will not be able to perform any deeds whatever, be they good or bad."

A large caravan comprised of the people of greater Syria and Medina were on their way to the House of God.[16] Imam Mūsā Kāẓim was also a member of this convoy, as were the Abbāsid caliph and tyrant Hārūn and other members of that damnable dynasty's gentry.

One day the Imam was passing by the side of Hārūn, when one of his henchmen posed a question to him as a way of taunting him. He said, "Is it permissible for a *muḥrim*[17] pilgrim on the Hajj pilgrimage to ride in a palanquin[18] and for its roof to cast a shade over his head?"

The Imam replied, "It is not permissible to do so voluntarily, but is permissible in an emergency where there is no choice in the matter."

The man asked again, "Is it permissible for a *muḥrim* pilgrim to walk under the shade [of a parasol] of his own free will?"

The Imam replied, "Yes."

The questioner then let out a loud peal of laughter, as if to mock the Imam by implying that there is no difference between the shade cast by the roof of a palanquin and that cast by a parasol.

---

[16] This is another name for the Masjid al-Ḥarām in Mecca with the Ka'ba at its center.

[17] *Muḥrim* is the participle form of a pilgrim who has entered *iḥrām*, which is the first stage of the pilgrimage (wherein the pilgrim changes his or her clothes in preparation for the pilgrimage and pledges allegiance to God). What is meant here is that the person referred to has formally entered into the state of the Hajj or greater pilgrimage.

[18] A covered litter for one passenger, consisting of a large box carried on two horizontal poles by four or six bearers.

The Imam turned to him and said, "The way of the Apostle of God was that when he was on the Hajj pilgrimage, he would take the top off the palanquin, but would avail himself of the shade [of a parasol] when on foot. Are you then surprised at the way of the Prophet, and do you then mock him and his ways?"

The Imam continued, "It is not permitted to apply one's reason by way of analogy (*qīyās*) in God's ordinances. Anyone who compares [the efficacy of] an ordinance with [that of] another, will surely stray from the Straight Path. The Straight Path is the one which dedicates itself to following the commandments and example of the Prophet." The person fell silent as he had nothing that he could say in response.

Faḍl ibn Rabīʿ, the guard of the palace of Hārūn or-Rashīd (the Abbāsid tyrant), reports: "One year, Hārūn or-Rashīd wanted to make the Hajj pilgrimage. In order to make a show of his power and grandeur, and especially for the benefit of the Ālids,[19] he set out from Baghdad to Mecca with an army of 100,000 men. The majesty and grandeur of this caravan was so great that no other caravan who had departed Baghdad with the same intention dared overtake the caliph's caravan on their way to making the Hajj pilgrimage.

The time for the Hajj pilgrimage arrived[20], and the caliph, while in a state of ritual consecration (*ihrām*),[21] entered the Masjid al-Harām[22] and started the ritual circumambulation (*tawāf*) of the House of God (the Kaʿba). Despite the fact that this was not a place for showmanship

---

[19] The House of Ali b. Abī-Tāleb.
[20] The pilgrimage occurs from the 8th to 12th (or in some cases 13th) of Dhū'l-Hijja, the last month of the Islamic lunar calendar.
[21] See footnote 17.
[22] The Sacred Mosque constructed around the Kaʿba in Mecca.

and self-conceit, and everyone is obliged to wear the same uniform of plain white robes (so as to be perfectly equal with everyone else in terms of their attire), Hārūn's guards pushed people aside in order to make room for him, and did not allow anyone to walk in front of the caliph.

In the midst of this, a pilgrim who was unknown to Hārūn and his entourage overtook him, and defied all of the efforts of the guards to have him fall back in line behind the caliph. When they reached the Black Stone (the *hajar al-aswad*), the stranger's hand touched the stone ahead of Hārūn, after which he kissed the stone and commenced his devotional prayers.

One of Hārūn's guards who had become vexed with the man's supposed effrontery said, "Get out from the presence of the caliph, you desert dweller!"

The stranger replied, "Everyone is equal to everyone else here, and there is no difference between the caliph and anyone else. God ﷻ has stated that [here in His House], desert dwellers and townspeople are equal to one another."

The caliph ordered his guards to let him be. During the ritual devotions at the Station of Abraham, the stranger again stood up to prayer ahead of the caliph. After the ritual was over, Hārūn, who had been impressed with the stranger's gumption, ordered him to be brought to his presence.

Rabīʿ saw the stranger busy in prayer in some corner. He approached him and after he had finished his devotions told him, "The Commander of the Faithful has summoned you."

The stranger said, "I have no business with him. Anyone who has something to say to me can come to me!"

The man's response was conveyed to the caliph who got up and went to him. After exchanging greetings, the caliph said, "Do I have permission to sit down?"

The stranger replied, "This place belongs neither to me nor to you; it is the House of God ﷻ and it is a sanctuary. You may sit or you may leave, as you desire."

Hārūn sat and asked, "O A'rābī (i.e., desert dweller, a condescending form of address), what was it that emboldened you to overtake me [in the circumambulation ritual]?"

The stranger said, "Whoever reaches here first has a right to complete his ritual first. And the plain white robe which is worn after which one enters the state of ritual consecration (*ihrām*) is worn in order for everyone to be equal to each other."

Hārūn said, "I will put a question to you. If you are able to answer it, then it will pass; otherwise, I will order you to be punished."

The stranger asked, "Is your question to be posed in the spirit of a student putting a question to a master, or is it for the purpose of boasting and self-aggrandizement?"

Hārūn said, "No! My question is one posed by a student questing for knowledge."

The stranger then said, "In that case, take a seat next to the master like a student and pose whatever question you might have with the respect and decorum due a student's master."

The face of the stranger and his manner of speech was familiar to the caliph, but try as he might, he could not recall his identity. Finally, the caliph asked, "What are the mandatory acts [ordained by the sacred law of Islam]?"

He heard the following in response: "1, 5, 17, 34, 94, 135, over 17; 1 out of 12; 1 out of 40; 1 out of 205; once a lifetime; one for one."

The caliph, who had not understood a word of what had been spoken, laughed loudly and said, "I ask you concerning the obligatory acts and you respond by reeling off a series of numbers??"

The stranger said, "Why, do you not know that the world is founded on numbers, and that the religion of Islam is based on numbers? Almighty God ﷻ measures the deeds of His servants with numbers, and the Day of Resurrection is a day of accounting. The whole order of creation is based on numbers, but the lack of order and chaos comes about as a result of the absence of the proper accounting [of one's intentions and words and deeds] …"

The caliph, who had become astonished, said, "You are right. So now tell me the meaning of these numbers, for if you have spoken without 'a proper accounting' of your words, you will have cost yourself your life!"

Rabīʿ added, "Show self-restraint and fear God, so that perchance the caliph will forgive you."

The stranger laughed. Hārūn asked, "What is there to laugh about?"

He said, "I am surprised by your lack of knowledge and awareness, and am at a loss as to decide which of the two of you is the more ignorant, the one who wants to hasten the event of [my] death, which in any event is certain, or the one who wants to postpone a death whose time has come. But as to what I meant when I said the number 1, it was the religion of Islam, in which there are 5 times in each day in which the offering of 5 ritual devotions is mandatory, which comprise 17 prayer cycles, 34 prostrations, 94 *takbīrs* and 135 *tasbīhs*.

"And as to the meaning of 1 out of 12, this refers to the fasting of the month of Ramaḍān, 1 out of the 12 months of the year of which is mandatory. And as to the meaning of 1 out of 40 and 1 out of 205, they refer to the mandatory alms tax and charitable poor due.[23] And as to the meaning of once a lifetime, it refers to the Hajj pilgrimage which is obligatory [upon those who are capable of performing it] once in one's lifetime. And 'one for one' refers to [the principle of] just retaliation (*qiṣāṣ*), concerning which God ﷻ has stated in the Quran, one for one [in equal measure]."

---

[23] *Zakāt wa sadaqa wājib.*

Hārūn, who had been impressed by the extent of the man's knowledge and learning, said, "I swear [upon my oath] to Allāh! You phrased it concisely, and I learned it well!"

He then ordered that a bag full of gold be brought over [and gave it to the stranger], who said, "O caliph! Why are you giving me this bag of gold, whereas I have not asked you for anything?"

The caliph replied, "It is the prize of the eloquence of your words of truth and that which I learned by them."

The man said, "Now I will put a question to you. If you answer correctly, I will give this bag of gold to you as your prize. And if you do not answer correctly, order another bag to be brought so that we can distribute them among the poor of Mecca."

The caliph made the order and said, "Ask whatever you will."

The man said, "Tell me, does the *khunfasā*[24] breastfeed its young or feed them by putting food in their mouths?"

Hārūn who was dumbfounded finally said, "O desert-dweller (*'a'rābī*)! You put such questions to the likes of me, the caliph??"

The man replied, "I have heard it reported that the Apostle of God ﷺ has said, 'One who becomes the leader and caliph of a nation must be the most preeminent of his people in terms of his knowledge and understanding.' Thus, it is incumbent on you, who are the leader of this nation and who fancy yourself to be the 'Commander of the Faithful', to be able to answer any question that is put to you."

The caliph said, "No, by Allāh. I do not know the answer. Do you know the answer yourself? If so, these two bags of gold are yours."

The man said, "The Lord of the [Two] Worlds[25] provides the sustenance of certain newborns of His creatures neither by way of suckling, nor by way of mouth-feeding; but does so by providing them with a source

---

[24] A species of beetle.

[25] The world of ordinary human perception and the collectivity of the domains of reality which are beyond the ken of ordinary human perception (*al-ghayb*).

of sustenance from within their bodies which is already with them when they are born. And such is the case with the newborn of the *khunfasā*, which abides under the soil."

Hārūn said, "Upon my oath to Allāh, I had not seen or heard of such things! Now these two bags of gold are yours. Your company was pleasing to me, and you imparted knowledge to me."

The man immediately divided the gold among the poor and left. Hārūn looked at him as he made his way and said in amazement, "A learned man in the form of a desert-dweller!" Later, he ordered his men to find out who he was and where he hailed from.

They told him that the man was not an *a'rābī* desert dweller, but was Mūsā ibn Ja'far ※, a progeny of the Prophet ※ who had come to Mecca from Medina to make the Hajj pilgrimage.

5. The Knowledge of the Imam

There is no doubt that our Immaculate Imams ※ – who are the legitimate successors of the final divinely-commissioned apostle, His Eminence the Prophet Muhammad ※– were also the inheritors of the knowledge of His Eminence the Prophet ※. The Prophet ※ himself had stipulated as much to the people on numerous occasions. One of the most famous and reliably-sourced of such hadīth reports is the following: "I am the City of Knowledge and Ali ※ is its Gate. Anyone who seeks knowledge must enter it through its gate."

Therefore, comprehensive and in-depth knowledge is an attribute which God ※ has granted His prophets and *awliā* (those who are spiritually proximate to God), and our Imams ※ are the great beneficiaries of this divine favor and grace.

The special form which this divinely-inspired attribute takes is a connection to the divine and being endowed with knowledge of domains of reality which are beyond the ken of ordinary human perception (*al-ghayb*). This knowledge is free from the possibility of defect and error, and is similar to prophetic revelation in the sense that it is immune from falsity and error. The difference, however, is that the *awsīā*[26] (i.e. the Imams ﷺ) are not prophets and are thus not the bringers of a new religion or dispensational order. Rather they are the guardians, expositors and demonstrators par excellence of the religion of the Prophet ﷺ and the leaders of his ministry and community after him.

The frequency of the hadīth reports that exist within the Islamic tradition concerning the supernatural knowledge of each and every one of the Imams ﷺ is to such an extent that there is no room left for any doubt for a Muslim who approaches the subject in an unbiased way and with an open mind. It becomes clear that these great men were indeed endowed with a profound and divinely-engendered knowledge which they evidenced and used as they saw fit for the guidance of the community of their faithful followers.

The displaying of the supernatural knowledge and power of the Imams ﷺ was of particular importance in the case of Imam Mūsā al-Kāẓim ﷺ because of Imam Ja'far as-Sādiq's ﷺ inability openly to proclaim his designation to his succession (due to the atmosphere of severe political suppression instituted by the Abbāsid tyrant al-Mansūr's repressive regime). Subsequently, the time would come when Imam Mūsā al-Kāẓim ﷺ would need to introduce himself to the people and to prove [the legitimacy of] his [claim to the] imamate, and to put an end to the confusion and uncertainty which would otherwise have reigned over the Shī'a community. We shall point to a few examples of such occasions in the passages which follow.

---

[26] *Awsīā* and *awlīā* or saints. (*awsīā* is the plural of *wasī* which is a word which refers to those who are the inheritors, legatees, executors and successors of prophets through the ages; the Shī'a refer to these as Imāms). Those of God's creatures who have spiritual proximity to Him; singular, *walīy*, inclusive of prophets and Imāms and, to a lesser degree, the *ulamā* and *fuqahā*, the magisters and scholars of Islam.

Hishām ibn Sālim reports: "After the martyrdom of Imam Ja'far as-Sādiq ﷺ, the people had gathered in Medina to see who his successor was. A rumor was making its rounds among them that Abdullāh, one of Imam Ja'far as-Sādiq's ﷺ sons, was the successor and Imam of the Muslims. As a result, people thronged to Abdullāh's house to offer their congratulations to him. Mu'min at-Tāq and I went along with the crowd to Abdullāh's house to see for ourselves what was going on.

"When the crowd had left the house, we went to Abdullāh with the intention of testing the question of whether or not the [special] knowledge of the Imams ﷺ had indeed been vested in him or whether this was not in fact the case. Mu'min at-Tāq put a few questions to him, including this one:

"How much is the *zakāt* alms tax on one's wealth?"

Abdullāh said, "Five out of every two hundred Dirhams."

We asked, "If a person only had one hundred Dirhams, how much zakāt alms tax would he be obliged to pay?"

Abdullāh said, "Two and a half Dirhams."

I said, "I swear [upon my oath] to Allāh! Even the Murji'ites[27] do not hold to what you just said!"

Abdullāh raised his hands heavenwards and said, "I swear [upon my oath] to Allāh that I do not know what the Murji'ites' position is on this matter."

We put several other questions to him but he was not able to answer them correctly. Thus, it was proven to us that he was not the Imam. We left him in indignant protest, and in a state of bewilderment as to where and how to find the Imam.

---

[27] The *murji'a* (or the Anglicized version, the Mūrji'ites) was the name given to the majority sect before they came to be known as the *ahl as-sunna wa'l-jamā'a*, or "Sunni" for short. This was on account of the fact that they "referred" the question of the sin of the third caliph Uthmān to God, preferring not to make a decision on it themselves. (*Mūrji'a* is derived from the verb *irjā'* or *rujū'*: to refer).

We were seated in one of the alleys in Medina, deep in thought, when we saw an old man pointing to me and beckoning me toward him. The fear came over us that he might be one of [the caliph] Mansūr's spies, because the caliph had embedded a large number of secret agents and infiltrators among the people in order firstly to identify Imam Ja'far as-Sādiq's ﷺ successor, and secondly, in order to monitor and report back on the affairs of the Shī'a community.

I told Mu'min ot-Tāq, "The old man is pointing only at me and does not seem to have any business with you, so get up and leave before you too get entangled in any trouble."

Mu'min ot-Tāq got up and put some distance between the two of us. I got up and went to the old man, who instructed me to follow him. I started to follow him and did not dare to ask any questions of him, being in fear of my very life.

After a while we stopped in front of a house besides whose door a manservant was standing. He gave instructions to the manservant and left me in his hands. The manservant took me inside the house. I saw that His Eminence Mūsā ibn Ja'far ﷺ, the honorable son of Imam Ja'far as-Sādiq ﷺ was seated in a chamber within the house. I entered the chamber and sat down in a corner after the exchange of greetings.

Mūsā ibn Ja'far ﷺ said, "If you have any questions, refer them only to me and not to aberrant groups and to those who have gone astray."

He repeated this last phrase three times. I took courage and said, "Would that I were sacrificed in your cause,[28] has Imam Ja'far as-Sādiq ﷺ passed from the earthly plane?"

He said, "Yes."

I asked, "Would that I were sacrificed in your cause, who is to succeed him and be our Imam and guide?"

He said, "If Almighty God ﷻ wills for you to be guided aright, He will do so by whatever means [He chooses]."

---

[28] An expression used to show deep reverence and respect.

I said, "Would that my father and mother were sacrificed in your cause, Abdullāh believes that he is the successor to your father."

He said, "Abdullāh desires that God ﷻ not be worshipped [as he ought to be worshipped]."

I said, "Are you then the Imam?"

He said, "I cannot answer this question of yours."

I thought to myself that I have not posed the question properly. And so I said, "Would that I were sacrificed in your cause, is there an Imam over you?"

He said, "No."

I asked, "Will you give me leave to put some questions to you, just as we used to put questions to your honorable father?"

He said, "Ask and listen to the answers, but do not broadcast [any of the information which you receive], as lives are in the balance."

I put several questions to His Eminence ﷺ and he answered them all correctly with reason, eloquence and poise. I realized that he was indeed an unlimited ocean of divine knowledge and wisdom, and I was so taken by his awe and grandeur that such a feeling had never overtaken me before. In closing I told His Eminence ﷺ, "A large number of your followers are bewildered and are searching for the [rightful] successor to your father. Should I disclose the fact of your [being vested in the office of the] imamate to them?"

He said, "Inform those whom you trust, but take a vow from them not to disclose this matter to anyone else, as lives are at stake in this matter." And he placed his hand on his throat when he said this.

I bid farewell to the Imam ﷺ and left the house, and I told my story to Mu'min at-Tāq, Abū-Basīr, Mufaḍḍal, and the other [close] companions of Imam Ja'far as-Sādiq ﷺ, who were privileged to enter into the presence of the Imam ﷺ and attain to certainty concerning his [investiture in the office of the] imamate. [The news of] this matter gradually made its rounds among the people, and Abdullāh's following waned as people abandoned him. Abdullāh looked into the reason as to why the people had abandoned him and was told that I had driven people away from him. He had therefore instructed some ruffians to be on the lookout for me and to give me a beating when they found me.

In a similar vein, it is reported that the Shīʿa of Neyshāpūr[29] had gathered to give a very large amount of money (which they owed [to the Imam] in accordance with the ordinances of the sacred law) to Muhammad ibn Ali Neyshāpūrī, so that he could ensure that it reached the hands of the Imam [safely]. They also gave him a fascicle consisting of seventy pages, each page of which contained a question, together with a blank space for the response. These sheets were in turn placed between two covers, which were wrapped with three ties which were sealed with wax so as to preclude anyone from being able to open the fascicle. They instructed Muhammad ibn Ali Neyshāpūrī to give the bundle to the Imam ﷺ in its present condition (with all of the seals intact), and to retrieve it from the Imam ﷺ on the following night so that he, Muhammad ibn Ali, could break the seals himself and see whether or not the questions had been answered. And if the questions had indeed been answered without the seals having been broken, then this would indicate that the person in question was indeed the Imam, after which he could place the entirety of the Imam's share (all of the money that the Shīʿa of Neyshāpūr had entrusted to him) at his disposal.

On the eve of the departure of the caravan [from Neyshāpūr to Madīna], an old woman who was indigent but God-fearing named Shatīta came to Muhammad ibn Ali and gave him one Dirham of money and a dress worth four Dirhams and said, "This is my due of the Imam's Share

---

[29] An ancient city close to present day Mashhad in northwestern Iran which was destroyed by the Mongol invasion.

(the religious tax previously mentioned), which I send to the Imam, although it is a pittance. But one should not refrain from paying one's Imam's due because it is negligible."

Muhammad ibn Ali entered Medina and heard the news of Imam Ja'far as-Sādiq's ﷺ martyrdom. He also heard it said that Imam Ja'far's ﷺ son Abdullāh was the successor to the sixth Imam. He went to Abdullāh and presented him with the bundle of questions. Abdullāh was unable to respond to all of the questions, and furthermore, he broke all the seals. Muhammad ibn Ali realized that he is not the Imam, and so left him without giving him the Imam's due funds entrusted to him.

He wandered the streets of Medina, muttering under his breath, "Guide me to Your path, Lord." And then a little boy called to him and said, "The person whom you are searching for is waiting for you. Follow me."

Muhammad ibn Ali followed the little boy, who took him to the house of His Eminence Mūsā ibn Ja'far ﷺ. Muhammad entered and greeted the Imam ﷺ, who said, "How soon you become disheartened, O Muhammad! [Do not despair, for] I am the *hujjat*[30] and *walī*[31] of God ﷻ."

He then said, "Bring the questions for me so that I can answer them without breaking the seals of the fascicle. Also bring Shatīta's Dirham and four-Dirham garment for me."

Muhammad complied with His Eminence's ﷺ request. When he opened the fascicle, he saw that the Imam ﷺ had provided written responses to all of the questions. Thus, he delivered all of the Imam's Due funds, as well as Shatīta's share, to the Imam ﷺ. The Imam ﷺ gave a pouch of forty Dirhams to Muhammad, together with a length of cloth and told him, "Give my regards to that pious woman [Shatīta] and give her this pouch as a gift from me. And this length of cloth is a piece of my

---

[30] *Hujjat*: see footnotes #6 and #7 for an explanation of this key word.
[31] *Walī*: 1. regent, sovereign, lord and master; 2. patron, guardian, protector, custodian.

burial shroud which my sister has woven for me. Give this to her too, and tell her that the time of her death will arrive nineteen days after her receipt of these gifts, and that she should put aside sixteen Dirhams for her burial costs, and to put the remaining twenty-four Dirhams aside so that it should be given in charity on her behalf [after her passing]."

After having said these things, the Imam ﷺ took some of the money which Muhammad ibn Ali had brought for him, and gave some of it back to him, instructing him to return those funds to their owners. He also instructed him not to divulge these matters [i.e. concerning his identity] to anyone until the political pressures against the House of the Prophet ﷺ which were being brought to bear by the tyrant al-Manṣūr were alleviated.

Muhammad ibn Ali returned to Neyshāpūr to find that all of the people whose money the Imam ﷺ had not accepted and which he had been instructed to return to their owners had exited the fold of the Shī'a faith. He thus returned their money to them, and did as he was instructed with respect to the old woman.

And just as the Imam ﷺ has foretold, the old woman died nineteen days later.

Hārūn ar-Rashīd's vizier (minister), Ali ibn Yaqṭīn, was a righteous and God-fearing man of faith who was a follower of Imam Mūsā ibn Ja'far ﷺ. He summoned two of his close and trusted aides and told them, "Purchase two strong and sturdy camels this very day and head for Medina indirectly. When you get there, call on His Eminence Imam Mūsā ibn Ja'far ﷺ and give him this money and these papers."

He cautioned them to beware of the caliph's agents and spies and not to be ensnared by them or to betray their secret to them, and not to talk to a single soul concerning this matter.

The two aids went to Kūfa and purchased two healthy camels and headed for Medina.

They had not yet put much distance between themselves and Kūfa when they saw two riders coming towards them. They were overcome with fear, and they thought that of a certainty, their lives were lost. But when the two riders approached, they saw that one of them was His Eminence Imam Mūsā ibn Ja'far ﷺ and the other was his attendant.

They greeted them warmly and with great relief. The Imam ﷺ told them to give him the papers which Ali ibn Yaqtīn had entrusted to them. The two aides complied and gave the Imam ﷺ the papers as well as the sum of money.

The Imam then withdrew a few letters from his sleeve and gave them to the aides, saying, "These are the answers to Ali ibn Yaqtīn's questions. Take them to him with due haste."

They obeyed the command of the Imam ﷺ and returned with speed. Ali ibn Yaqtīn was very pleased and grateful that the answers to his questions had reached him in less than a day's time, adding to the faith he had [in his Imam].

Mūsā ibn Bakīr reports: Imam Mūsā ibn Ja'far al-Kāżim ﷺ gave me a manuscript and said, "Carry out the instructions contained in this letter and report the results back to me."

I took the scroll and placed it under my prayer mat. A few days passed and I forgot about the document. Sometime later, I called on the Imam ﷺ on some other business and he asked me what I had done with the scroll. I told him that it was in my house.

He said, "O Mūsā! Whenever I instruct you to do something, be sure to comply with my instructions!"

He then drew out a manuscript from his side and gave it to me, and I realized that it was the same scroll which he had given me previously and which I had placed under my prayer rug and forgotten about.

When the Abbasid tyrant Hārūn had locked Imam Mūsā ibn Ja'far al-Kāẓim ﷺ in his dungeons, two of the preeminent students of Abū-Ḥanīfa (both of whom were famous in their own right as scholars in the Quranic sciences) decided to pay the Imam ﷺ a visit and to discuss some religious questions with him in order to defeat him [in this debate] and thereby to discredit him.

When the two arrived at the dungeon, the prison guard went to the Imam ﷺ and said, "My shift is over and I am heading home. If there is anything that I can do, or if there is anything that you need, let me know so that I can procure it and bring it for you in the morning."

The Imam ﷺ said, "Go with God ﷻ. I do not need anything."

When the guard left, His Eminence the Imam ﷺ turned to the two scholars who had witnessed the exchange and said, "Are you not surprised at a man who will die tonight but who wants to see to my affairs of the morrow?"

The two scholars got up and left the prison without saying a word, but later confided in each other: "We came to engage him in matters of sacred jurisprudence and the ordinances of the sacred canon, and he talks about occurrences from domains of reality which are beyond the ken of ordinary human perception (*al-ghayb*)! Let us send someone to the house of the guard to stand watch until morning and see what will happen; to see if what he said is true."

It was just past midnight when their agent returned. He was excited and reported with panting breath that the guard had died at midnight. They went to the guard's house and discerned that he had died despite the fact that he was young and healthy.

They went to Imam Mūsā Kāżim ﷺ in the morning and said, "We would like to know how you acquired this [supernatural] knowledge."

The Imam ﷺ said, "This knowledge is of that species of science which the Apostle of God ﷺ taught Ali ibn Abī-Tālib al-Murtaḍā ﷺ, and is not one that can be acquired by others."

The two scholars were bewildered and became silent, as they did not have anything else to say. And that is why they got up and left the prison humiliated and shamefaced.

Shu'ayb reports: One day I had the privilege of being at the service of Imam Mūsā Kāżim ﷺ. His Eminence said, "Tomorrow a man from the Maghrib[32] will come to you and will ask you about me. When he does so, say, 'Mūsā ibn Ja'far ﷺ is the *walī*[33] of God ﷺ and the successor to Imam Ṣādiq ﷺ.'"

"The name of that man is Ya'qūb (Jacob). He is tall and broad-chested. He is the most learned man of his people. Whatever questions he puts to you concerning matters of sacred jurisprudence and the ordinances of the sacred law you should respond to on my behalf. If he wants to meet with me, that is fine too, you may bring him to me."

The next day I was engaged in the ritual circumambulation (*tawāf*) of the Ka'ba when a brawny man approached me and said, "I'd like to enquire as to the health of your master."

I said, "And who might my master be?"

---

[32] The region of North Africa west of Egypt.
[33] *Walī*: 1. regent, sovereign, lord and master; 2. patron, guardian, protector, custodian.

He said, "Mūsā ibn Ja'far ﷺ," and continued, "I have some questions concerning matters of the sacred law, which I would like to know his answers to."

I said, "I am authorized to act on his behalf in these matters. What is your name?"

"Ya'qūb."

"Where do you hail from?"

"From the Maghrib."

"And how did you identify me?"

"In a dream someone told me to go to Shu'ayb and ask him whatever I wanted to ask." When I awoke, I asked after you. They told me what you looked like and told me to look for you here."

"Kindly sit here and wait for me to complete my circumambulations."

Having completed my circumambulations, I went to him and sat down, and answered all of the questions that he put to me. I found him to be a sensible and learned man. At the end of our conversation, he said that he would like to meet Imam Kāẓim ﷺ. I took his hand and brought him to His Eminence's ﷺ house. We entered the house and exchanged greetings, and when the Imam ﷺ looked at the man he said, "O Ya'qūb! You and your brother came here yesterday and fell into a dispute over something on your way over. The dispute escalated into an argument wherein you imprecated each other and are no longer on speaking terms. This state of affairs is not in our tradition or in the tradition and creed of our fathers and forefathers before us. We never encourage our followers to engage in such acts. Have fear of the One God ﷻ Who is without partners or equals. It will not be long before death separates you and your brother and you will regret [your words and deeds]. Your brother will die in this journey before he reaches his home. And this will be on account of the fact that you have severed your relationship to your close kin[34], as a consequence of which Almighty God has shortened your lifespans."

Ya'qūb said, "Would that I was sacrificed for your cause! What about the time of my own death?"

The Imam said, "The time of your death had also been reached, but because you stopped to pay a visit to your aunt on your way over here, Almighty God added twenty years to your life."

That man left the presence of His Eminence the Imam and returned to his homeland. I saw him again on the way to Mecca the following year. I asked him how he was doing, and I also asked about his brother. He said, "My brother passed away last year on the way back [to the Maghrib], and was buried *en route*."

Another special feature of our Imams which stands out and which history has attested to in good measure is the debates and formal scholarly exchanges which they held with their detractors. The Imams continually engaged in and consistently defeated and put their detractors to shame in formal debates by applying unassailable logic and irrefutable proofs and establishing the verities of the teachings of the Shī'a and of the House of the Apostle of God.

Our noble Imams always provided correct and comprehensive answers to each and every question that was put to them with the aid of the divine knowledge with which they were endowed. They did so at different levels of complexity and understanding which were appropriate to the level of understanding of their interlocutors. Their knowledge was such that anyone who engaged them in debate, including their detractors

---

[34] The severing of relations with one's close kin is strictly forbidden in the sacred canon of Islam.

and sworn enemies, ultimately confessed to his defeat and to the power and depth and breadth of the mind of the Imams ﷺ and to the comprehensiveness of their learning and knowledge.

One day, the Abbāsid tyrant Hārūn ar-Rashīd summoned Imam Mūsā Kāẓim ﷺ from Medina to Baghdad and engaged him in discussion.

Hārūn said, "I want to ask you about some things which have been preoccupying my mind for some time but which questions I have not posed to anyone else. I have been told that you never utter any falsehood, so kindly answer my questions properly and truthfully."

The Imam ﷺ said, "If I am given leave to speak freely, I shall inform you of whatever knowledge I have in the fields of the questions you have."

Hārūn said, "You are at liberty to speak freely. Say whatever you will. And now to proceed to my first question: Why do you and the general populace believe that you, the sons of Abū-Tālib, are more preeminent than we, the sons of Abbās, whereas we are both [branches] from the same tree? Abū-Tālib and Abbās were both uncles to the Prophet ﷺ, and are equal to each other in terms of their ties of kinship with the Prophet ﷺ."

The Imam ﷺ replied, "[It is on account of the fact that] we are closer to the Prophet ﷺ than you."

Hārūn said, "And how is that?"

The Imam ﷺ replied, "Because our forefather Abū-Tālib was a blood brother of the father of the Most Noble Prophet ﷺ (having the same father and mother), but Abbās was a step brother (having ties of kinship only from his mother's side)."

Hārūn said, "I have another question. Why do you claim that you inherit from the Prophet ﷺ, whereas we know that when the Prophet ﷺ died, his uncle Abbās (our forefather) was alive, but his other uncle Abū-Tālib (your forefather) was deceased, and it is evident that while an uncle is alive, a nephew cannot be the beneficiary of any inheritance?"

The Imam ﷺ said, "Do I have leave to speak freely?"
Hārūn said, "I stipulated that you do at the beginning of our conversation."

The Imam ﷺ said, "Imam Ali ibn Abī-Tālib ﷺ has stated, 'With children being extant, no one can be the beneficiary of any inheritance except the mother and father and the husbands and wives [of the children].' With children being present, no inheritance obtains for an uncle, either by way of the Quran or by way of the prophetic hadīth corpus. Thus, those who consider the uncle to be equivalent to the father [for purposes of inheritance law], do so on their own account and their position has no basis [in scripture].[35] In addition to this, it is reported that the Prophet ﷺ has stated about Imam Ali ﷺ, 'Ali is the best judge amongst you.'

"And it is reported from Omar ibn al-Khattāb [the second caliph], 'Ali is our best judge.' This sentence is a general truth that has been established for his eminence Ali ibn Abī-Tālib ﷺ, because all of the knowledge on account of which the Prophet ﷺ has praised his associates, such as knowledge of the Quranic text and its proper recitation, knowledge of the ordinances of Islam, and so on, are all contained in the concept of Islamic judgement and judgeship. Therefore, when we say Ali ﷺ is the best judge among us, it means that he is preeminent in all of the Islamic sciences."

[The Imam ﷺ is arguing – when Imam Ali ibn Abī-Tālib ﷺ states, 'With children being extant, no one can be the beneficiary of any inheritance except the mother and father and the husbands and wives [of the children];' his word is final and must be accepted, and the position that the uncle is considered to be equivalent to the father [for purposes of inheritance law] must necessarily be rejected, for as the Prophet ﷺ has explicitly stated, Ali ﷺ is more familiar than everyone else with the ordinances of Islam.]

---

[35] Thus, given the fact that the Prophet's daughter Lady Fātima' az-Zahra ﷺ was alive at the time of her father's death, the Prophet's uncle Abbās does not inherit from him.

Hārūn said, "I have another question: Why do you allow the people to make a connection between you and the Prophet ﷺ and refer to you as 'Children of the Apostle of God', whereas you are the children of Ali ؑ and not of the Prophet ﷺ, as everyone's [lineage] is classified in accordance with their father [and not their mother], and the Prophet ﷺ is your maternal forefather [and not your paternal one]?"

The Imam ؑ replied, "If the Prophet ﷺ were to come back to life and ask for your daughter's hand in marriage, would you give your daughter in marriage to him?"

Hārūn said, "Glory be to Allāh! Why ever not?? To be sure, it would be a point of pride and honor for me before all Arabs and non-Arabs and before the Quraysh too!"

The Imam ؑ then said, "But if the Prophet ﷺ were to come back to life he would never ask for my daughter's hand in marriage, neither would I give my daughter in marriage to him [in the impossible event that he was to do so]."

Hārūn said, "Why not??"

The Imam ؑ said, "Because he is my [fore-]father [albeit from my mother's side], but the Prophet ﷺ is not your father." [Thus, we can rightly refer to ourselves as the children of the Prophet ﷺ].

Hārūn said, "But then why do you think of yourselves as the seed (*dhurīya*) of the Prophet ﷺ, whereas the seed is from the side of the son and not the daughter?"

The Imam ؑ said, "Excuse me from having to respond to this question."

Hārūn said, "Certainly not! You must respond, and you must respond with evidence from the Quran!"

The Imam ؑ said, "The Quran says,

وَتِلْكَ حُجَّتُنَا آتَيْنَاهَا إِبْرَاهِيمَ عَلَىٰ قَوْمِهِ ۚ نَرْفَعُ دَرَجَاتٍ مَّن نَّشَاءُ ۗ إِنَّ رَبَّكَ حَكِيمٌ عَلِيمٌ ﴿٨٣﴾ وَوَهَبْنَا لَهُ إِسْحَاقَ وَيَعْقُوبَ ۚ كُلًّا هَدَيْنَا ۚ وَنُوحًا هَدَيْنَا

$$\text{مِن قَبْلُ ۖ وَمِن ذُرِّيَّتِهِ دَاوُودَ وَسُلَيْمَانَ وَأَيُّوبَ وَيُوسُفَ وَمُوسَىٰ وَهَارُونَ ۚ وَكَذَٰلِكَ نَجْزِي الْمُحْسِنِينَ ﴿٨٤﴾}$$

[6:83] And this was Our argument which We vouchsafed unto Abraham against his people: [for] We do raise by degrees whom We will. Verily, thy Sustainer is wise, all-knowing. [6:84] And out of his seed, [We bestowed prophethood upon] David ﷺ, and Solomon ﷺ, and Job ﷺ, and Joseph ﷺ, and Moses ﷺ, and Aaron ﷺ: for thus do We reward the doers of good, [6:84] and [upon] Zachariah ﷺ, and John ﷺ, and Jesus ﷺ, and Elijah ﷺ: every one of them was of the righteous.

"I now ask you: is Jesus ﷺ, who is stipulated to be of the seed of Abraham ﷺ, so stipulated by way of his father or by way of his mother?"

Hārūn said, "According to the letter of the Quran, Jesus ﷺ did not have a father."

The Imam ﷺ said, "Therefore, he is considered to be of the seed of Abraham from his mother's side. And we too are considered to be of the seed of the Prophet ﷺ from our mother's side, Lady Fāṭimaᵗ al-Zahrā ﷺ. Should I cite another verse from the Quran?"

"Please."

"I shall recite the Verse of the Mubāhala (The Mutual Imprecation), which reads,

$$\text{فَمَنْ حَاجَّكَ فِيهِ مِن بَعْدِ مَا جَاءَكَ مِنَ الْعِلْمِ فَقُلْ تَعَالَوْا نَدْعُ أَبْنَاءَنَا وَأَبْنَاءَكُمْ وَنِسَاءَنَا وَنِسَاءَكُمْ وَأَنفُسَنَا وَأَنفُسَكُمْ ثُمَّ نَبْتَهِلْ فَنَجْعَل لَّعْنَتَ اللَّهِ عَلَى الْكَاذِبِينَ ﴿٦١﴾}$$

[3:61] And if anyone should argue with thee about this [truth] after all the knowledge that has come unto thee, say: "Come! Let us summon our sons and your sons, and our women and your women, and ourselves and yourselves; and then let us pray [together] humbly and ardently, and let us invoke God's curse upon those [of us] who are telling a lie."

"No one has denied that the Prophet ﷺ brought anyone other than Imam Ali ؑ, Lady Fāṭimaᵗ al-Zahrā ؑ, and their sons, Imams Hasan ؑ and Husain ؑ to the ritual mutual imprecation of the Mubāhala with the Christians of Najrān. Therefore, the subject of the sentence 'Let us summon our sons and your sons', in the aforementioned verse must necessarily be Imams Hasan ؑ and Husain ؑ, and this is irrespective of the fact that they are related to the Prophet ﷺ by way of their maternal bond and are the children of His Eminence's daughter [and not of his son]."

Hārūn said, "Is there anything you want from me?"

Imam Mūsā Kāẓim ؑ said, "No, I want nothing but to be able to return to my home."

And Hārūn said, "We will have to think about that."

6. The Imam's Role in the Cultivation of the Muslims

The knowledge and exemplary model provided by Imam Mūsā Kāẓim ؑ was a reflection of the knowledge and paradigmatic example set by the Prophet ﷺ and his purified progeny. Anyone who was thirsting for knowledge and for finding the right path to their self-development and perfection could drink their fill at the well of his wisdom, and their thirst would be sated so completely that they would attain to excellences of virtues in learning and faith in the briefest periods of time.

About twenty years had passed from His Eminence Imam Mūsā Kāẓim's ؑ noble life when his honorable father passed away, and the majority of his father's students and alumni turned to him and benefitted from his wisdom for over thirty-five years.

Those who had been trained in the school of the noble Imam ﷺ were incomparably superior to others in their mastery of the Quranic sciences such as sacred jurisprudence, hadīth, and dogmatics; and in their practice too, their piety and devotions and their mode of righteous conduct and service to the Muslim community was exemplary. Master theologians with a specialty in apologetics and debating the finer points of creedal belief and dogma could not go up against any of them in debate without being crushed by the eloquence of their rhetoric before long and having no choice but to confess to their defeat.

The grandeur of the spirit and character of these students of the Imam ﷺ astonished their detractors, and especially caught the eye of the rulers of the day. They feared that they would use their charisma to muster their devoted, following in the cause of an insurrectionary movement against them, or at a minimum, they feared that the wisdom of their teachings which inveighed against injustice would shed light on their own wrongful and wicked practices and illegitimate power, thereby exposing their ignominy and turning the opinion of the masses against them and agitating them to insurrection against their illegitimate reign.

We will now proceed to provide a brief biography of some of the students of the school of Imam Mūsā Kāẓim ﷺ and of the other Imams of the Ahl al-Bayt ﷺ.

1. Ibn Abī-Umayr (d. 217 AH)

Ibn Abī-Umayr was a celebrated student and great companion of the Imams ﷺ of the Purified House of the Prophet ﷺ, having witnessed and benefitted from the presence of three Imams (Imam Kāẓim, Imām Riḍā, and Imām Jawād, unto all of whom be God's peace). Many hadith reports have reached us from him concerning various subjects. His lofty station was proverbial among Shīʿa and Sunni alike, and he was also considered a reliable and trustworthy transmitter of hadith reports by the scholars of both sects.

Jāḥiz, a Sunni scholar, writes about him: "Ibn Abī-Umayr was the foremost [scholar] of his age in all fields."

Faḍl ibn Shādhān states, "It was reported to the ruling powers of the day that Ibn Abī-Umayr knows the names of all of the Shī'a of Iraq. The authorities told him to name all of their names, but he refused. So they stripped him of his clothes and hung him between the trunks of two palm trees and gave him one hundred lashes. They also robbed him of a hundred thousand dirhams of his wealth."

Ibn Bakīr states, "Ibn Abī-Umayr was imprisoned and subject to much harsh treatment. They robbed him of all his wealth. It is said that it was during this same period of imprisonment and confiscation that his books of hadith were lost [or destroyed]."

Shaykh Mufīd writes, "Ibn Abī-Umayr spent seventeen years in prison, and his property was confiscated. Someone owed him ten thousand dirhams. When he heard what had become of Ibn Abī-Umayr's wealth, he sold his house in order to repay his debt to that great scholar. When Ibn Abī-Umayr was presented with the money, he asked him, 'Where did you get this money? Did you come into an inheritance or come across a hidden treasure??' The man said, 'I sold my house.' Ibn Abī-Umayr said, 'But Imam Ṣādiq has told me that one's residence is excepted from the demands of lenders and the rules of borrowing. Thus, I cannot accept this money, although I am in need of the first dirham from it.'"

2. Safwān ibn Mahran

Safwān was a righteous and trustworthy man. The great scholars of the science of hadith considered him to be an important transmitter of reports from the Imams of the School of the Ahl al-Bayt. In the proper mode of courteous ethical conduct (*akhlāq*) he had reached a station that enjoyed the endorsement of the Imam. As will be pointed out later, immediately upon being told that it is a sin to cooperate with oppressors, he ceased all of his operations that were associated with the regime, selling the camels he used to rent to Hārūn so that he would not be in a position to have to refuse doing so.

3. Safwān ibn Yahyā

Safwān ibn Yahyā was one of the great companions of Imam Kāżim ﷺ. Shaykh Tūsī writes, "The scholars of the science of hadith considered Safwān ibn Yahyā to be the most reliable and trustworthy person of his time, and to be the most pious among them." Safwān ibn Yahyā also benefitted from being in the presence of the Eighth Imam (Imam Riḍā) ﷺ, who held him in high esteem and honor. Imam Jawād ﷺ also remembered him fondly, saying, "May God ﷻ be pleased with him and with our contentment with him. Never once did he take a position against either my father or myself."

Imam Kāżim ﷺ stated, "The damage that a pair of predatory wolves can inflict on a flock of unprotected sheep is not more that the damage that is inflicted by the love of power and authority to the religion [i.e. to the way of life] of the Muslim." He then continued, "Safwān ibn Yahyā – may the soothing shade of God's mercy continue to be cast upon him – is not one who lusts for power."

4. Ali ibn Yaqtīn

Ali ibn Yaqtīn was born in Kūfa in the year 124 AH. His father was a Shī'a and a financial contributor to Imam Ja'far as-Ṣādiq ﷺ, for which crime he was wanted by [the Umayyad caliph] Marwān. He fled to Medina with his wife and two sons, Ali and Abdullāh. In the Umayyad/ Abbāsid interregnum, Ali ibn Yaqtīn returned to Kūfa with his family.

Ali ibn Yaqtīn established relations with the Abbāsids, and headed various high offices of state, which enabled him to act in the interest of and as the guardian of members of the Shī'a community.

When Hārūn or-Rashīd appointed Ali ibn Yaqtīn as his vizier (minister), the latter asked Imam Kāżim ﷺ what he thought of his being involved in the affairs of state [of the usurping Abbāsid power], to which the Imam ﷺ responded, "If you have no choice, [there is no objection], but refrain from expropriating the wealth and property of the Shī'a." The reporter of this hadith says, "Ali ibn Yaqtīn told me that I make a show of expropriating the wealth and property of the Shī'a, but [later] return it to them in secret."

Once Ali ibn Yaqtīn wrote the following to Imam Kāżim ﷺ, "My patience is at an end with the business of the caliph. May God ﷻ sacrifice me for your cause, if you give me leave, I will [= I would like to] quit this job." The Imam ﷺ replied, "Permission is not granted. Fear God ﷻ [and stick with the task at hand]."

He also told him at one time, "Make a commitment to do this one thing, and I will ensure three things for you: that you will not die by the sword, that you will not become indigent, and that you will not see the inside of a prison."

Ali ibn Yaqtīn asked, "What is it that I must commit to?"

The Imam ﷺ replied, "That whenever one of our friends and followers comes to you, that you will honor [his request]."

Abdullāh Kāhalī states, "I was at the service of Imam Kāżim ﷺ when Ali ibn Yaqtīn came towards us. The Imam ﷺ turned to his companions and said, "Anyone who wishes to see a Companion of the Apostle ﷺ of God, let him look to the person who is approaching us."

One of those present asked, "Is he then one who is of the People of Heaven?"

The Imam ﷺ said, "I bear witness that he is one of the People of Heaven."

Ali ibn Yaqtīn never slackened in carrying out the Imam's orders. Whatever he was commanded to do, he would carry out the command, although he did not know the reasons which lay behind the orders or their rationale.

One day, Hārūn or-Rashīd gave some expensive clothes to Ali ibn Yaqtīn as a gift, among which was a robe fit for a king. Ali ibn Yaqtīn sent all of the clothes and the prize robe, together with some other goods to Imam Kāżim ﷺ. The Imam ﷺ accepted all of the goods except for the kingly mantle, and wrote to Ali ibn Yaqtīn saying, "Keep this robe safely and do not let it out of your possession, as you will soon be in need of it."

Ali ibn Yaqtīn did not know why the mantle had been returned, but he kept it as instructed as he knew that there was a good reason for the Imam's instructions. A few days passed. Then one day, Ali ibn Yaqtīn became distraught at a bondsman who was also his confidante and sent him away. The slave who was privy to Ali's closeness to Imam Kāżim ﷺ and to the fact that he had sent the clothes to the Imam decided to go to Hārūn and tell him what he knew. Hārūn became angry and said, "I shall certainly get to the bottom of this. If it is as you say it is, then I shall kill him!"

Hārūn summoned Ali ibn Yaqtīn that very minute and asked, "What have you done with the robe that I gave you?"

Ali ibn Yaqtīn said, "I have kept it safe, placing it with some fragrant musk in a special chest."

"Bring it to me at once!"

Ali ibn Yaqtīn sent one of his servants, who brought the robe and placed it before Hārūn. When Hārūn saw the robe, his temper faded and his anger toward Ali ibn Yaqtīn receded. He told him, "Return the robe to its chest and return to your duties in peace. After this, I shall never take anyone who lodges a complaint about you at their word." And he ordered the unfortunate but treacherous slave to be given a thousand lashes of the whip. The slave had not survived five hundred lashings when he expired, which was a fitting end for his treachery.

It is also related that one day, Ali ibn Yaqtīn wrote the Imam ﷺ a letter in which he asked, "Nowadays, the ritual ablution (*wuḍū*) is made in various different ways among the different sects within Islam. What is the correct way of making one's ritual ablutions?"

In response, the Imam ﷺ recalled the way in which most non-Shī'a made their ritual ablutions, and instructed him to make his ablutions in this manner and not in the manner of the Shī'a.

A little later, one of Ali ibn Yaqtīn's enemies went to Hārūn in order to denigrate him. He told Hārūn that Ali ibn Yaqtīn was a Shī'a and swore an oath to that affect. Hārūn asked him how it could be ascertained whether Ali ibn Yaqtīn was or was not a Shī'a.

Ali ibn Yaqtīn's sworn enemy said, "There is a substantial difference between the Shī'a and non-Shī'a in the way in which the ritual ablution is made. If the caliph secretly monitors the way in which Ali ibn Yaqtīn makes his ritual ablutions, he will easily see that he is in fact a Shī'a."

Hārūn and the ill-wisher secretly made their way to Ali ibn Yaqtīn's home and watched through a window as he made his ablutions. But contrary to their expectations, they saw that he made his ablutions unlike the way the Shī'a make theirs, but made his ablutions as do the Sunnis. The man who had failed in his conspiracy asked Hārūn to secretly monitor the way in which Ali ibn Yaqtīn made his ablutions a few more times. Hārūn did so, but Ali ibn Yaqtīn continued to make his ablutions in the way he was instructed to do by his Imam ﷺ.

Hārūn who had not seen any positive results from his efforts, punished the ill-wisher. A while later, a letter arrived from the Imam ﷺ telling Ali ibn Yaqtīn that the danger has passed and that he can revert back to making his ablutions in the way of the Shī'a rite.

Ali ibn Yaqtīn died in the year 182 AH, at a time when Imam Mūsā Kāẓim ﷺ was in prison. He has authored several books, the names of which are mentioned by Shaykh Mufīd and Shaykh Sadūq.

5. Mu'min al-Tāq

Muhammad ibn Ali ibn Nu'mān's patronymic was Abū-Ja'far and he was known as Mu'min al-Tāq. He was a companion of Imam Sādiq ﷺ and Imam Kāżim ﷺ. Imam Sādiq ﷺ thought very highly of him, and has mentioned him in the context of the great dignitaries among his close companions.

Mu'min al-Tāq had this unerring ability to prevail over whosoever he engaged in debate with [concerning creedal matters]. Imam Sādiq ﷺ had forbidden certain of his companions from engaging in dogmatics and apologetic debates on account of their inability and lack of talent in this area of activity, but he encouraged Mu'min al-Tāq to enter into this arena.

In describing Mu'min al-Tāq, Imam Sādiq ﷺ told Khālid, "Mu'min al-Tāq engages in debate with our detractors and lands on them like a bird of prey [of a sudden and out of nowhere]. And if your wings are clipped, you will never take flight."

Concerning the reason for his title, it is said that Mu'min al-Tāq's shop in Kūfa was under an arched vault (*tāq*), [adding this to the prefix which means "true believer"].

When Imam Sādiq ﷺ passed away, Abū-Hanīfa taunted Mu'min al-Tāq by telling him in a mocking manner that his Imam died, to which Mu'min al-Tāq quickly retorted, "But your Imam has been reprieved until the Day of Judgment."[36]

6. Hishām ibn. Hakam

Hishām ibn. Hakam was a genius in debating creedal beliefs and in dogmatics and apologetics, being undeniably superior to his contemporaries in this field. Ibn Nadīm writes, "Hishām ibn. Hakam was a Shī'a theologian who had mastery of the subject of the imamate (the

---

[36] The reference is to Satan, who was given leave until the Day of Judgement according to the Quran.

religio-political leadership of the community). He was an expert at apologetics, always having answers [to the objections of his opponents] at the ready."

Hishām ibn Hakam authored many books and engaged in many interesting discussions with the theologians and scholars of other religions and sects. Yahyā ibn Khalid al-Barmakī, Hārūn ar-Rashīd's prime minister, put a question to Hishām in the caliph's presence: "Is it possible for truth to be present in two mutually contradictory positions?"

Hishām said, "No."

Yahyā said, "Is it not the case that when two people differ on a point of discussion, that either they are both right, both wrong, or that one is right and the other one is in the wrong?"

Hishām said, "Yes, those are the three possibilities [which obtain logically]. But [in reality] it is not possible for both to be in the right [if their positions are mutually contradictory]."

Yahyā said, "If you accept that two people cannot both be in the right when it comes to the ordinances of religion when their positions are contradictory, then what was the case with Ali ؑ and Abbās who went to Abū-Bakr and disputed with each other concerning the inheritance of the Prophet ﷺ of God? Which one was in the right?"

Hishām said, "They were both in the right and they did not disagree with each other; their dispute was superficial, and their intention in putting on this show was to make the judge between them [Abu-Bakr] realize the error of his ways. They wanted to make him understand that when he said that he had heard the Prophet ﷺ say that prophets do not leave a [material] heritage to their inheritors, that he was lying, and that both of them were in fact [legally entitled] to inherit from the Prophet ﷺ."

Yahyā became bewildered and was unable to respond, and Hārūn al-Rashīd praised Hishām.

Yūnus ibn Yaʿqūb reports: A group of the companions of Imam Ṣādiq ﷺ were with the Imam (including Hamrān ibn Aʿyān, Muʾmin al-Ṭāq, Hishām ibn. Sālim, Tayyār, and Hishām ibn. Hakam). Hishām ibn. Hakam was young.

Imam Ṣādiq ﷺ told him, "Will you then not tell us what you did to Amr ibn. Ubayd, and how you twisted him with your questions?"

Hishām ibn Hakam said, "My modest reserve in your presence will not allow my tongue to function properly."

The Imam ﷺ said, "When you are instructed to do something, you should comply with your instruction."

Hishām ibn Hakam said, "I had heard that Amr ibn Ubayd had a habit of positioning himself in the [congregational] mosque of Basra, and would make speeches for the Basrans, and this did not sit well with me. I entered Basra on Friday and went to the mosque. I saw that Amr ibn Ubayd was seated in the mosque and that people had gathered around him and were putting questions to him. I broke through the throng and sat close to him and said, "O Scholar, I am a stranger to these parts. Allow me to put a question to you."

When he gave me leave, I asked, "Do you have eyes?"

He said, "What kind of a question is this, boy?"

I said, "Such is the nature of my question."

He said, "Go ahead and ask it then, even if it is a stupid question."

I asked again, "Do you have eyes?"

"Yes."

"What do you see with them?"

"Colors and shapes"

"Do you have a nose?"

"Yes."

"And what do you smell with it?"

"Odors and scents"

"Do you have a mouth?

"Yes."

"What do you do with it?

"I taste the taste of food with it."

"Do you have a brain?"

"I do."

"What do you do with it?"

"I recognize everything that interacts with the limbs of my body and my senses with it."

"Do the limbs of your body not make you independent of your brain?"

"No."

"And how is that, whereas all of your limbs and senses are sound and whole?"

"Whenever any of these limbs and senses entertain a doubt about anything, they refer the issue to the brain in order that the doubt be resolved and for certainty to obtain."

"So God ﷻ has created the brain in order to resolve the doubt of the limbs and the senses of the body, is that right?"

"That is so, yes."

"So human beings are definitely in need of their brains, correct?"

"Indeed."

Hishām ibn Hakam then said that he said, "God ﷻ has not let the limbs and the senses of your body to wander aimlessly without a sense of leadership and without the need for a leader or Imam who can correctly distinguish between what is right and what is wrong, but He has let the whole of His creation of humanity to wander around aimlessly, bewildered and in doubt and confusion, each person at odds with every other person, and has not appointed an Imam for them to refer back to when they are in doubt or fall into dispute about something?!"

Amr ibn Ubayd fell silent and did not say anything. He then turned to me and asked, "Where are you from?"

"From Kūfa."

"Are you not Hishām ibn Hakam?"

"Yes, I am Hishām."

He got up, took me by the hand and seated me in his position, and did not speak another word until I got up and left."

Imam Sādiq ﷺ smiled and said, "Who taught you this argument?"

Hishām said, "O son of the Apostle of God ﷺ. This argument came to my tongue suddenly and without any preamble."

The Imam ﷺ said, "O Hishām! Upon my oath to God, this argument appears in the scriptures of Abraham and Moses."

7. Mufaddal ibn Omar

Mufaḍḍal ibn Omar was one of the great companions of the Imams Sādiq ﷺ and Kāẓim ﷺ, who was a great magister (theologian cum doctor of sacred jurisprudence) as well as a trusted transmitter of hadith reports. He was close to Imam Sādiq ﷺ and was in charge of some of his affairs.

A group of the followers of the Ahl al-Bayt ﷺ (the Members of the Household of the Prophet ﷺ) entered Medina and asked Imam Sādiq ﷺ to introduce them to someone to whom they could refer their religious matters when they needed to do so. The Imam ﷺ said, "Let anyone who has a question come to me and put his question to me personally."

But they insisted that a person [other than the Imam himself] be deputized, so the Imam ﷺ said, "I deputize Mufaḍḍal for you. Accept whatever he says, for he speaks nothing but the truth."

Imam Sādiq ﷺ gave several sessions of private lessons on *Tawḥīd*[37] to Mufaḍḍal, whose contents have been collected in one volume under the

---

[37] *Tawḥīd*: the Islamic conception of monotheism: 1. The unicity of the creatorship of the universe; 2. The unicity of the order of creation; 3. The exclusivity of providential lordship (*tawḥīd-e rubūbīat*). God's integral (*tawḥīd*) order of creation. Fidelity (*tawḥīd*) and Infidelity (*shirk*) to the Exclusivity of God's Providential Lordship in the Social Order. *Tawḥīd* is the first principle of the Islamic faith and is usually translated as Monotheism or as the unicity of God. *Tawḥīd* refers to the unicity of ﷺ not just in His capacity as Creator (i.e. unicity

title *Tawḥīd al-Mufaḍḍal* (The *Tawḥīd* of Mufaḍḍal). These special instructions are a testimony to the special attention which the Imam ﷺ gave to Mufaḍḍal, and the importance he placed in his prize student.

Mufaḍḍal was so well-liked by the Imam ﷺ that he once said about him, "Upon my oath to God, I like you, and like anyone who likes you."

Imam Kāẓim ﷺ says about Mufaḍḍal, "Mufaḍḍal is my boon companion and the cause of my comfort."

When Mufaḍḍal passed away, Imam Kāẓim ﷺ was very saddened, and said the following about him: "May God ﷻ have mercy on his soul. He was a father [to me] after my father. He is now at peace."

8. Hammād ibn Īsā

Hammād ibn Īsā is considered to be one of "the People concerning whom there is Consensus" (*aṣḥāb al-ijmāʿ*).[38] He was privileged to take in the life

---

of Creatorship), but also refers to the seamlessness of the order within creation (including man's social order) as a corollary of that act of creation. Thus, *tawḥīd* refers to the integrality of creation with the social order that is intended for that creation by God: the integral (*tawḥīdic*) Islamic society. The *tawḥīdic* worldview is the Islamic vision of monotheism; it is an integral vision of the universe where belief in the unicity of creatorship is seamlessly intertwined and combined with the belief that providential lordship over the world and the individual and collective affairs of man are the exclusive domain of God. It is belief in the unicity of creatorship and the integrality of the order of creation with the will of the One Creator, which is the necessary corollary of this unicity. *Tawḥīd* is the primary creedal tenet of Islam which holds that Allah ﷻ is the sole creator of the world, and that He has exclusivity of providential lordship over His creation, i.e. the exclusive right to sovereignty and control over it.

[38] *Aṣḥāb al-ijmāʿ*: This term applies to a number of companions and students of the Imams ﷺ who benefitted from being witnesses to the presence of the Imams al-Bāqir ﷺ, as-Ṣādiq ﷺ, al-Kāẓim ﷺ, and ar-Riḍā ﷺ, and concerning whose reliability and trustworthiness as transmitters of hadith reports there is consensus

and times of the four Imams, and was a witness to the presence of the Imams as-Sādiq ﷺ, al-Kāżim ﷺ, ar-Riḍā ﷺ, and al-Jawād ﷺ, passing from the earthly plane in the year 209 AH.

He was one of the greatest magisters and scholars of hadīth science of the city of Kūfa. He was well-versed in [all aspects of] the science of hadith and was cautious as a practitioner of the science. He asked Imam Kāżim ﷺ to make a supplication on his behalf, and Imam Kāżim ﷺ supplicated to God ﷻ to provide him with a home, a wife, children, an attendant, and with fifty Hajj pilgrimages. The prayer of the Imam ﷺ was granted and Hammād attained to all his desires and made the Hajj pilgrimage fifty times, meeting his death by drowning on the occasion of his fifty-first Hajj pilgrimage when he was preparing to make his *ihrām*[39] ritual ablutions in a river.

9. Yūnus ibn Abdur-Rahmān

Yūnus ibn Abdur-Rahmān was a righteous servant of God, a scholar of high standing, a perfected human being, and an ascetic devotee, and is considered to be one of "the people concerning whom there is consensus" (*ashāb al-ijmāʿ*).[40]

He was born during the reign of the tyrannical Umayyad caliph Hishām ibn Abdul-Malik. He met Imam Bāqir in Mecca between the stations of Safā and Marwā but has not transmitted any hadith reports from His Eminence. He also met Imām Sādiq ﷺ in the Prophet's mosque and cemetery while the Imam ﷺ was busy performing devotional acts between the Prophet's grave and his pulpit. Therefore, he was not able to put any questions to the Imam ﷺ.

---

among Shīʿa scholarship, considering reports transmitted by them to be *sahīh* (sound).

[39] See footnote #17
[40] See footnote #38

Yūnus ibn Abdur-Rahmān has transmitted a large volume of hadith reports from the Imams al-Kāżim ﷺ, ar-Riḍā ﷺ, and al-Jawād ﷺ. His celebrity among the ordinary populace was to such an extent, and his affiliation with a given sect amongst the various sects that existed at the time was so consequential that an affluent dignitary of another sect placed a very large sum of money at his disposal on condition that he adopt the rich man's rite (*madhhab*); but Yūnus ibn Abdur-Rahmān returned the money, refusing to part company with his Imam and with the teachings of the House of the Prophet ﷺ.

Abū-Hāshim al-Ja'farī writes, "I offered one of Yūnus ibn Abdur-Rahmān's books to Imam Hasan al-Askarī ﷺ. The Imam asked, "Whose writing is this?"

I said, "It is written by Yūnus ibn Abdur-Rahmān."

He said, "God ﷻ the Sublimely Exalted will give him a [luminous] light for every word in this book on the Day of Judgement."

In a related report, it is related that Imam Hasan al-Askarī ﷺ read through the book page by page until its end, then said, "This [book] represents [or contains the teachings of] my religion and the religion of my father and forefathers before me, and all of it is [nothing but] truth."

One of the magisters (*fuqahā*) asked Imam Riḍā ﷺ, "I am at a great distance from you, and do not have access to you at all times in order to put my religious questions to you. So to whom should I refer such questions?"

His Eminence ﷺ said, "Put your questions to Yūnus ibn Abdur-Rahmān."

It is also reported that Imam Riḍā ﷺ stated concerning Yūnus ibn Abdur-Rahmān that he is the Salman the Persian of our time.

And it is further reported that when Imam Mūsā ﷺ attained to martyrdom, there was a large amount of funds which belonged to the Shī'a which were entrusted with the Imam's representatives (*wakīl*, pl. *wukalā*), and that Satan (*shayṭān*) deceived some of these representatives who coveted these funds [and were thus ensnared by Satan]; and this was the reason that they denied the death of Imam Mūsā ﷺ and became known as the Wāqifites.⁴¹

One of these erstwhile representatives had seventy thousand Dinars in trust, and another had thirty thousand Dinars. When Yūnus ibn Abdur-Rahmān propagated the imamate of Imam Riḍā ﷺ, they feared that he would drive people away from them, and so they offered him ten thousand Dinars to stop his agitation against their cause.

In response, Yūnus ibn Abdur-Rahmān said, "I have heard Imam Bāqir ﷺ and Imam Sādiq ﷺ say, 'Whenever reprehensible innovations (*bid'a*) appear among the people, it is incumbent on the Imam to display his [supernatural] knowledge [of the domains of reality which are beyond the ken of ordinary human perception (*al-ghayb*)], for if he does not do so, the light of faith will be taken from him.' And I will not cease to struggle in the way of God's religion and of His commandments."

The response of Yūnus ibn Abdur-Rahmān brought about a great enmity toward him in the hearts of the Wāqifites and caused them to be at war with him.

Finally, it is reported that Yūnus ibn Abdur-Rahmān would visit forty of his brothers in faith every morning and give them greetings of peace. Only after performing this daily ritual would he return to his home and eat his breakfast and make his prayers and work on his writings.

10. Yūnus ibn Ya'qūb

Yūnus ibn Ya'qūb was an especially close companion of Imam Sādiq ﷺ and Imam Kāẓim ﷺ who initially believed in the imamate of Abdullāh

---

⁴¹ The Wāqefites were a small sect who denied the death of Imam Mūsā b. Ja'far ﷺ, considering him to be the Mahdī ﷺ (the universal savior who is to appear in the end days according to Islamic hadith scripture.) They believed that Imam Mūsā b. Ja'far ﷺ was alive and that he would not die before he filled the world with equity and justice.

(Imam Kāẓim's ﷺ brother); but he soon realized his mistake and joined the ranks of the companions and followers of Imam Kāẓim ﷺ.

Yūnus ibn Yaʿqūb passed away in Medina during the imamate of Imam Riḍā ﷺ, who instructed his followers to ritually prepare and enshroud his body for burial, and to participate in his burial ceremony. He was buried in the Baqīʿ cemetery next to the pure bodies of the Shīʿa Imams ﷺ, despite the fact that he was from Iraq.

Muḥammad ibn Walīd states, "One day I had gone to the Baqīʿ cemetery in order to make pilgrimage to the graves of the Purified Imams ﷺ and to those of their great followers. At the end of my pilgrimage, I went to the grave of Yūnus ibn Yaʿqūb in order to recite the Sūra al-Fātiha of the Quran for him. At this time, the cemetery guard came up to me and asked, "Who is this man whom Imam Riḍā ﷺ instructed me to pour water once a day on his tombstone for forty days?"

7. The Imam and his Relations with the Authorities

Imam Mūsā ibn Jaʿfar was four years old when the oppressive Umayyad dynasty imploded. The policy of the Umayyads which showed favoritism toward the Arabs, their policy of suppression through brute force, and the anti-Iranian bias of the Umayyads caused the general masses, and particularly the Iranian masses who thirsted for the just rule of true Islam, to agitate and revolt against them. In the midst of all this, the political operatives and statesmen of the day took advantage of the people's proclivities and desires for a government that was based on the model that Imam Ali ﷺ provided in his five years' reign as caliph; and this was particularly the case among the Iranian populace whose love of the Ālids and of the People of the House of the Prophet ﷺ was particularly strong. These disingenuous statesmen deposed the Umayyads with the help of Abū-Muslim of Khorāsān in the name of establishing a just and equitable order, but instead of handing the reins of state to Imam Jaʿfar as-Ṣādiq ﷺ,

they positioned Abul-Abbās as-Saffāh the Abbāsid pretender on the throne of the caliphate and in fact on the throne of a hereditary kingship.

The leaders of the anti-Umayyad revolt did a grave injustice to the cause of Islam and the Muslims by their duplicitous revolution, in so far as they pretended to rise up against the Umayyads in favor of the cause of the Ālids, whereas in fact they were agitating and conspiring in favor of the cause of the Abbāsid, thus preventing the caliphate from returning to its rightful center.

Abū-Salma and Abū-Muslim of Khorāsān initially called the people to the Ālids, but from the very beginning, they were planning to bring about the oppressive kingship and tyrannical rule of the Abbāsid dynasty; and this is why Imam Ja'far as-Sādiq ﷺ, in a display of his deep political insights, did not believe their words or lend them his support. Because he knew that they had not risen up in revolt against the Umayyads in favor of his cause but had something entirely different in mind.

Thus, another usurping and oppressive dynasty came to power in the year 132 AH as claimants to the caliphate and the legitimate succession to the Prophet ﷺ, and this dynasty was no better than the Umayyads in its wanton despotism, hypocrisy, and its trampling under foot of every precept and tenet of the religion which they claimed to uphold; and in certain respects, the Abbāsids far surpassed the Umayyads in their dastardly deeds. And what is worse, while the Umayyads' oppressive reign lasted ninety years, the Abbāsids protracted their reign of repression and domination with their policy of duplicity and deception until the collapse of Baghdad in the year 656 AH at the hands of the Mongol hordes, that is, for a grueling 524 years.

During his lifetime, the Seventh Imam ﷺ was witness to the full range of inequities, suppression, and political pressures which the ruling authorities could muster, from the short caliphate of the Umayyad Marwān to the autocratic reigns of Saffāh, Mansūr al-Dawāniqī, Mahdī, Hādī and Hārūn ar-Rashīd.

The mere breath of these satanic despots would have sufficed to cast a murky patina on the pure and crystalline mirror of the Imam's spirit and to make him grief-stricken, let alone all of the nefarious damage which each and every one of them – from Marwān and Mansūr to Hārūn ar-Rashīd – inflicted on the body and spirit of that precious soul; and if there was any wickedness which they refrained from, it was only because of their inability to accomplish it, and not for a want of their trying.

Abul-Abbās as-Saffāh died in the year 136 AH and was succeeded by his brother Mansūr al-Dawāniqī. Mansūr founded the city of Baghdad as the capital of the Abbāsids and killed Abū-Muslim, and after the consolidation of his power was accomplished, he did not rest for a moment in his murderous rampage, imprisonment, and torture of the progeny of Ali ☙ or in his subsequent expropriation and pillage of their property. He martyred most of the great dignitaries of this august House, foremost among them being Imam Ja'far as-Sādiq ☙.

Mansūr al-Dawāniqī was a bloodthirsty and cunning murderer with a vicious combination of treachery, envy, miserliness, and avarice. His treachery with respect to Abū-Muslim who devoted his whole life in an ultimately successful effort to bring him to power, and who had ensured the consolidation of his power base, has become the stuff of legend in the annals of history.

At the time that Mansūr martyred the noble father of Imam Mūsā al-Kāẓim ☙, His Eminence was twenty years old, and was in conflict and contention with the oppressive reign of Mansūr until the age of thirty. He organized his followers in secret and saw to their needs. He protected the pure Islamic creed from the corrupting hands of distortion and falsification at the hands of unqualified "scholars" who had sold themselves to the interests of the Abbāsid court, and he taught the noble principles of the sacred canon of Islam to those who thirsted for its truths.

Mansūr died in the year 158 AH, and was succeeded by his son al-Mahdī, who continued his father's policies of chicanery and deception. With a few exceptions, al-Mahdī freed all of the political prisoners which he had inherited from his father, who were for the most part the partisans or *Shī'a* of Imam Kāżim ﷺ and returned to them the property which had been expropriated from them. But he kept a close eye on them and held them in suspicion and enmity.

In his duplicity and pretention at being a supporter of the Ālid line, he would even give large sums of money to poets who sang the praises of Ali ﷺ and the noblemen of his progeny. For example, he once gave Jabbār ibn Bard seventy thousand Dirhams, and Marwān ibn Abī-Hafs one hundred thousand Dirhams. He was a profligate spender of the public purse when it came to wining and dining and debauchery at the expense of the people. For example, he wasted fifty million Dirhams on the wedding ceremony of his son Hārūn – an unprecedented sum.

Imam Kāżim's ﷺ celebrity bloomed during al-Mahdī's reign and shone as brightly as a full moon against the full darkness of night, revealing in the firmaments what virtue, piety, and knowledge in leadership can and should be. The people would secretly turn to him in groups to quench their spiritual thirst from the wellspring of its original source.

Mahdī's agents and spies who roamed throughout all of the territories of Islam but who were especially present around Imam Kāżim ﷺ, reported everything back to him. And because Mahdī was insecure in his usurped caliphal office, he ordered Imam Kāżim ﷺ to be brought from Medina to Baghdad, where he was kept under lock and key.

Abū-Khālid az-Zubālaī reports, "In the course of carrying out this command, the agents who had gone to Medina to arrest Imam Kāżim ﷺ stopped by the town of Zubāla on the way back and entered my home. In a brief stolen moment away from the eyes of these agent, the Imam ﷺ told me to procure certain items for him. I was very distraught at his arrest and told him that I was concerned for his safety, now that he was being taken over to that savage.

He said, "I am not concerned about that. But you should await me at our appointment on such and such a time and place."

That nobleman went to Baghdad and I anxiously counted the days until the appointed time arrived. I hastened to the appointed place, my heart aflutter with anxiety, jumping at the smallest sound.

The sun started to set and its glow became ruddy as it disappeared past the horizon and into the darkness of night when I saw a wraith appear from afar. I wanted to fly towards it, but I feared that it might not be the Imam ﷺ and that I would give myself away.

I stayed put, and the Imam ﷺ finally approached. He was mounted on a mule. As soon as his precious and penetrating eyes fell upon me, he said, "Doubt not, O Abā-Khālid." He continued, "They will take me to Baghdad later, and at that time, I will no longer return."

Alas, it happened just as that nobleman predicted.

During this same journey whereby the Imam ﷺ was brought to Baghdad for his imprisonment, al-Mahdī saw Ali ibn Abī-Tālib ﷺ in a dream in which he recited the following verse from the Quran to him:

[47:22] Would ye then, if ye were given the command,
work corruption in the land and sever your ties of kinship?

Rabi', the caliph's chamberlain and adjutant, says, "Mahdī sent for me at midnight. I became very apprehensive and rushed toward him and saw that he kept on reciting this verse. He then told me, 'Go and fetch Mūsā ibn Ja'far ﷺ from prison and bring him to me.'"

"I went and brought the Imam ﷺ. Mahdī stood up and kissed his cheeks, sat him next to him and told him about his dream.'"

And at that very moment he ordered that the Imam ﷺ be taken back to Medina. Rabīʿ says, "Because I feared that some obstacle might arise, I prepared the provisions for the journey that very night, and put the nobleman on his way to Medina by the morning's first light.

In Medina, the Imam ﷺ continued the guidance of the people by expounding the teachings and the principles of the faith to the Shīʿa in defiance of the Abbāsid repression and did so until the caliph al-Mahdī died in the year 169 AH and was succeeded by his son al-Hādī.

Hādī was a tyrant like his father before him, but unlike his father, he did not put up a pretense of amity towards the House of the Prophet ﷺ, taking away in one sweep all of the accommodating measures which his father al-Mahdī had instituted in favor of the Ālids and their Shīʿa in a mock show of his solidarity with them.

Hādī also summoned Imam Mūsā Kāżim ﷺ to Baghdad and imprisoned him in his dungeon, but he died not long after that, and the Imam ﷺ was freed and returned to his home in Medina.

But the most shameful of Hādī's outrages was his waging of the heart-rending Battle of Fakh. At the beginning of the reign of the Abbāsids, Abdullāh, a grandson of Imam Hasan ﷺ, together with two of his sons, Muhammad (who was known as an-Nafs az-Zakīya (the Pure Soul)), and Ibrāhīm, rose up in insurrection against the Abbāsid caliphs. They hoped to wrest control of the state from the hands of the Abbāsids and take matters into their own hands. But they were defeated after a series of unsuccessful battles and put to death in a deplorable manner inside the Abbāsid dungeons.

On one hand, their deaths caused insurrectionary ripples among the supporters of the Ālids, who rose up against the Abbāsids; and on the other, it caused the Abbāsids to bring more repressive measures to bear against the Ālids, whom they feared more than ever as a result of this insurrection, decreasing their freedom of movement, increasing the monitoring of their activity and generally instituting any and all measures they deemed necessary in order to preclude the possibility of the occurrence of any further insurrection.

Husain ibn Ali was an Ālid based in Medina who had become wearied from the tyranny of the Abbāsid oppression. After having informed Imam Mūsā Kāżim ﷺ of his intentions, he rose up in resurrection against the caliph al-Hādī. [While documentary evidence to the effect is scant,] we can certainly imagine the Imam ﷺ predicting Husayn ibn Ali's defeat and advising him against his fateful decision.

Nonetheless, Husayn ibn Ali left Medina for Mecca with a group of about 300 men in arms. Hādī's army surrounded them in an area known as Fakh and martyred him and all of his men. They then repeated what the Umayyads had done in the plain of Karbalā; that is, they severed their heads from their bodies and took them to Medina, where they put them on display in a gathering where a group of Ālids including Imam Mūsā ﷺ was present. No one said a word except Imam Mūsā ﷺ who, having seen the head of the leader of the insurrection, said, "Verily, we belong to God, and verily, we shall return to Him. I swear [upon my oath] to Allāh! He was martyred despite the fact that he was a righteous Muslim. He fasted often and spent many of his nights in worship and devotion to God and was one who regularly enjoined the doing of that which is right and forbade the doing of that which is wrong. Within the ranks of his family, he was peerless."

In addition to his dark political personality, the caliph Hādī's personal qualities left much to be desired. He was a drunkard and a degenerate debauchee. On one occasion he gave a camel's load of the public purse's gold and silver coins to the poet Yūsuf Sayfal simply because he recited a few melodious verses of poetry.

Ibn Dab an-Nāmī reports, "I once [had occasion to] call upon al-Hādī. His eyes were bloodshot from drink and lack of sleep. He asked me to relate a tale about wine. I did so in verse. He wrote the verses down and gave me forty thousand Dirhams.

Ishāq al-Muwassilī, the famous Arab musician, says, "If Hādī had survived, we would have raised the walls of our houses with [bricks of] gold."

Hādī died unexpectedly in the year 170 AH, which was at a time when he had decided to murder Imam Kāżim ﷺ, along with his brother Hārūn, and his mother. He was succeeded by Hārūn ar-Rashīd, who became the absolutist dictator of all of the territories of Islam.

Imam Kāżim ﷺ was forty-two at this time.

The reign of Hārūn ar-Rashīd was the era of the peak of the autocratic power of the Abbāsids. At the end of the pledge of allegiance ceremony, Hārūn ar-Rashīd appointed the Iranian statesman Yahyā the Barmakid as his prime minister and granted him absolute authority in ministering to the affairs of state, including the power to appoint and to dismiss anyone from any position as he pleased. As a symbolic gesture to seal this deputation, he gave him his signet ring, which was something that was done in accordance with the customs which were prevalent at the time; after which he busied himself with wine-drinking and the pillage of the public treasury with large expenditures on the purchase of gems and fine jewels, and on debauchery and licentiousness more generally.

The annual income of the public treasury at that time, when a two- to four-year old sheep was sold for one Dirham, was five hundred million, two hundred and forty thousand Dirhams. Hārūn began to spend freely of this immense wealth. He gave a million Dirhams to a poet by the name of Ashja' un account of a panegyric which he composed in his honor. To the poet Abul-'Atāhīya and the musician Ibrāhīm al-Muwassilī he gave a hundred thousand Dirhams each, simply for composing a few lines of verse and putting them to music, respectively.

There was a large contingent of female singers and performers gathered in Hārūn's palace, where all sorts of musical instruments were available. He had an exorbitant liking for jewelry. Once he paid one hundred thousand Dirhams for the purchase of a ring. The daily expense of his kitchen was ten thousand Dirhams, and it is said that at times up to thirty different stripes of food were prepared for a single meal.

One day Hārūn desired to have camel-meat for his dinner. When the meal was served, Ja'far Barmakid asked him, "Does the caliph know the cost of the meal that has been brought to him?"

"Three Dirhams."

"No, by God! It has cost four thousand Dirhams so far, because for a long time a camel has been slaughtered daily so that camel-meat would be at the ready in the event that the caliph desires to have it!"

Hārūn gambled and drank wine. Yet these things notwithstanding, he carried on a pretense of being a Muslim in order to fool the ignorant and uninformed masses of people. He would make the Hajj pilgrimage, and at times would ask preachers to preach to him and would even break out in crocodile tears!

Hārūn was extremely irritated at what he perceived to be the recalcitrance of the Members of the Household of the Prophet ﷺ (or the Ahl al-Bayt ﷺ) relative to the demands of the Abbāsid regime. He thus looked to take advantage of any opportunity which availed itself to crack down on them or to try to abase and demean them.

He would pay exorbitant sums to poets and eulogists who had sold themselves to his court for them to lampoon and parody the Ahl al-Bayt ﷺ. For example, in the case of the poet Mansūr an-Nimrī, who had composed an ode disparaging and denigrating the Ālids, he ordered that he be taken to the treasury vault and allowed to take whatever he wanted from it.

He exiled all of the Ālid residents of Baghdad to Medīna and killed countless numbers of them and their supporters. He was even unhappy about the fact of the general population's love of the grave of the Lord of the Martyrs, Imam Husayn ﷺ, which had become a shrine to which pilgrimage was made. He thus ordered the shrine and the dwellings which had sprung up in its environs to be levelled to the ground, and to cut down the Cedar tree which had grown over his tomb. Prior to this, the

Apostle of God ﷺ had repeated three times: "May God ﷻ curse the one who cuts down the Cedar tree."

There is no doubt that His Eminence Imam Mūsā Kāẓim ؑ could never agree [to cooperate] with such an unjust and despotic regime. Rather, he was continually in touch with his followers and partisans (*shī'a*) with whom he maintained both outward and secret contact in order to determine what their respective positions should be relative to the oppressive regime, and in order to secure as much as was possible under the current circumstances, the survival of the teachings and practice of the authentic Islam of his forefather, the Most Noble Apostle of Islam.

The Imam ؑ told Safwān ibn Mehrān, who was one of his companions, "You are righteous in every respect save that you rent your camels to Hārūn."

Safwān ibn Mehrān said, "I rent them for the purposes of the Hajj pilgrimage, and I do not accompany them on the journey."

But the Imam ؑ replied, "Do you then, on this account, at a minimum not inwardly hold out the hope that Hārūn should return safely from his journey, so that your camels are not lost and your rent gets paid?"

He said, "Yes, this is true."

And the Imam ؑ concluded, "Anyone who desires the sustenance and longevity of the life of a tyrant will be counted among their numbers [on the Day of Judgement]."

While it is true that His Eminence the Imam ؑ at times allowed some of his followers to maintain their contacts and employment with the Abbāsid court, this is because he evaluated these cases on an individual basis and deemed such contact and employment to be politically expedient and in the greater interest of the community of faith. He would appoint persons to such positions whose presence in the tyrannical regime he knew would be necessary and beneficial to the Shī'a cause, and whose presence in the court would act to inform the Ālids of any of the conspiracies and plots against them that they happened to become aware of. A prominent example of this was when the minister Ali ibn Yaqtīn wanted to resign from the Abbāsid court, but was not allowed to do so by His Eminence Imam Mūsā Kāẓim ﷺ.

It so happened that one day during the time that Imam Mūsā Kāẓim ﷺ was held in the dungeons of the Abbāsids, the caliph sent his vizier Yaḥyā to him to convey the message from the caliph that if the Imam ﷺ were to ask for clemency, that a pardon would be granted and that he would be freed. But the Imam ﷺ was unwilling to make such a request. Even in the most trying of times, the Imam ﷺ maintained a courageous and heroically uncompromising position against Hārūn's illegitimate and anti-Islamic regime, because he knew that any kind of compromise with Hārūn was a step which would lead in the direction of the demise of Islam and of the community of those who had attained to faith in it.

One day, the Imam ﷺ wrote a letter to Hārūn from his prison cell; a letter in which his grandeur and fortitude of belief in the righteousness of his position and purpose can be seen: "A day does not pass in which I am subject to hardship unless it be a day that you are subject to peace and comfort; but remain [as you will] in wait for the time in which the both of us will be ushered to a day which has no end and in which the practitioners of villainy and criminality will be the losers..."

Hārūn kept the Imam ﷺ in prison for several years, not just because he envied his spiritual station and place of honor among the people, but even more so because he knew that as long as the Imam ﷺ was present in the social arena, he would not be able to uproot the tree of Islam and to plant in its stead the tree of ignorance, unbelief, and hypocrisy in the hearts and minds of the people.

Hārūn closely monitored and was informed of the continual contacts which the Imam's followers had with him by the vast network of spies and the secret intelligence apparatus which he had at his disposal. He knew that the Imam's courageous spirit would not countenance the least compromise, and that the quietist or apolitical posture of the Imam ﷺ was a measure of expedience adopted to ensure that the honor and long-term security of Islam is maintained. Hārūn therefore thought he would take the upper hand and stood with an unmitigated and shameless duplicity at the grave of the Prophet ﷺ. Ignoring his family's dynastic usurpation of the office of the imamate, his various and sundry crimes against the people, his own expropriating and stealing of the people's property and wealth and his turning the caliphate into a hereditary kingship of oppression by brute force... addressed the Prophet ﷺ and stated, "O Apostle of God, I apologize for the decision that I have made concerning your son Mūsā ibn Ja'far ﷺ. Deep inside, I do not desire to imprison him. But I do so because I fear that if I do not, a civil war will ensue and there will be bloodshed in your community!"

Hārūn then ordered his guards to arrest Imam Mūsā ibn Ja'far ﷺ, who was preoccupied with prayer and his ritual devotions at the side of the grave of the Prophet ﷺ, and to take him in secret to Basra and to keep him there under lock and key.

The Imam ﷺ spent one year in the prison of Īsā ibn Ja'far, who was the governor of Basra and Hārūn's kin. The excellences of Imam Mūsā ibn Ja'far's ﷺ many virtues had such a profound effect on Īsā ibn Ja'far that this hangman wrote to Hārūn: "Take him away from my ward, or else I will release him!"

And so Hārūn ordered that the Imam ﷺ be brought to Baghdad, where he was imprisoned under the watch of Faḍl ibn Rabī'. After that, he spent some time as Faḍl ibn Yaḥyā's prisoner. And because none of these three men were willing to bloody their hands with the pure blood of the Imam ﷺ, His Eminence was eventually transferred to the dungeon of Sindī ibn Shāhak.

The reason for these transfers was clear: none of these wardens were willing to be directly involved in the killing of the Imam ﷺ and to become aiders and abettors to Hārūn's terrible crime.

But the last of these hangmen, Sindī ibn Shāhak, carried out Hārūn's order and poisoned that precious man. Prior to murdering the Imam ﷺ, Hārūn gathered a group of famous dignitaries so that they would testify that the Imam ﷺ had not been subjected to ill treatment or been the victim of foul play and that he died a natural death in prison. His intention was to exonerate himself and the Abbāsid regime from the murder of that great Imam, and to avoid or at least to mitigate the likely insurgency which he feared would take place when news of the premature death of the leader of the Shī'a reached their ears.

However, the Imam's courage and intelligence nullified all of Hārūn's efforts, for as the witnesses who were to testify to the Imam's natural death came to see him, he managed to say, despite his having been severely poisoned, "They have poisoned me with nine poisoned dates. My body will turn green tomorrow and I will die on the following morning."

So it came to pass, and two days later, on the 25th of the month of Rajab in the year 183 AH, the heavens and the earth sat in mourning, in commiseration with the Shī'a faithful who had lost their righteous and legitimate leader.

8. A Sampling of the Words of the Imam

There are many precious words and gems of wisdom which have reached us from our great Imam, His Eminence Mūsā ibn Ja'far ﷺ, familiarity with which acts as a beacon for those who are on the true path of the Apostle of God ﷺ and the honorable program which he brought, with which one can transact one's life in a way that is pleasing to God, the Sublimely Exalted. We shall now take a small cup from the deep and limitless ocean of the wisdom of the Imam ﷺ:

- Humility is to act with others as you would have them act with you.
- The best way to gain proximity to God ﷻ after attaining knowledge of Him is worship, kindness to one's parents, and the abandonment of self-conceit and pride, and envy of others.
- Anyone who is duplicitous or deceptively hides a fault from another Muslim or deceives him or tricks him in another way is worthy of God's damnation.
- The worst of God's bondsmen is one who is two-faced and two-tongued; one who sings the praises of his brother in faith to his face, but talks ill of him when his back is turned; or one who becomes envious of a fellow Muslim when he happens to be the beneficiary of God's graces, but who refuses to lend a helping hand to his fellow Muslim who has fallen on hard times.
- Anyone who becomes enamored with [the glitter and the carnal pleasures of] the world, will forfeit the fear of [losing his interests and station in] the hereafter.
- The best actions are those which are moderate and which take the middle path.
- Protect your wealth by paying the poor due (or alms tax: *zakāt*).

Imam Muhammad ibn Ali al-Jawād

1. Prelude

There can be no doubt that the most astonishing story within the whole of creation is the story of man's vice-regency [of God] on Earth. And if we look with insight into this matter, man's superiority and dignity over the other creatures within creation is on account of this great bounty of God's having endowed man with the honor of being His vice-regent on Earth.[42] Almighty God ﷻ adorned mankind with the faculty of intellection and the ability to reason, and after testing him before the angels, entrusted him with the Trust of His vice-regency on Earth – A Trust the burden of responsibility of which the heavens, and the earth, and the mountains could not endure and therefore refused to take on.[43]

---

[42] It should be noted that not all humans, of course, are representatives of God ﷻ on Earth, but only those which have attained to perfection, i.e., the prophets and Imams (unto all of whom be God's peace).

[43] This is the Quranic verse that is being referenced: [33:72] *Verily, We did offer the trust [of reason and volition] to the heavens, and the earth, and the mountains: but they refused to bear it because they were afraid of it. Yet man took it up – for, verily, he has always been prone to be most wicked, most foolish.*

God ﷻ entrusted His Trust to the Chosen Ones, to those who were the pinnacles of knowledge and wisdom and who are the limitless ocean of faith and piety, whose minds are immune to error and to the commitment of any iniquity, whose hands have never been polluted by sin, and from whose mouths an unkind word was never uttered.

This pure and sacrosanct chain, from the Prophet ﷺ Adam ﷺ to the Seal of the Prophets, His Eminence the Prophet Muhammad ﷺ, and from the last Prophet ﷺ to the last *wasi*,[44] His Eminence the Mahdi[45] (may God ﷻ hasten the advent of his noble person), are the intermediaries between God ﷻ the Sublimely Exalted and His creatures and are the everlasting wellsprings of His Super-Abundance and Grace.

Anyone who discovers this spring and drinks his fill from it will end up in God's Heaven, will be numbered among the righteous and will attain to a felicity that is everlasting.

The Chosen Ones are the greatest of God's creatures and have acted as leaders for the rest of humanity. Because they were in possession of supernatural knowledge and because of their divinely inspired words and deeds, the lives of each of these Chosen Ones was unique in their respective ages and was accompanied with various wonders and miracles that were suited to different contexts and occasions.

His Eminence the prophet Noah ﷺ lived for almost a thousand years until Almighty God ﷻ unleashed the flood on his recalcitrant enemies. Almighty God ﷻ also sent down fire and brimstone from the heavens onto those who would not heed the warnings of the prophets Hūd ﷺ and Sālih ﷺ. The prophet Abraham ﷺ entered into a pyre, and at God's command the fire became cool to him, and it was as if he was in a garden. The prophet Moses's ﷺ staff turned into a serpent by God's command and

---

[44] See footnote #26

[45] The Mahdī ﷺ: the awaited universal savior of humanity whose advent is awaited by all Muslims and who is believed will appear at the end of time to establish a reign of justice on Earth.

chased Pharaoh's magicians. The prophet Solomon ﷺ commanded the winds and spoke to the birds. The prophet ﷺ Jesus ﷺ brought the dead back to life. The honorable Prophet ﷺ of Islam had all sorts of wonders and miracles [to establish the divine origin and legitimacy of his mission].

When the Prophet ﷺ was born, the Ka'ba, which was filled with stone and wooden statues worshiped as gods by idol-worshipers, trembled for two days causing all the idols to come crashing down. A fire which had not been put out for over a thousand years and which was held as sacred by the Zoroastrians in the Sāsānid court of the Persians was miraculously extinguished; and the palace of the Persian king at the Kasrā fortress trembled so strongly that cracks appeared in the stone structure causing fourteen of its huge columns to buckle and crash down.

The Prophet's ministry brought about huge changes in the world, ushering in a new era for humanity. This is how the story of man, God's vice-regent on Earth, became the most astonishing story in the history of the world, and how this great bounty of God's was accompanied with impossible wonders and marvels in each of its unique epiphanic iterations.

Among these many marvels and miracles is the fact that none of the prophets or Imams ﷺ were schooled or received an education under any human tutelage, but rather, drank their fill from the timeless fount of divine knowledge. For this reason, age did not play a role in the commissioning of the divinely-commissioned leaders of humanity, or in their ability to minister to their ministry. Rather, if it was God's will, these Chosen Ones could and would be commissioned at any age to their heavenly mission of prophethood or to the imamate and dispatched for the guidance of mankind. Thus, some of these Chosen Ones were commissioned to their respective divine missions in middle age or older, and some were commissioned to their exalted positions in their youth or even in their childhood years. We can thus conclude that if it is God's will, the age of the leaders and guides chosen by Him will not 'enter the equation', so to speak.

And this is why we see it affirmed in the Quran that the prophet John (*yahyā*) ﷺ was commissioned to his ministry in childhood and the prophet Jesus ﷺ was commissioned while he was still in his cradle. Almighty God ﷻ states in the Quran:

$$
\text{يَٰيَحْيَىٰ خُذِ ٱلْكِتَٰبَ بِقُوَّةٍ ۖ وَءَاتَيْنَٰهُ ٱلْحُكْمَ صَبِيًّا ﴿١٢﴾ وَحَنَانًا مِّن لَّدُنَّا وَزَكَوٰةً ۖ وَكَانَ تَقِيًّا ﴿١٣﴾}
$$

[19:12] [And when the son was born and grew up, he was told,] "O John ﷺ! Hold fast unto the divine writ with [all thy] strength!" – for We granted him wisdom while he was yet a little boy, [19:13] as well as, by Our grace, [the gift of] compassion and purity; and he was [always] a God-fearing man.

And concerning His Eminence the Christ ﷺ, God ﷻ states in the Quran:

$$
\text{فَأَتَتْ بِهِ قَوْمَهَا تَحْمِلُهُۥ ۖ قَالُوا۟ يَٰمَرْيَمُ لَقَدْ جِئْتِ شَيْـًٔا فَرِيًّا ﴿٢٧﴾ يَٰأُخْتَ هَٰرُونَ مَا كَانَ أَبُوكِ ٱمْرَأَ سَوْءٍ وَمَا كَانَتْ أُمُّكِ بَغِيًّا ﴿٢٨﴾ فَأَشَارَتْ إِلَيْهِ ۖ قَالُوا۟ كَيْفَ نُكَلِّمُ مَن كَانَ فِى ٱلْمَهْدِ صَبِيًّا ﴿٢٩﴾ قَالَ إِنِّى عَبْدُ ٱللَّهِ ءَاتَىٰنِىَ ٱلْكِتَٰبَ وَجَعَلَنِى نَبِيًّا ﴿٣٠﴾ وَجَعَلَنِى مُبَارَكًا أَيْنَ مَا كُنتُ وَأَوْصَٰنِى بِٱلصَّلَوٰةِ وَٱلزَّكَوٰةِ مَا دُمْتُ حَيًّا ﴿٣١﴾ وَبَرًّۢا بِوَٰلِدَتِى وَلَمْ يَجْعَلْنِى جَبَّارًا شَقِيًّا ﴿٣٢﴾ وَٱلسَّلَٰمُ عَلَىَّ يَوْمَ وُلِدتُّ وَيَوْمَ أَمُوتُ وَيَوْمَ أُبْعَثُ حَيًّا ﴿٣٣﴾ ذَٰلِكَ عِيسَى ٱبْنُ مَرْيَمَ ۚ قَوْلَ ٱلْحَقِّ ٱلَّذِى فِيهِ يَمْتَرُونَ ﴿٣٤﴾}
$$

[19:27] And in time she returned to her people, carrying the child with her. They said: "O Mary ﷺ! Thou hast indeed done an amazing thing! [19:28] O sister of Aaron ﷺ! Thy father was not a wicked man, nor was thy mother a loose woman!" [19:29] Thereupon she pointed to him. They exclaimed: "How can we talk to one who [as yet] is a little boy in the cradle?" [19:30] [But] he said: "Behold, I am a servant of God ﷻ. He has vouchsafed unto me revelation and made me a Prophet ﷺ ... [19:33] "Hence, peace was upon me on the day when I was born, and [will be upon me] on the day of my death, and on the day when I shall be raised to life [again]!" [19:34] Such was, in the words of truth, Jesus ﷺ the son of Mary ﷺ, about whose nature they so deeply disagree.

Therefore, it can only be out of ignorance when some people discredit the possibility of some of our Immaculate Imams ﷺ attaining to the office of the imamate during their childhood years.

His Eminence Imam Abū-Ja'far Muhammad ibn Ali al-Jawād[46] ﷺ attained to the office of the imamate after the martyrdom of his father Imam Riḍā ﷺ at the age of eight or nine. He was designated as the imam and leader of the community of the faithful by way of the explicit designation of the Prophet ﷺ of God ﷻ, by way of the Imams ﷺ who followed in the wake of the Prophet ﷺ, and by his father before him, Imam Riḍā ﷺ; thus shouldering the burden of the imamate and of God's vice-regency on Earth. It so happened that the enemies of Islam and those who were ignorant of the truth tested him on numerous occasions, but his being endowed with knowledge that could only have been divinely inspired epiphanized in him in such an absolute and indubitable way that, in truth and in all fairness, one should cite the imamate of Imam Jawād ﷺ in his childhood as the [non-scriptural] affirmation and proof of the

---

[46] Pronounced Javād in Persian.

prophethoods of the Prophet ﷺ John (*yahyā*) ؑ and the Prophet ﷺ Jesus ؑ in their childhood, rather than the other way around.[47]

2. Birth

Forty some odd years had passed from the noble life of the eighth Imam, Imam Riḍā ؑ, but he was still without any descendants. This was a matter of concern for the Shīʿa because they believed, on the basis of hadīth[48] reports of the Prophet's and of the Imams ؑ that a son will be born to Imam Riḍā ؑ who will continue the line of the imamate[49] for the Muslims and will continue the perfection of the unfinished ministry of the Apostle of God ﷻ. For this reason, they anxiously awaited the day when God the Sublimely Exalted would grant a son to Imam Riḍā ؑ. This period of waiting was a trial for those of little faith and belief to fall victim to the devil's temptations and to fall by the wayside on the straight path. But those whose hearts and souls had been infused with faith in their Lord and Cherisher considered His promise of a son for their Imam to be definite and categorical and unimpeachable, and counted the days for the day in which the promised event would occur. Those who had become restless in their waiting would ask their Imam to pray to God ﷻ to grant him a son when they were honored to visit His Eminence ؑ, who in response would say, "God ﷻ will [indeed] give me a son who will be my heir (*wārith*) and who will be the Imam that succeeds me."

---

[47] This is especially the case as there exist numerous historical documentary evidence from Sunni sources for the former, while the proof for the latter is limited to being scriptural in nature.
[48] *Hadīth*: See footnote #5
[49] Religio-political leadership of the community.

Eventually on the 10th day of the month of Rajab in the year 195 AH[50], the divine promise was fulfilled and Imam Muhammad ibn Ali ﷺ opened his eyes onto the world. His *kunya* or patronymic is Abū-Jaʿfar and he is known as Imam al-Jawād and as at-Taqī.

The birth of that brilliant light was a happy day for the Shīʿa; it was a faith-affirming day for them and confirmed them in their beliefs because it dispelled any lingering doubts which had found their way into the hearts of some of the faithful due to the tardiness of the birth.

Imam Jawād's ﷺ mother was called Sabīka. Imam Riḍā ﷺ named her Khīzarān. The lineage of this pious and honorable woman went back to Māria the Copt, who was one of the wives of the Prophet ﷺ and who gave birth to a son for the Prophet ﷺ named Abraham. Imam Jawād's ﷺ mother was one of the most virtuous women of her era. The Prophet ﷺ had referred to her as "the best of women" in a hadīth report. Many years prior to her entering into the House of Imam Riḍā ﷺ in wedlock, Imam Mūsā Kāẓim ﷺ had spoken of some of her characteristics and had sent his regards to her by way of Yazīd ibn Salīt, one of his companions.

Hakīma, one of Imam Riḍā's ﷺ sisters, says, "At the time of the birth of Imam Muhammad at-Taqī ﷺ, my brother asked me to stay with Khīzarān. On the third day after his birth, the newborn child opened his eyes heavenward, looked to the left and to the right, and said, 'I bear witness that there is no deity except Allāh, and I bear witness that Muhammad is His messenger.'"[51]

I became alarmed at [the utterance of] these words and went to my brother and told him what I had seen. He said, "The marvels which

---

[50] i.e. of the lunar Hijra calendar (the date of the migration of the Prophet and his Meccan followers from Mecca to Medina, which is the beginning of the Islamic calendar and which occurred in the year 622 of the Christian era).

[51] This account and all of the accounts which follow are sourced from the most reputable and reliable Shīʿa sources, which have been referred to (with the sources cited) in the original Persian.

you will see from him shall be more unusual than what you have seen so far."

Abū-Yaḥyā as-Sanʿāī reports, "I was at the service of Imam Riḍā ﷺ when they brought Imam Jawād ﷺ to him, who was only a small child at that time. The Imam ﷺ said, 'This is a newborn whose bounty to the Shīʿa community is unprecedented.'"

Perhaps this stipulation of Imam Riḍā's ﷺ is on account of the reason which we alluded to before, because Imām Jawād's ﷺ birth dispelled the community's anxiety about Imam Riḍā ﷺ not having had any offspring to succeed him so that his issue saved their faith from the pollution of skepticism and doubt.

Nawflī reports: When Imam Riḍā ﷺ was journeying to Khorāsān I asked His Eminence ﷺ, "Do you not have any business with me today?" He said, "It is a duty that is incumbent upon you to follow [and obey] my son Muhammad ﷺ. I shall be going on a journey that is without return."

Muhammad ibn Abī-Abbād, Imam Riḍā's ﷺ scribe, reports: That nobleman (Imam Riḍā ﷺ) used to refer to his son by his patronymic as a sign of respect, and when a letter arrived from Imam Jawād ﷺ, he would say, "Abū-Jaʿfar has written me..." And whenever Imam Riḍā ﷺ would direct me to write a letter to Abū-Jaʿfar Imām Jawād ﷺ, he would address him in terms [appropriate to men] of honor and greatness, and the letters which we received from Imam Muhammad at-Taqī [Imam Jawād ﷺ] were written with a style that was at the peak of eloquence and expressive beauty.

Muhammad ibn Abī-Abbād also reports: I heard Imam Riḍā ﷺ state, "After me, Abū-Jaʿfar [Imam Jawād ﷺ] shall be my *waṣī*[52] and successor from among my House."

Muʿammar ibn Khallād reports: While remembering something, Imam Riḍā ﷺ stated, "What need do you have of hearing this matter from

---

[52] Inheritor, legatee, executor and successor. See footnote #26

me? It is Abū-Jaʿfar [Imam Jawād ﷺ] whom I have designated as my successor. We are a family whose sons inherit our knowledge completely."

What is meant here is that the entirety of the sacred knowledge and the spiritual and worldly stations of the imamate are inherited from the previous Imam ﷺ to the next one, and this transference of special knowledge is specific to the Imams ﷺ and does not apply to their other children.

Khayrānī reports that his father related: I was with the Imam ﷺ in Khorāsān. Someone asked His Eminence ﷺ, "Who should we refer to if something befalls you?"

The Imam ﷺ said, "To my son Abū-Jaʿfar."

It seems that the questioner did not consider the age of Imam Jawād ﷺ to be sufficient and questioned how a child could shoulder the responsibilities of the office of the imamate. Imam Riḍā ﷺ who had sensed the questioner's doubt asked, "God the Sublimely Exalted commissioned Jesus ﷺ to prophethood and gave him a ministry when his age was less than Abū-Jaʿfar's current age."

Abdullāh ibn Jaʿfar reports: We were honored to be at the service of Imam Riḍā ﷺ together with Safwān ibn Yaḥyā. At that time, Imam Jawād ﷺ was three years old and was present [with us]. We asked Imam Riḍā ﷺ, "Who is your successor in the event that something should happen to you?"

Imam Riḍā ﷺ pointed to Abū-Jaʿfar ﷺ and said, "This son of mine."

We persisted, "With him being so young?"

The Imam ﷺ replied, "Yes, [even] with him being so young. Almighty God ﷻ appointed [the prophet] Jesus ﷺ as his *hujjat*[53], even though he was not yet three years of age."

---

[53] *Hujjat*: see footnotes #6 and #7 for an explanation of this key word.

3. Imam Jawād's ﷺ Imamate

The investiture to the institution and office of the imamate, like that of the institution of prophethood, is a grace of God ﷻ the Sublimely Exalted, who bestows it on the righteous and deserving servants of His choosing. The age of such servants is not a factor in His decisions in this regard. Perhaps those who consider the prophethood and/ or the imamate of divine agents who are in their childhood to be highly improbable or impossible have equated and are therefore confusing these categories with ordinary offices and with functions which are carried out by ordinary people. Whereas the stations of prophethood and the imamate are offices whose functions are fulfilled by people who are chosen by the will of God ﷻ Who grants such offices to those of His servants who have been deemed worthy and deserving of receiving His infinite knowledge and wisdom. Thus, there is no question of any problem arising logically if such an office is granted by God ﷻ to a minor for whatever reason He might deem to be expedient; for reasons which only He is privy to and which certainly might include a divine desire to test humanity and to separate the true believers from the ordinary believers, unbelievers and hypocrites.

The ninth Imam, Imam Jawād ﷺ, attained to the exalted station of the imamate when he was eight or nine years of age (the dating of the reports varies). Muʻallā ibn Muhammad reports: "I saw Imam Jawād ﷺ after the passing of Imam Riḍā ﷺ, and paid careful attention to his physical stature so that I could report what I had seen accurately to the Shīʻa community. As I was making my observations, His Eminence sat down and said, "O Muʻallā, Almighty God ﷻ has provided a reason for the imamate just as He has done for prophethood, and has stated that He appointed [the prophet] John (*Yahyā*) ﷺ to [the station of] prophethood when he was a child."

Muhammad ibn Hasan ibn ʻAmmār reports: When I was in Medina for two years, I used to visit with Ali ibn Jaʻfar (Imam Riḍā's ﷺ uncle), and he would relate to me hadith reports which he had heard from his father Imam Mūsā Kāẓim ﷺ. One day I was seated next to him in the

Mosque of the Prophet ﷺ when Imam Jawād ؏ entered. Ali ibn Ja'far jumped to his feet and, leaving his sandals and robe behind, leapt to kiss his hand and to bow down before him and honor him.

The Imam ؏ said to him, "Be seated, O Uncle. May God ﷻ have mercy on you."

Ali ibn Ja'far said, "How can I be seated, my lord, when you are standing?"

When Ali ibn Ja'far returned to his seat, his companions reproached him, saying, "Why do you show him such respect whereas you are his father's uncle!"

Ali ibn Ja'far became irritated and said, "Be silent! Do you want me to deny the excellences of his virtues while Almighty God ﷻ has not seen fit to appoint this white-beard – and he drew his hand over his face – to the imamate, whereas He has seen this youth to be worthy and appointed him to this station? I seek refuge with God ﷻ from [the evil of] that which you say. I am His servant."

Umar ibn Faraj reports: We were standing on the bank of the Tigris with Imam Jawād ؏. I told him, "Your partisans (*Shī'a*) claim that you know the weight of the water of the Tigris River"

Imam Jawād ؏ said, "Is Almighty God ﷻ capable of granting this knowledge to a fly?"

I said, "Certainly, God ﷻ is capable of doing so."

The Imam ؏ replied, "I am dearer to God ﷻ than a fly and dearer to Him than most of His creatures."

It is related from Ali ibn Hassān al-Wāsitī who reports: Because Imam Jawād ؏ was only a child, I took a few toys with me, thinking that I would give them to him as a gift. I entered into the presence of that nobleman. People were putting their questions to him, and he was responding to their questions in turn. When all of their questions had been answered, the Imam ؏ got up and left. I too left and followed him and obtained permission for a meeting with him through his adjutant. When I entered [into his chambers], I offered him my salaams. His Eminence ؏

returned my greetings but seemed troubled; nor did he give me leave to sit down. I went forward and placed the toys in front of him. His Eminence ﷺ looked at me in anger and pushed the toys aside and said, "Almighty God ﷻ has not created me to play with such playthings. What business do I have with toys?!" I gathered up the toys and begged His Eminence's ﷺ forgiveness. His Eminence accepted my apology and forgave me, and I made my exit.

4. The Imam and his Relationship with the People

After the heart-rending martyrdom of Imam Riḍā ﷺ, his honorable son Imam Muhammad at-Taqī (Imam Jawād ﷺ) took on the perilous responsibilities and heavy burden of the office of the imamate by the command of God ﷻ in order to guide the Shī'a to the right path in a tumultuous era where false memes concerning their beliefs were put out by the enemies of the religion and [whose nefarious affects] rained down on the Shī'a who were its main victims. The Imam ﷺ lived out his short but fruitful life in the city of his noble ancestor the great Prophet ﷺ of Islam, and in Baghdād, which was the newly-founded capital of the usurping and tyrannical Abbāsid dynasty. The Imam ﷺ used every possible opportunity for disabusing the true believers (the Shī'a) and the Muslims more generally of errors in their thinking. He instructed them in the teachings of the religion, proving and establishing the legitimacy of his claim to the imamate or to the political and religious leadership of the community, which leadership was nothing more or less than the continuation of the movement and ministry of the Apostle of God ﷻ. By applying his divinely-inspired knowledge, Imam Jawād ﷺ convinced and humbled his adversaries and polished away the patina of doubt that existed in the minds of the skeptics and led them to the straight path whose attributes and direction he explicated.

During the length of his luminous life, the Imam ﷺ had numerous encounters with the scholars and thinkers of his era, as well as with the people of other faiths and their elders and representatives, who would come to see him from near and far. He would take these opportunities to guide those who were searching for truth to the right path by expounding on the truths of the message of Islam. We shall refer to a sampling of such encounters in what follows.

After the Eighth Imam, Imam Riḍā ﷺ, was martyred, eighty people from among the scholars and magisters (*fuqahā*; doctors of sacred jurisprudence) of Baghdad and other cities gathered in a large caravan to head to Mecca in order to make the Hajj pilgrimage. On their way, they stopped by Madina and met with Imam Muhammad at-Taqī al-Jawād ﷺ. They stayed in Imam Jaʿfar as-Ṣādiq's house ﷺ, which was empty. The Imam ﷺ, who was still quite young, joined their assembly and was introduced to everyone by a man named Muwaffaq. Everyone arose and offered their salaams, and the Imam ﷺ in turn offered his salaams to the visitors. Once the formalities were out of the way, questions were put to the Imam ﷺ, who responded to all of them correctly, displaying a very high level of expertise. Everyone was very pleased to see the obvious signs [of one worthy of the office] of the imamate in him, and they attained to certainty in [the rightfulness of] his [claim to the office of the] imamate; they became very happy and praised His Eminence ﷺ and supplicated [God ﷺ for his continued health and leadership].

One of those people who went by the name of Isaac (*Isḥāq*) reports: I too wrote ten questions down to ask His Eminence ﷺ and promised myself that if His Eminence ﷺ provided the correct answers to these ten questions, that I would ask him to supplicate God ﷺ to make the baby which my pregnant wife was carrying to be a boy. The meeting went on for hours; people kept asking questions and the Imam ﷺ kept answering them. It was getting late so I got up to leave, intending to come back the next day and to give His Eminence ﷺ the letter then. As soon as the Imam ﷺ saw me, he said, "O Isaac! Almighty God ﷻ has fulfilled my prayers. Name your son Ahmad."

I became incredibly happy at what the Imam ﷺ had said, and told him, "Praise be to Allāh! There is no doubt that this man is God's proof (*hujjat*)[54]."

Isaac returned to his own country, and God ﷻ granted him a son whom he named Ahmad.

Umrān ibn Muhammad al-Ash'arī reports: I had the honor of being at the service of Imam Jawād ﷺ. After taking care of some business, I told the Imam ﷺ, "Umm al-Hasan sends her salaams to you and asked that you do her the favor of giving her one of your robes so that it can act as her burial shroud."

The Imam ﷺ said, "She is no longer in need of this."

Without knowing exactly what he meant by this, I took my leave and made my way back to my township [sometime later]. When I got there, I heard that Umm al-Hasan had passed away thirteen or fourteen days before the time that I had visited the Imam ﷺ.

Ahmad ibn Hadīd reports: We were with a group of Shī'a and other Muslims making our way to Mecca for the Hajj pilgrimage. Some bandits stopped us and robbed us of our belongings. When we got to Medina, I came across Imam Jawād ﷺ in an alley and went to his house where I told the Imam ﷺ what had befallen us. He ordered his aids to bring some

---

[54] *Hujjat*: see footnotes #6 and #7 for an explanation of this key word.

money and clothing for me and told me to divide the money up between my fellow wayfarers to match the amount that the bandits had robbed from each person. I went back and divvied up the money between everyone. The money that the Imam ﷺ had given me was exactly the amount which the bandits had robbed us of, not a single coin more or less.

Muhammad ibn Sahl al-Qummi reports: It had been a while since I had settled in Mecca. I went to Medina and entered Imam Jawād's ﷺ house with the intention of asking His Eminence ﷺ to grant me one of his robes, but the opportunity did not avail itself for me to put my request to him while I was still in Medina. I thought that I would put my request to him in writing in a letter. I wrote the letter, but before dispatching it, I resolved to go to the Mosque of the Prophet ﷺ and offer two cycles of ritual devotions and to supplicate God ﷻ one hundred times to tell me what was in my best interest: if I were inspired to send the letter, I would do so, and if not, I would tear it up. I did so and I was inspired not to dispatch the letter. I therefore tore the letter up and headed for the House of God ﷻ.[55] On my way there I saw someone who had a kerchief in hand and was looking for me among the people of my caravan. I went to him and introduced myself to him. He gave me the kerchief and told me, "Your lord Imam Jawād ﷺ has sent this for you."

I opened the kerchief to find that the Imam ﷺ had sent me one of his robes.

---

[55] The Ka'ba, or the Great Mosque.

Ma'mūn, the wily Abbāsid caliph, invited Imam Jawād ﷺ to his capital Baghdad and married one of his daughters to him in accordance with his prearranged plans. Imam Jawād ﷺ stayed in Baghdad for a short while, after which he returned to Medina.

When he was leaving Baghdad, a group of people escorted the Imam ﷺ to outside the city limits in order to bid him farewell.

At sunset, they reached a village in which there was an old mosque, and the Imam ﷺ went to the mosque in order to offer his evening ritual devotions. In the mosque's courtyard there was a lote[56] (*sedr*) tree which had not borne any fruit up to that time. His Eminence ﷺ asked for some water in order to make his ritual ablutions, and made his ablutions at the foot of that tree, after which he led the congregational devotions, after which he offered four additional (supererogatory, *nāfila*) cycles of the ritual devotions and closed his offerings with a prostration of thanksgiving. He then bid everyone farewell and left [for Madina].

The following day the tree gave a healthy weight of fruit. The people were astonished at this occurrence, and the event only added to their certainty about [the legitimacy of] the Imam's ﷺ [claim to the office of the] imamate. Shaykh Mufīd, one of the very great scholars of Shī'a Islam, relates that close to two hundred years later, he personally saw that tree and ate of its fruit.

Umīyat ibn Ali reports: When Imam Riḍā ﷺ was in Khorāsān, I lived in Medina and had dealings with Imam Jawād's ﷺ house. It was usual that when I went to visit Imam Jawād ﷺ, his household would come [to the exterior quarters of the house reserved for entertaining visitors; outside the inner sanctuary of the house where the womenfolk could go about without

---

[56] A species of plum.

having to veil themselves] and offer their salaams. One day His Eminence told his maidservant to tell the womenfolk to prepare themselves for a mourning ceremony. The next day the Imam ﷺ again told his womenfolk to enter into mourning. When they asked him who they should be mourning for, he said, "For the best person on the face of the earth."

Sometime later, the news of the martyrdom of Imam Riḍā ﷺ reached Medina; and it became evident that Imam Riḍā ﷺ had been martyred at the order of the caliph Ma'mūn the same day that Imam Jawād ﷺ had ordered his House into mourning.

Yaḥyā ibn Aktham, the Chief Justice of the Abbāsid caliph, was a wicked and morally corrupt debauchee. He was a diehard enemy of the House of the Prophet ﷺ. But this fact notwithstanding, he had admitted that one day he had seen Imam Jawād ﷺ next to the tomb of the Prophet ﷺ of God ﷻ and entered into a discussion and a debate with him concerning various matters. "Imam Jawād ﷺ answered all of my questions and objections, at the end of which I said, I swear [upon my oath] to Allāh! I want to ask you something, but I am ashamed to do so."

The Imam ﷺ replied, "I will answer your question without your having to utter it with your tongue. You want to ask who the Imam is."

I said, "By Allāh, that was indeed my question!"

He said, "I am the Imam."

And so I asked, "Do you have any evidence to prove such a claim?"

At that instance the staff that was in the hands of His Eminence ﷺ began to speak and said, "He is my lord and master (*mawlā*), the Imam of this era, and God's proof (*ḥujjat*) [to mankind]."

The Unknown Imams

Ali ibn Jarīr reports: I was at the service of Imam Jawād ﷺ. A sheep had been lost from among the sheep of the Imam's ﷺ house. They had dragged one on the Imam's ﷺ neighbors to the Imam's presence, accusing him of theft. His Eminence ﷺ said, "Woe unto you! Set him free! He has not stolen the sheep. It is presently in such and such a house; go and fetch it!"

The people went to the house which the Imam ﷺ had identified and found the sheep and charged the owner of the house with theft and arrested him and roughed him up and tore his clothing, even though the fellow swore that he had not stolen the sheep.

They took him to the Imam ﷺ, who reproached them [again], saying, "Woe unto you! You have done him a grave injustice. The sheep entered his house on his own accord and the man was not aware of the sheep's presence.

After enlightening everyone, the Imam ﷺ apologized on the people's behalf and gave him some money to pay for the damage to his clothes.

Ali ibn Khālid reports: When I was in Sāmarrā I heard that they had brought a man from Greater Syria (*ash-shām*) in chains and leg-irons and imprisoned him here, his charge being that he had claim to be a prophet.

In order to find out what the story was, I went to the prison and made nice with the prisoner guards until they allowed me to go to the prisoner. When I met the prisoner, I found him to be an intelligent and educated man. I asked him, "What is the real story behind your arrest?"

He said, "In Syria there is a place called Ra's al-Husain, which is where they had displayed the sanctified head of His Eminence Imam Husain ﷺ [after they massacred him at Karbalā]. I had gone there and was offering my ritual devotions. One night, when I was occupied with the ritual invocation (*dhikr*) of our Lord, I suddenly saw someone [standing] in front of me. The man told me to arise. I got up and without saying a word began to follow him. After having travelled a few steps, I found myself in the Mosque of Kūfa [in southern Iraq]. The stranger asked, "Do you recognize this mosque?"

I said, "Yes, this is the Kūfa [Congregational] Mosque."

I offered my ritual devotions there together with that great man after which we exited the mosque. We started walking again, and after a little while I saw that we were in the Mosque of the Prophet ﷺ in Medina. We made pilgrimage to the sacred shrine of His Eminence the Prophet ﷺ, offered our ritual devotions in the mosque, and then left. We walked a little distance more, after which I suddenly found myself to be in Mecca, in the House of God ﷻ. We made the ritual circumambulations of the Ka'ba and left. We walked a little distance more, after which I suddenly found myself to be back in Ra's al-Husain, after which that great man disappeared from my sight.

I was astonished at what I had seen and did not disclose my secret to anyone until a year had passed. One night that same nobleman appeared to me again and told me to follow him.

I got up and followed him and we repeated the same pattern of events that had happened the previous year. But this time, I beseeched him to identify himself before he parted. When he saw how insistent I was, he introduced himself, saying, "I am Muhammad ibn Ali ibn Mūsā ibn Ja'far ibn Muhammad ibn Ali ibn al-Husayn ibn Ali ibn Abī-Tālib ؑ."

I related this tale to a number of my friends. Before long the news of my adventure had made all the rounds and had gotten to the notice of Muhammad ibn Abdul-Mālik az-Zayyāt, the Abbāsid caliph Mu'tasim's vizier. He ordered that I be arrested and be brought here in chains and shackles, and that I be kept under lock and key under the false allegation that I have claimed to be a prophet.

Ali ibn Khālid says, "I asked him if he would like me to write a letter informing Abdul-Mālik az-Zayyāt of the truth of the matter, so that if he is not aware of it, he can be properly informed and order your release?"

He said that he had no objection, so I wrote the whole story to Abdul-Mālik az-Zayyāt. The vizier replied on the reverse of my scroll as follows: "Tell him to ask the person who has taken him from Syria to Kūfa and Madīna and Mecca and back again to let him out of prison."

I was saddened by the vizier's reply. I went to the prison on the following morning to tell the man the bad news and to advise him to be patient. When I got here, I found the prison guards to be in a state of agitation and the prisoners to be restless and astounded. When I asked what was going on I was told that the man who claimed to be a Prophet ﷺ escaped from prison last night and no one knows how he did it; whether he was swallowed up by the earth or took flight to the heavens; and that no matter where they searched, they found no trace of the man.

Abū-Salt al-Herāwi was a companion and close friend of Imam Riḍā's ﷺ. After the martyrdom of the Eighth Imam of the Shīʿa, he was arrested and taken to prison under the orders of Maʾmūn, the wily Abbāsid caliph. He relates the following tale:

I was in prison for a year. It was a very difficult time for me and I was constantly miserable and dejected. I had stayed awake one night and was busy with my devotions and prayers in which I took intercessory recourse with the Most Noble Prophet ﷺ and his noble family, supplicating God ﷻ to free me for the sake of their dignity and honor. My supplications had not yet been completed when I saw that Imam Muhammad al-Jawād at-Taqī ﷺ was standing over me there in my prison cell. His Eminence said, "O Abū-Salt! Is your confinement ailing you?"

I said, "Yes, by Allāh!"

He said "Arise!"

That nobleman then placed his hands on my shackles and they immediately fell apart and I was freed. His Eminence ﷺ took my hand

and took me out of the prison with him. The guard saw me, but he dared not speak from the awe that His Eminence ﷺ inspired in him. When we had put some distance between us and the prison, His Eminence ﷺ said, "Go with God's peace; you will not see Ma'mūn after this, nor will he [or his henchmen] ever see you." And so it came to pass, as foretold by the Imam ﷺ.

It was a practice of Imam Jawād's ﷺ to teach his companions and the Shī'a community at large about the ways of asceticism, God-fearing piety, being content with one's lot in life, and the avoidance of the fool's gold of the world, by way of teaching stories from the Prophet ﷺ, the past Imams ﷺ, and their companions. For example, Abdul-Aḍīm al-Hasani, the great companion of His Eminence Imam Jawād ﷺ relates how the great nobleman told the story of a day when Abū-Dharr al-Ghaffārī was invited to Salmān the Persian's house. When the time for the meal arrived, Salmān spread a tablecloth [on the floormat] and placed what he had in the way of food on the spread. His food was dried bread, which he dipped in water and ate.

Abū-Dharr took a piece of bread and placed it in his mouth. It was not very appetizing as it had been made without any salt, and so he said, "What good bread. It would be improved with some salt."

Salmān said, "That's true."

He then got up and took the jug of water and left the house. Because he did not have any money, he left the water jug as a bond (or "in hawk", as they say) with the grocer, got some salt from him, and returned and placed the salt on their spread. His guest ate the bread with the salt provided, after which Abū-Dharr said, "Praise be to Allāh for giving us this level of contentedness."

Whereupon Salmān responded, "Yes, all praise is due to Allāh, but if there was [a sufficient degree of] contentment, the jug would not be in hawk to the grocer right now!"

After the martyrdom of Imam Riḍā ﷺ, Ma'mūn transferred his capital in the year 204 AH from Marv in Khorāsān to Baghdād. One of the reasons for this was his effort to reconcile his side of the family with the rest of the Abbāsids who were based in Baghdad [and who had sided with his brother Amīn in the fratricidal war that had erupted between them after the death of their father, Hārūn ar-Rashīd]. After settling down in Baghdad and quelling any unrest which remained within the Abbāsid clan, Ma'mūn decided to invite Imam Jawād ﷺ to Baghdad in order to try to appease the Shī'a and absolve himself of the murder of Imam Riḍā ﷺ of which he was rightly accused. A few days before he was to meet with the caliph, His Eminence ﷺ passed by a street in which there were children playing. It so happened that on that day, Ma'mūn left the palace to go hunting and passed by that same street. When the children saw the caliph and his entourage, they ran away in all directions, fleeing the caliph and leaving him to look at a street that was now empty except for the presence of the Imam ﷺ, who was nine years old at the time.

Ma'mūn was surprised at the fact that this one child had not moved from where he was standing. He therefore bade him to come forward and asked him, "The rest of the children fled, what caused you to stay put and not to have any fear of us?"

His Eminence ﷺ replied, "I stood because my path was not restricted so that I should have a need to widen it by my departure; nor did I have any sin on account of which I should fear anyone; and neither did I think badly of you, that you would question an innocent person without just cause."

Ma'mūn who had been taken aback by the eloquence of the youth's words said, "How well you speak. What is your name?"

"Muhammad."

"And whose son are you?"

The Imam ﷺ said, "I am the son of Ali ibn Mūsā ar-Riḍā ﷺ."

Ma'mūn pretended to be happy to meet him, and said, "Well done! No one but you could have given such an appropriate answer. I shall return from my hunt shortly and shall meet with you."

Ma'mūn went in pursuit of game but failed to hunt anything that day. A bird of some kind flew overhead and Ma'mūn released his hawk to hunt it. But the bird escaped the talons of the hawk, who flew out of sight in its pursuit. A long time passed before Ma'mūn's hunter hawk returned, carrying nothing but a small fish in its clutches. Irately Ma'mūn started back to his palace, but met Imam Jawād ﷺ on his way back. While he was still holding the fish in his hand, Ma'mūn decided to test the Imam ﷺ. So he put a smile on his face and said, "I bet you can't guess what I am holding in my hand."

His Eminence ﷺ replied, "God ﷻ the Sublimely Exalted has created small fish in the endless ocean of His mercy and grace which birds of prey hunt down and by means of which sultans put the sons of the prophets to the test."

Ma'mūn was astounded by this response and realized that the Imam ﷺ was much more knowledgeable than he had hitherto conceived; and he felt belittled compared to the grandeur and the greatness of the [supernatural] knowledge of the Imam ﷺ. He then had the Imam ﷺ ride with him and took him to his court, where he honored him and showed him so much respect that it caused his courtiers to envy the attention that was being lavished on the youth, leading them to conspire against him.

Mahziyār the Persian was a Christian scholar who entered into Islam after having studied and pondered the religion. He also adopted the Shī'a rite within Islam. His son, Ali ibn Mahziyār, was a companion and a close and loyal friend to three Imams: Imam Riḍā ﷺ, Imam Jawād ﷺ, and Imam Hādī ﷺ. He wrote several books on the subject of Shī'a sacred jurisprudence (*fiqh*), and was the deputy (*nāyib*) of the Imams ﷺ in the southeast city of Ahvāz. His shrine is still extant in Ahvāz and is a pilgrimage destination for the devotees of the Ahl al-Bayt ﷺ (the Members of the Household of the Prophet ﷺ) to this day.

One day, one of the Christian residents of Tarsus sent eight gold Dirhams as a gift to Imam Jawād ﷺ. Khayrān, Ali ibn Mahziyār's manservant took delivery of the gift and presented it to his master Ali ibn Mahziyār. Ali was unsure as to whether he should accept the gift or to return it. He thus wrote a letter to Imam Jawād ﷺ asking whether he is able to accept the gift or not.

In response, the Imam ﷺ wrote, "When you receive a gift from him, be it in Dirhams [i.e. gold coins] or in any other form, accept it, because the Apostle of God ﷺ did not turn down gifts from Christians and Jews."

By the grace of God, Imam Jawād ﷺ was able to read people's minds and to look into their past and future. At times, he would respond to their questions before they had given voice to them, shining the bright light of certainty on the hearts of his questioners. For example, it is reported that someone came to the Imam ﷺ and started to ask his question:

"Would that I was sacrificed for..."

The Imam interrupted: "He should not 'break'⁵⁷ his ritual devotions!"

The man arose, paid his departing respects, and left. The people who were around the Imam and who had no idea what had just taken place said, "Would that we were sacrificed for your cause⁵⁸, what just happened??"

The Imam replied, "The man wanted to know whether a mariner who works on a ship and travels with it wherever it goes should offer his devotions in the normal way or whether he should shorten the number of cycles [after the ship has travelled the minimum distance for this rule to take effect]. And I told him that he should not 'break' [the number of the cycles of] his ritual devotions."

Muhammad ibn Maymūn reports: Before the Abbāsid caliph al-Ma'mūn had summoned Imam Ridā to Khorāsān, His Eminence made a journey to Mecca on which I accompanied him. One day something happened which decided me to return to Madina. And so I went to Imam Ridā and told him that I had decided to return to Madina and that if there was any message or letter which he would like me to deliver to his son, that he should give it to me so that I could deliver it.

---

⁵⁷ When travelling a long distance, the sacred law of Islam states that one must "break" the number of the cycles of the ritual devotions offered to ﷲ in half (to ease the burden of the traveler), so that only two cycles are incumbent on a believer in lieu of a four-cycle devotion. This is a simplified explanation, and the details are more complex, which is why the questioner had a question in his mind as to whether or not even to 'break' the number of cycles.

⁵⁸ A formal expression of respect, and a supplication to God to keep the Imam safe.

A slight smile came over the Imam's face, after which he wrote a letter and gave it to me. When I returned to Madina, I paid a visit to the Imam's house, even though I was in poor health and had completely lost my eyesight. I knocked on the door and Imam Jawād's manservant opened it and ushered me to his presence. When I presented the letter to him, the Imam ordered his manservant to break the letter's seal. The Imam read the letter and then looked at me and said, "O Muhammad! How is your eyesight?"

I said, "O son of the Apostle of God, as you can see, my eyes have lost their strength and have lost their ability to see."

The Imam stroked my eyes with his blessed hands, and my eyes were cured from the grace (*baraka*) which his hands were charged with, and I was able to see my surroundings again. I then fell to the Imam's feet and kissed his hands and feet.

When I left his presence, my eyesight was better than it had ever been.

The Abbāsid caliph Ma'mūn invited Imam Jawād to Baghdad and gave the hand of his daughter Umm al-Faḍl to him in marriage, placing the couple in one of his palaces and ordering his staff to see to the Imam's every need, and to lavish them with all sorts of fine clothing and the best of foods. He believed that by entertaining the Imam in this way, the Imam would ease up and eventually release his high Islamic ideals and values and give way to earthly temptations, thereby losing his credibility with the people.

Husain Makkārī reports: I came to this town at a time when Imam Muhammad at-Taqī (Imam Jawād) was in Baghdad, and I heard that the Imam is living in the lap of luxury and honor under the care of the caliph. I went to see him and when my eyes fell upon the blessed countenance of His Eminence ﷺ, I said to myself that it is not possible for the Imam ﷺ to return to Madina, because he is treated with the highest honor and dignity, and the best food and clothing is placed at his disposal.

As these thoughts were crossing my mind, His Eminence lowered his head and some moments passed. He then raised his blessed head and looked at me and addressed me while his pallor had turned pale: "O Husain! [Eating] barley bread with coarse salt in the vicinity of the shrine of the Apostle of God ﷺ is more pleasing to me than what you see here…"

Qāsim ibn Abdur-Rahmān was a sworn enemy of the Ahl al-Bayt of the Prophet ﷺ and was affiliated to the Zaydī rite. He reports: At one time I had paid a visit to Baghdad. I was walking the streets of the city when all of a sudden I saw a big commotion among the people who were all rushing in one direction. I became curious and followed them. Along the way I asked one of them, "What has caused everyone to rush in this direction in such a hurry?"

The man said, "Imam Ridā's ﷺ son is passing by a street here, and we all want to see him."

I was surprised and upset by the people's devotion but decided to go along to see if I could figure out the mystery behind the people's devotion to the man. I got to where the Imam was supposed to be and found a good spot from which to witness the event. The Imam ﷺ gradually came into view while he was mounted on horseback, together with an entourage of people who were following him. He came close to me and I saw that he was a youth of not many years of age. I thought to myself, "May Allāh deprive the Shī'a of His mercy for believing that this youth has been appointed by God ﷺ and that obeying him is a religiously incumbent duty. Was there no one better than him to be found??"

As these thoughts were running through my mind, the Imam ﷺ came up to me and called me by my name and quoted a verse from the Noble Quran that referred to the Thamūd people who denied the prophet Sālih's ﷺ prophethood, reasoning that they should not be expected to follow the dictates of one who is from them, and is of flesh and blood like them, and who had no power or retinue or dynastic lineage.

I realized that the Imam of the Shī'a is aware of my inner thoughts, which is why he responded to the questions that I had [in mind] but had not given outward expression to. But nonetheless, I said to myself, "He must be some sort of magician or sorcerer, and it is through these dark arts that he has become aware of people's thoughts."

The Imam ﷺ looked at me again and this time recited the following blessed verse from the Quran: Is it the case that he has been given revealed knowledge from among the people, whereas there exists among them those who are more powerful and wealthier? It is not the case that revelation has been given to him; rather, he is a self-conceited and arrogant liar.

At this point I became certain that he knows all of the secrets in God's creation. I therefore repented from my past deeds and attained to faith in him and came to believe that he was God's appointed proof (*hujjat*) among mankind.

Ahmad ibn Ali ibn Kulthūm reports: I went to see one of the Shī'a by the name of Abū-Zaynaba, who was a close friend of Ahkam ibn Bashshār and was fully informed about the latter's affairs and life story. I told Abū-Zaynaba, "I have seen a knife scar on Ahkam ibn Bashshār's throat and have asked him about it several times, but he has avoided my question each time. Do you know what happened to him?"

Abū-Zaynaba replied, "During the time when Imam Muhammad at-Taqī ﷺ resided in Baghdad, Ahkam ibn Bashshār and I lived in a house in Baghdad together with five other of the Shīʿa faithful. One afternoon, Ahkam ibn Bashshār left the house without us being aware that he had left and did not come back that night. We became very concerned and started to search for him when a letter reached us from the Imam ﷺ. In it, the Imam ﷺ had written that our friend from Khorāsān (meaning Ahkam ibn Bashshār) was at death's door. His enemies have cut his throat and have wrapped him in a blanket and thrown him in some dilapidated ruin. The Imam ﷺ had given the address of the place and ordered us to go and find him and to bring him back to health with such and such a medicine. So, we left for the place immediately and found him dying there and saved his life. Aktham is alive and well now and owes his life to the Imam ﷺ.

5. The Imam's Marriage

In the history of the life of Imam Riḍā ﷺ it is stated that the caliph Maʾmūn strove to portray himself as a friend and benefactor of the Ahl al-Bayt of the Prophet ﷺ in order to quell the various pro-Ālid insurrectionary movements which were undermining and threatening the very foundations of his regime, as well as for the purposes of attracting the support of the Iranian Shīʿa of Khorāsān, where his capital was located. By forcing the heir-apparency on Imam Riḍā ﷺ, the caliph wanted to bring about these objectives as well as to be able to monitor the affairs of the Imam ﷺ from close range.

On the other hand, the Abbāsid clan was none too happy with this plan of his, as they feared that it would backfire, causing the caliphate to shift from their hands to the hands of the Ālids after Maʾmūn's death. They thus rose up in rebellion against the caliph [in Baghdad and in the Hijāz], urging him to kill the Imam ﷺ and lending an urgent dynamic which militated for this outcome to their agitation. Their agitation was quelled after Imam Riḍā ﷺ was martyred by poisoning at the hands of Ma'mūn's assassins, after which the Abbāsid clan in Baghdad turned to him and were reconciled.

Ma'mūn's poisoning of the Imam ﷺ was quick and secretive, and the caliph made every effort for the truth of the Imam's death not to get out, attempting to cover up his crime with ostentatious public displays of mourning for what was supposedly a "natural" death. He even took the pretense of his mourning to the extreme of secluding himself in the Imam's cemetery for three days during which he ate nothing but salt-bread and water and cried a river of crocodile tears. But despite all of this pretense and subterfuge, the truth eventually came out and it was known to the Ālids that their Imam ﷺ had been poisoned and that his assassin was none other than Ma'mūn. They thus became very angry and distanced themselves from the caliph. Consequently, Ma'mūn saw his reign facing another grave danger, and conspired to come up with another scheme in order to confront and uproot this new threat: he instituted a policy of amity and brotherhood with Imam Jawād ﷺ, whom he invited to Baghdad and to whom he gave the hand of his daughter Umm al-Faḍl in marriage, hoping to get the same benefits from this union that he hoped to get from the appointment of Imam Riḍā ﷺ to his heir-apparency.

In the year 204 AH, that is, a year after the martyrdom of Imam Riḍā ﷺ, Ma'mūn brought that great Imam's young son from Madina to Baghdad and suggested the marriage of his daughter to him. The Imam ﷺ accepted this marriage, which was to the advantage of the Shī'a. By doing so, he also provided Umm al-Faḍl the opportunity to change the course of her life which was spent hitherto in the palace of the caliph, and to join the ranks of the pious and righteous servants of God ﷻ. The simple and unostentatious lifestyle of the Imam ﷺ was modeled after that of the Most Noble Prophet ﷺ, and taking that example to heart could enable Ma'mūn's daughter to join the ranks of the true followers of the Prophet ﷺ of Islam.

Additionally, this opportunity presented the Imam ﷺ with the chance to establish contacts with the people and to instruct them in the true teachings of Islam and to familiarize them with the way in which the Apostle of God ﷺ lived his life, without having to be as concerned with the atmosphere of political repression, exile, imprisonment, and murder which was the stock in trade of the absolutist Abbāsid regime. The Abbāsid clan was well aware of the respite that this arranged marriage provided to someone who they considered to be a dangerous rival to their throne, so that they were none too happy about the arrangement and started their complaints to Ma'mūn.

Rayyān ibn Shabīb reports: When the Abbāsids became aware of Ma'mūn's decision to wed his daughter to Imam Jawād ﷺ, they became concerned lest the reins of power be taken out of their hands and fall into the hands of their Ālid rivals; and this was a repetition of the concern that they had previously when Imam Riḍā ﷺ was appointed as the caliph's heir-apparent. They therefore took their complaint to Ma'mūn and foreswore him of his decision. They said, "You well know that which has gone before between us and the Ālids. You also know that the caliphs before you would exile them and treat them with contempt. Before this, we were much concerned about the fact that you had bequeathed your heir-apparency to [the Imam] ar-Riḍā ﷺ, but God ﷺ solved that problem [for us]. Now we swear you [upon your honor] to Allāh not to worry us unduly any further and to reconsider your decision about this marriage, and to give the hand of your daughter to one of the Abbāsids who is worthy of this bond [of marriage] …"

In reply, Ma'mūn said, "Concerning that which occurred between you and the Ālids, it was you who was at fault. If you look at the matter in all fairness, they are more worthy than you [for this office], and what the caliphs before me did was [committing the sin of] cutting one's ties with one's kin, from which [sin] I seek refuge in Allāh [to prevent me from committing]. Nor do I harbor any regrets about [my having designated Imam Riḍā ﷺ as] my heir-apparent: I asked him to accept the heir-apparency, but he did not accept it, and so, God's will was done. Concerning Abū-Jaʿfar Muhammad ibn Ali ﷺ, I must say that I chose him [as a suitable candidate] for marriage to my daughter because he has mastery over and is preeminent to all other people of virtue despite his young age, and this is a cause for consternation. I hope and trust that this fact becomes clear for everyone just as it has become clear for me, so that they will come to the correct conclusion, which is in accord with my own opinion, which is that the Imam ﷺ is the worthiest person to take my daughter's hand in marriage."

The Abbāsids replied, "No matter how astounding this youth's knowledge and wisdom is, the fact remains that he is yet a child and has not learned *adab* (i.e. how to comport himself in accordance with the worldly culture of the polite classes) or diplomacy. Wait until he learns *adab* and becomes familiar with the rudiments of the religious sciences, then put your plan into effect."

The caliph responded, "Woe unto you! I know this youth better than you do. He is from a family whose knowledge is God-given so that they are not in need of being educated. His father and forefathers before him were never in need of the people for their mastery of the ways of *adab* and the religious sciences. If you would like, you can put him to the test yourselves so that what I have told you is obviated and proven to you."

They replied, "This is a very good idea. We will test him, and put to him questions in theology and sacred jurisprudence (*fiqh*). If he answers our questions correctly, we will withdraw our complaint, and the veracity of the caliph's decision will be shown in its full light for all [to see]; but if he is not able to answer our questions correctly, our problem will be resolved by the caliph's reconsidering his decision concerning the marriage."

Maʿmūn accepted and said, "You can test him whenever you please."

They thus ordered Yahyā ibn Aktham, the great magister and scholar of the era to appear before al-Maʿmūn, promising the latter that

Yaḥyā ibn Aktham would humiliate Imam Jawād ﷺ, and promising the former a great financial reward if he were able to come up with a question which the Imam ﷺ could not answer. And so it was arranged. They seated Imam Jawād ﷺ in a place of honor, and Yaḥyā ibn Aktham proceeded to put his questions to the young Imam.

Yaḥyā said, "My lord, what do you say concerning someone who is on the Hajj pilgrimage and is in a state of *ihrām*[59] (a state of ritual consecration) who happened to kill a game [animal]?"

The Imam ﷺ replied, "This question has several possibilities. Was the person in question within the boundaries of the sanctuary or outside the boundaries? Was he aware of the ban against doing such a thing [during the Hajj ritual] or was he ignorant of this prohibition? Was the killing intentional or accidental? Was he a bondsman or a freeman? Was he a minor or had he reached the age of majority? Was it the first time that he committed such an offense or the second? Was his kill a bird or something other than a bird? Was it large or small? Does he regret his deed or does he intend to repeat the offense? Did the kill take place during the day or at night? And was his *ihrām* for the major or minor pilgrimage?"

Yaḥyā ibn Aktham was flabbergasted that a nine-year old child could dissect his question so expertly, and he was at a loss for words. Seeing that Yaḥyā had nothing further to say, al-Ma'mūn then turned to Imam Jawād ﷺ and told him that he had done well, and asked him if he, in his turn, had any questions for Yaḥyā ibn Aktham?

The Imam then ﷺ asked Yaḥya: "What do you say about [the case of] a man who looks at a woman in an unlawful manner in the early

---

[59] *Muhrim* is the participle form of a pilgrim who has entered *ihrām*, which is the first stage of the pilgrimage (wherein the pilgrim changes his or her clothes in preparation for the pilgrimage and pledges allegiance to God). What is meant here is that the person referred to has formally entered into the state of the pilgrimage.

morning, who then becomes lawful to him [to look at] before noon, and become unlawful to him [again] at noon, only to become lawful to him [yet again] in the afternoon, and becomes unlawful to him [for a third time] at sunset, who becomes lawful to him [for a third time] at the time of the night (*ishā*) ritual devotions (*salā'*), and becomes unlawful to him [for a fourth time] at midnight, and becomes lawful to him [for a fourth time] at daybreak?"

Yahyā said, "I do not know!"

Imam Jawād ﷺ said, "The person is a slave-girl (*kanīz*) which a non-Arab (*ajnabī*) man looked upon with lust, which was unlawful to him; the man then buys the slave-girl before noon, only to free her at noon; he then marries her in the afternoon; and divorces (*zihār*)[60] her at sunset; [and regrets his action] and pays the atonement price (*kaffāra*), at night, [thereby making her lawful to him again]; at midnight, he makes a *raj'ī*[61] divorce with her, and "returns" to her at daybreak."

At this point, Ma'mūn praised God ﷻ for making his opinion to be the correct one and turned to his kinfolk and said, "Now do you see that which you were bent on denying?"

Ma'mūn then suggested before the same assembly that Imam Jawād ﷺ marry his daughter Umm Faḍl and asked him to pronounce the wedding sermon. The Imam ﷺ accepted and began the sermon as follows:

---

[60] This is the most final form of divorce, where the man proclaims his wife to be unlawful unto him "as my mother is unlawful unto me". As such, it does not require a "waiting period" [of three menstrual cycles] during which she cannot be remarried (*'idda*) before the two can marry again, but a marriage can take place again (immediately) if the man repents of his action and pays the atonement price (*kaffāra*).

[61] A *raj'ī* divorce is a divorce in which the man can 'return' (*raj'a'*) to his (erstwhile "divorced") wife during the wife's waiting period (*'idda*), and continue marital relations without the need for a new marriage contract (*nikāh*).

"I am grateful to the Lord for [my] having confessed to His bounties; and pronounce the Words of Unicity (*kalimāt at-tawhīd*; i.e. *lā illāha illā Allāh*) in order [to assure] sincerity in [the proclamation of] His unicity; and send greetings of peace unto Muhammad, the lord of created beings, and unto the Chosen Ones from among his progeny.

"Without doubt it is due to the grace and mercy of God ﷻ upon His creatures that He has made them free of the need to resort to the illicit things in life by providing them with licit alternatives, ordaining the necessity of marriage, and He has stated:

$$وَأَنكِحُوا الْأَيَامَىٰ مِنكُمْ وَالصَّالِحِينَ مِنْ عِبَادِكُمْ وَإِمَائِكُمْ ۚ إِن يَكُونُوا فُقَرَاءَ يُغْنِهِمُ اللَّهُ مِن فَضْلِهِ ۗ وَاللَّهُ وَاسِعٌ عَلِيمٌ ﴿٣٢﴾$$

[24:32] And [you ought to] marry the single from among you as well as such of your male and female slaves as are fit [for marriage]. If they [whom you intend to marry] are poor, [let this not deter you;] God ﷻ will grant them sufficiency out of His bounty - for God ﷻ is infinite [in His mercy], all-knowing."

And then, by determining a *mahrīya*[62] equivalent to that which Imam Ali ؑ gave to Her Eminence Lady Fātimaᵗ az-Zahrā ؑ (five hundred Dirhams), Imam Jawād ؑ agreed to his marriage to Ma'mūn's daughter. After the festive meal had been served and the guests had departed and only a small group of the Abbāsids and Ma'mūn's courtesans had remained, the caliph asked the Imam ؑ to explain the correct juridical

---

[62] *Mahrīya* - The bride price or marriage portion or bridal gift. The price a man would have to pay his bride as a condition of being granted her hand in marriage; it is the opposite of a dowry, which refers to money or property brought by a bride to her husband at marriage.

position concerning the various possibilities of the hunt during the Hajj pilgrimage, which the Imam ﷺ accepted and proceeded to explain in detail. The caliph was surprised and delighted with the Imam's erudite and scholarly performance and praised him profusely before the gathering.

It must be borne in mind, of course, that despite his hypocritical pretenses to friendship and respect for the Imam ﷺ, Ma'mūn had no aim in this sham marriage other than to further his political objectives, some of which we shall enumerate:

1. By placing his daughter within the Imam's ﷺ household, Ma'mūn would always be able to closely monitor the affairs of that household and to keep track of the Imam's ﷺ affairs. Ma'mūn's daughter, in her turn, faithfully carried out her job of spying for and reporting to her father, as attested to by the annals of history.

2. Another one of Ma'mūn's objectives of this marriage was to make a solid connection between the Imam ﷺ and the caliphal palace wherein there was all sorts of debauchery and scandalous behavior taking place on a nightly basis (such as drinking, gambling, womanizing, etc.), thereby bringing about a sort of guilt by association for the Imam ﷺ and damaging his reputation and reducing his eminence and stature in the minds of the general population, thereby tainting his reputation of purity and immaculacy. As Ma'mūn hoped, this brought about a concomitant reduction in the legitimacy of the Imam's ﷺ claim to the office of the imamate – a hope of the caliph's which of course remained frustrated and unfulfilled.

Muhammad ibn Rayyān reports: As much as Ma'mūn tried to involve Imam Jawād ﷺ in depravity and sin, he was never successful. In the festivities which followed the wedding ceremony, Ma'mūn appointed a hundred [beautiful] slave girls, each carrying a goblet full of gems, to welcome him [i.e. to offer themselves to him], and this they did. But the Imam did not pay any of them any attention, demonstrating in practice to all present that he loathed such practices.

In these same festivities, they had brought a [female] singer and performer [to engage in the sin of belittling and mocking the dignity of the female persona by acting as an amusement for men by singing and dancing for them]; but just as she started her performance the Imam accosted her, saying, "Have fear of God ؼ [concerning what you are about to do]!"

The minstrel was so intimidated by the awesome power of the Imam's ؼ imperative (which was charged with His Eminence's ؼ authority whose source was the deep spiritual well of sacred dominion [over the affairs of mankind]) that he lost his grip on his musical instrument and was never able to take up the playing of any musical instrument with his hands after that.

3. As we have pointed out earlier, the wily Abbāsid caliph strove to mitigate the protests and insurrectionary tendencies of the Ālids by means of this marriage, and to project an image of himself as their friend and benefactor.

4. What Ma'mūn intended to do with this marriage was to fool the masses of the people. Thus he would occasionally say things like "I brought about this union so that Abū-Ja'far [Imam Jawād ؼ] would be given a child by my daughter so that I would become the grandfather of a child who is the progeny of the Prophet ؼ and of Ali ibn Abī-Tālib ؼ."

But fortunately, this ruse of Ma'mūn's also did not pan out as his daughter never gave birth to any children, and the children of Imam Jawād ؼ, including the tenth Imam, Imam Hādī ؼ, were all conceived by another wife who was a virtuous and honorable bondswoman by the name of Samʿāna Maghrabīya.

Over all, this marriage which Maʾmūn was so insistent about, was political in nature. Thus, although the marriage potentially entailed a life of prosperity, this aspect of it was of no importance to Imam Jawād ﷺ who, like his great forefathers before him, placed no importance in such things, and for whom the material benefits of this life were of no value. The truth of the matter was the exact opposite: living life in and around Maʾmūn's palace and the caliphal court was a tortuous imposition for His Eminence ﷺ.

We had provided an example of the nature of this imposition earlier when we quoted a report from Husayn Makkārī, where he believed that the Imam ﷺ had attained to a life of affluence next to the caliph and would never return to his hometown of Medina, but the Imam ﷺ turned to him and addressed him with a pale pallor, saying: "O Husayn! [Eating] barley bread with coarse salt in the vicinity of the shrine of the Apostle of God ﷺ is more pleasing to me than what you see here…"

For this reason, the Imam's tarrying in Baghdad did not last, and he returned very quickly to Medina with his wife Umm al-Faḍl, where he remained until the year 220 AH.

6. The Imam's Companions

Like their forefather the Apostle of God, our Immaculate Imams ﷺ were constantly engaged in teaching and instructing and cultivating the people [in the ways of Islam]. We must be cognizant of the fact that their ministry cannot be compared with the work of teaching institutions, who have set times for their classes outside of which they are closed and do not offer any teaching services. However, our immaculate leaders were engaged in their ministry at all times. The manner of their comportment, their actions and reactions, their words and their interactions with different people, and even the various aspects of their everyday lives acted as exemplary models and paradigmatic examples for those who were in contact with these precious souls. Anyone who kept their company, no matter how briefly, was afforded the opportunity to learn from their manner of comportment and ethical posture, as well as from their knowledge [of the Quranic sciences]. They were afforded the opportunity to ask any questions that they might have and to receive a response. Nor was the scope of the questions which could be asked limited: they would ask their Imam about any and all problems that they had and would receive a response which was commensurate with the limits of their own understanding.

It goes without saying that a ministry such as this, where men were guided and trained [in the way of God], is unique and without parallel anywhere except where it is led by those who have been sent by the Lord of Providence. And it is natural that the essence and rich fecundity of such a ministry should be attractive and appealing, which is why the usurping Abbāsid tyrants did everything in their power to place obstacles in the path of the people's free access to their true leaders because they knew that if the people became aware of these special attributes of their Imams', they would be drawn to their true and divinely-appointed guides, causing an imminent threat to their oppressive regime.

The people were only afforded a relatively free access to their Imams ﷺ during the short reign of Umar ibn Abdul-Azīz, who was exceptional among the Umayyad caliphs in that he was a righteous man, and in the interregnum between the decline of the Umayyads and the time of the consolidation of the Abbāsid absolutism (both of which coincided roughly and respectively with the imamates of Imam Muhammad al-Bāqir ﷺ and his son, Imam Ja'far as-Sādiq ﷺ). And this is why we see the number of the students of Imam Ja'far as-Sādiq ﷺ (and those who have related hadīth reports from His Eminence) reach the vicinity of four thousand, but that in other eras where the usurping caliphs had an absolute hold on power and where their absolutism reigned supreme, the number of the students of the Imams ﷺ and of those who have related hadīth reports from them are extremely limited.

For example, the number of the companions and students and hadith transmitters of Imam Jawād ﷺ were limited to about one hundred and ten, a number which speaks to the extremely limited nature of the possibility of the Imam's ﷺ contact with his followers during the time of His Eminence's ﷺ imamate. At the same time, brilliant personages can be found among this limited number, some of whom we shall enumerate by way of example.

1. Ali ibn Mahziyār al-Ahvāzī

Ali ibn Mahziyār was a close companion and a representative of Imam Jawād ﷺ. He is also counted among the number of the close companions of Imam Riḍā ﷺ and Imam Hādī ﷺ as well. He was known as someone who would spend much time in the ritual devotions to God, and his forehead was callused as a result of the frequency and duration of his prostrations. It is said that he would enter into prostration at sunset and would raise his forehead from the ground only after having supplicated God ﷻ on behalf of a thousand true believers (*mu'min*, plural: *mu'minīn*), asking Him to grant each of these that which he wanted for himself.

Ali ibn Mahziyār lived in Ahvāz and is the author of over thirty books. He attained to such heights of [fidelity to the tenets of the] faith and righteous conduct that Imam Muhammad at-Taqī ﷺ has praised him in the following terms: "In the name of Allāh, the Merciful, the Beneficent. O Ali! May God ﷻ grant you a goodly reward and place you in [a lofty station of] Heaven; and to secure you from misery and abjection in both worlds, and to resurrect you [among the number of people who are resurrected] with us. O Ali! I have tried and tested you in the goodness of your intentions, in your obedience and compliance with the ordinances of the sacred law, and in carrying out that which has been made obligatory to you [by the ordinances of God's religion], and if I say that I have not found anyone [to have passed the test as successfully] as you, I have hope that I have spoken the truth. May God ﷻ grant you His Heaven. Your services [to our cause] in the heat of the day and in the cold of night are not hidden from us. I beseech God ﷻ to grant you of His special mercy when He gathers everyone on the Day of Resurrection, such that you will be the envy of others. Verily, God ﷻ is All-Hearing [and hears the prayers] of all those who pray to Him.

2. Aḥmad ibn Muḥammad ibn Abī-Naṣr al-Bazantī

Aḥmad ibn Muḥammad was a resident of Kūfa and was a companion of Imam Riḍā ﷺ and Imam Jawād ﷺ, both of whom had great respect for him. He is the author of several books, including al-Jāmi'. All of the scholars within Shī'a Islam acknowledge his mastery in the religious sciences and consider him to be completely trustworthy in terms of his transmittance of hadith reports. This great scholar is one the four scholars who were at the service of Imam Riḍā ﷺ and who were subject to the special respect and favor of that Imam (the story of which we have related in the book pertaining to Imam Riḍā ﷺ).

3. Zakarīya ibn Ādam

Zakarīya ibn Ādam was a resident of the city of Qom (in north-central Iran), and his shrine there is to this day a pilgrimage destination for the believers and the devotees of the House of Immaculacy and Purity. Zakarīya was a very close companion of Imam Riḍā ﷺ and Imam Jawād ﷺ, concerning the latter of whom we know that he prayed for him and considered him to be a loyal companion.

It is reported that once when he was visiting Imam Riḍā ﷺ, His Eminence the Eighth Imam spent the whole evening until the break of dawn instructing him [in the mysteries of the religion]. One day someone asked Imam Riḍā ﷺ, "I live far from you and am unable to visit you in person. Who should I refer my questions to regarding the teachings of our religion and its ordinances?" His Eminence ﷺ replied, "Ask Zakarīya ibn Ādam, for he is trustworthy in the affairs of religion as well as in the affairs of the world."

4. Muhammad ibn Ismāīl ibn Bazīʿ

Muhammad ibn Ismāīl was a close companion of Imam Kāżim ﷺ, Imam Riḍā ﷺ and Imam Jawād ﷺ, and all of the scholars within Shīʿa Islam acknowledge his mastery in the religious sciences and consider him to be completely trustworthy in terms of his transmittance of hadith reports. He was a righteous man who was dedicated to the ritual devotions to God, and has also written several books. At the same time, he worked as a courtier in the court of the Abbāsid caliphs. As a consequence of his employment, one day Imam Riḍā ﷺ told him, "Almighty God ﷻ has certain servants of His who are employed in the court of tyrants by means of whom He manifests his arguments or proofs (*burhān*), and empowers them in various cities [where the Shīʿa reside] in order to prevent His friends and *awlīā* (those who enjoy spiritual proximity to God) from being subjected to tyranny and iniquity, and to help facilitate the affairs of the Shīʿa. These servants of God are the sanctuaries of the believers during times of trouble and danger, and those among our followers who fall on hard times turn to them for help and seek the solutions to their problems from them. Almighty God ﷻ gives peace and security to the believers from the reach of oppressors through them. They are true believers in whom God ﷻ places His trust [in order to accomplish certain of His goals] on Earth. The Resurrection is illuminated [in part] by their light. I swear [upon my oath] to Allāh that Heaven has been made for them and they have been made for Heaven, and may they ever enjoy its bounties." The Imam ﷺ then said, "Any one of you who has a mind to it can attain to such stations."

Muhammad ibn Ismāīl asked, "Would that I was sacrificed in your cause, attain to what kind of stations?"

His Eminence ﷺ replied, "To the station where you are [employed] with [the court of] tyrants, and please us by pleasing our Shīʿa." In other words, that whatever office or official position you attain to, that your ultimate objective should be the alleviation of the onus of oppression and iniquity from the shoulders of the believers.

In conclusion, Imam Riḍā ﷺ told Muḥammad ibn Ismāʿīl (who was a vizier in the Abbāsid court), "Be thou one such [believer], O Muḥammad!"

Ḥusayn ibn Khālid reports: I was with a group [of my fellow Shīʿa believers] and we were at the service of Imam Riḍā ﷺ when talk of Muḥammad ibn Ismāʾīl ibn Bazīʿ came up. His Eminence ﷺ said, "It would be pleasing to me if there were among you someone such as him."

Muḥammad ibn Aḥmad ibn Yaḥyā reports: I went to Fayd, which is a place on the road to Mecca, with Muḥammad ibn ʿAlī ibn Bilāl in order to make pilgrimage to the grave of Muḥammad ibn Ismāʾīl. Muḥammad ibn ʿAlī sat facing the qibla[63] at the head of the grave and said, "The one who is buried here related to me that Imam Jawād ﷺ said, 'One who makes pilgrimage to the grave of his brother in faith, and sits facing the qibla at the side of his grave, and places his hand on the grave and recites the Surat al-Qadr[64] seven times, will become immune to the great fear, the great fear of the Day of Resurrection.'"

Muḥammad ibn Ismāʾīl ibn Bazīʾ reports: I asked Imam Jawād ﷺ to send me one of his shirts so that I could use it as my burial shroud. His Eminence ﷺ sent me one of his shirts and instructed me to remove its buttons."

---

[63] The direction of prayer (i.e. facing the Kaʿba in Mecca).

[64] The 97th Sūra (or "chapter") of the Quran. (The word chapter is placed in quotes because it implies that the Quran is a book in the sense of a book that is divided into chapters, each of which supports a thesis in a progressive fashion. But of course, the Quran is not such a book but a compilation of a series of revelations which were revealed over a period of twenty-three years to the Prophet Muḥammad, each revelation of which has its own historical context, and whose meaning cannot be properly understood without understanding the contexts which are the ground of each respective revelation.)

7. The Martyrdom of the Imam

The devious Abbāsid caliph al-Ma'mūn died in the year 218 AH. He was succeeded to the throne by his brother al-Mu'tasim. Mu'tasim did not have the cunning and perspicacity of his brother al-Ma'mūn. He summoned Imam Jawād ﷺ to Baghdad from Medina in the year 220 AH so that he would be close at hand where he could keep an eye on him. At the same time, the physical proximity of the Imam ﷺ gave al- Mu'tasim the opportunity to carry out some of his hare-brained schemes which were devised supposedly to make a fool of the Imam ﷺ in the eyes of the public.

One such scheme was to force the Imam ﷺ to participate in complex theological and juridical discussions (where the Imam ﷺ, it was assumed, would be caught off-guard and unprepared). But contrary to the wish of the oppressor, victory was always with the Imam ﷺ, and the light of the divine which was with the Imam ﷺ at all times would shine all the more brightly in these sessions. One of these sessions which has become very famous and whose story has been related and repeated in many books is 'the Episode of the Cutting off of the Hand of the Thief'.

Ibn Abī-Dawwād was the Chief Justice of Baghdad during the reign of al- Mu'tasim. He held this exalted station during the reins of four caliphs, namely, al-Ma'mūn, al- Mu'tasim, al-Wāthiq, and al-Mutawakkil; and he resided over the fates of men in all of these governments. He was a corrupt and licentious reprobate. The following report reaches us from Zarqān, who was a close friend of Ibn Abī-Dawwād:

One day Ibn Abī-Dawwād returned from the court of al-Mu'tasim and was visibly distraught. I asked him the reason for his distress.

He replied, "Today something happened to me that made me wish that I had died twenty years ago so that I would have avoided this fate that has befallen me."

I asked, "But why??"

He said, "Because of what happened to me in al-Muʿtasim's court thanks to Abū-Jaʿfar [Imam Jawād] ﷺ."

I asked, "What happened?"

He replied, "Someone came to the caliph, admitted that he had stolen something, and asked to be submitted to the just punishment of the sacred law in order to be absolved of the onus of the crime. The caliph gathered all of the magisters and doctors of the sacred law, as well as Muhammad ibn Ali [Imam Jawād ﷺ], and asked us from which point the hand of the thief should be severed."

I said, "From the wrist."

The caliph asked, "What is the reason for this?"

I replied, "Because Almighty God ﷻ stated in the Noble Quran in the Āya of Tamayyum[65] to wash your face, and your hands. And that what is meant by hands is up to the wrist.

"Some among the doctors of the sacred law agreed with me that the hand of the thief must be severed from the wrist, but there were others who said that it is necessary to sever the thief's hand from the elbow, and when al-Muʿtasim asked them for their reason, they replied, 'Because Almighty God ﷻ stated in the Noble Quran in the Āya of Tamayyum to wash your face, and your hands [and arms up to the elbow]. Therefore, what is meant by God ﷻ by hands here is up to the elbow.'

"At this point al-Muʿtasim turned to Muhammad ibn Ali al-Jawād ﷺ and asked, 'What is your opinion?'

"The Imam ﷺ replied, 'These people here present all have their opinions; therefore, excuse me from having to present mine.'

"But the caliph insisted that the Imam ﷺ state his position, and so the Imam ﷺ said, 'I will state my position [only] because you have insisted [that I do so]. These [people] are [all] mistaken, because it is only

---

[65] [5:6] *O you who have attained to faith! When you are about to pray, wash your face, and your hands and arms up to the elbows, and pass your [wet] hands lightly over your head, and [wash] your feet up to the ankles.*

the four fingers of the thief that must be severed, and the rest must be left intact.'

The caliph asked, 'On what basis?'

The Imam ﷺ said, 'Because the Apostle of God ﷺ has stated, "Prostration before God ﷺ is done using seven members of one's body: the forehead, the two palms of one's hands, the two knees, and both feet [the two thumbs of the feet must be in contact with the ground]. Therefore, if a thief's hand is severed from the wrist or elbow, he will not be left with any hand with which to make a proper prostration [in the performance of his obligatory ritual devotions]. Furthermore, God ﷺ the Sublimely Exalted has stated, [72:18] *The [seven] places of worship belong to Allāh, so do not invoke anyone along beside Allāh.* Therefore, that which belongs to God ﷺ must not be severed.'

"The caliph accepted Abū-Ja'far Muhammad ibn Ali's [Imam Jawād's] ﷺ position and ordered the thief's fingers to be severed. I thus lost face in front of all who were present to the point where I wished I was dead from the force of the shame I felt."

A few days after this incident, Ibn Abī-Dawwād went to al-Mu'tasim out of spite and envy and said, "Out of goodwill toward you, I caution you that the incident of a few days ago was not to the benefit of your government because you gave preference to the authoritative legal opinion (*fatwa*) of Abū-Ja'far Muhammad ibn Ali ﷺ over the opinion of others in front of the best scholars and highest dignitaries of the land, whereas he is someone whom half of your subjects consider to be the legitimate leader of the community of Muslims and consider you to have usurped the office which should legitimately be his. [The news of] this event has made its rounds among the people and has become [yet another] reason for [the affirmation of] the legitimacy [of the Imam's ﷺ claim to the office] of the imamate among his supporters.

These words riled up al-Mu'tasim who had already harbored thoughts of the Imam's ﷺ murder in his heart on numerous other occasions and harbored all sorts of enmity for him; and these latest words of his Chief Justice finally made up his mind to murder the Imam ﷺ.

Some days later the caliph summoned a number of his ministers and told them, "It has become necessary that you perjure yourselves against Abū-Jaʿfar Muhammad ibn Ali ﷺ and provide me a written statement that he intends to revolt against me and take back the reins of state from the Banī-Abbās."

The ministers all proclaimed their readiness to do so and presented their written statements to al-Muʿtasim, who summoned the Imam ﷺ and while pretending outrage, shouted, "Why do you want to rise up in rebellion against me?"

His Eminence ﷺ said, "I swear [upon my oath] to Allāh, no such thought has crossed my mind."

Many people have testified against you in this regard, and I shall presently summon them so that they can present their testimony to you in person and to provide you with the reasons [for their testimonies]."

The ministers were summoned and appeared before the caliph and the Imam ﷺ and said, "Abū-Jaʿfar Muhammad ibn Ali ﷺ intends to rise up in rebellion against the state and has written letters in this regard to his bondsmen and followers, some of which we have been able to confiscate from his bondsmen."

They then presented some letters to the caliph. The Imam ﷺ, who was seated in the gallery, raised his arms heavenward and said, "If these people are putting the lie to me, Lord, give them their just punishment."

At this point, the ground began to shake. The shaking was so violent that whoever stood up from their seated position would fall back down. Al-Muʿtasim, who was overcome by fear, asked the Imam ﷺ beseechingly: "O son of the Apostle of God, I am sorry for what I said and turn [to God] in repentance. Pray God ﷻ to stop this earthquake!"

The Imam prayed to God, and the earth stopped shaking. Eventually al-Muʿtasim carried out his vile plan and poisoned the Imam on the last day of the month of Dhī-Qaʿda of the year 220 AH.

The Imam's ﷺ pure body was laid to rest next to the grave of his grandfather, Imam Kāẓim ﷺ, in the Quraysh cemetery in Baghdad. May God's peace be upon him and upon his pure ancestors. The shrine of these two great Imams have become known as the Shrine of the Kāẓimain [i.e. the Shrine of the Two Kāẓims], and has been a pilgrimage destination of Muslims from the time of their burial.

8. A Sampling of the Words of the Imam

The words of the Immaculate Imams ﷺ, which are rays from the sun of knowledge and droplets from the endless ocean of divine wisdom which are their presence here on Earth, are sure signposts on the journey back to God ﷻ for those of His bondsmen who are on this salvific journey. This is because these great and divinely-inspired men were immune to any and all kinds of error and deviations from the correct beliefs of God's religion of truth.

Their constructive guidance is not limited to a single dimension of human behavior and individual and communal life; rather, it covers every possible aspect of human existence. Nor is its efficacy and applicability limited to a specific group or type of people. All of these words of theirs drives everyone toward the peak of their respective individual perfections, awakening one's true and primordial dispositions (which are directed toward the recognition and appreciation of God) in every phase of one's life journey.

We will now present a sampling of the words of wisdom of Imam Muhammad ibn Ali at-Taqī al-Jawād ﷺ, all of which are taken from Sunni sources.[66]

1. One who turns to God ﷻ for his needs and away from reliance on people [for his daily sustenance and worldly needs] will become

---

[66] The majority of these quotes are taken from the following two books: Shablanjī's *Nur al-Absār* and Ibn Sabbāq al-Mālikī's *Fusūl al-Muhimma*.

the subject of the needs of the people; and anyone who makes a habit of piety and living in a righteous manner will become beloved by the people.
2. The perfection of mankind is in wisdom.
3. The peak of generosity (*muruwwa'*) is not to behave towards others as one would not have others behave towards oneself.
4. Do not act on a deed whose time has not yet come, as it will only bring regret.
5. Do not harbor unreasonable expectations as this will bring about a hardening of the heart.
6. Have mercy on those who are less able than you, seeking God's mercy for yourself by way of your mercy towards them.
7. One who considers a wicked deed to be acceptable is a partner in committing that sin.
8. The sinner, the partner and enabler of the sinner, and he who is complacent concerning the sin; these are all partners in the act of committing that sin.
9. One who gives [good] advice to one's brother in faith in private has adorned him [with his good deed], and one who gives out advice in public and in the presence of others has darkened that person's public image.
10. It is more effective to be conscious of God ﷻ in one's heart than to command one's limbs into action [in His cause].
11. The Day of Judgment and [the Day when] Justice [shall be Served] is harder for the oppressor than the day of oppression is for the oppressed.
12. At the head of the Record of Deeds of the Muslim on the Day of Judgment shall be the kindness of his character and temperament.
13. Three character traits will endear man to God:
    a. Asking for His forgiveness in earnest.
    b. Kindness and gentleness toward others.
    c. Giving generously in charity.

14. There are three character traits which will not disappoint those who foster them:
    a. Not being impatient in carrying out one's duties.
    b. Consulting others concerning one's affairs.
    c. Trusting in God ﷻ once one has decided on a course of action.
15. The least of anyone's punishment who places his hope in one who has a corrupt moral disposition (*fāsiq*) is privation and frustration.
16. Anyone who places his hope in anyone other than God ﷻ shall have his fate assigned to that other person or entity by God ﷻ.
17. He who acts on something without being fully informed about the consequences of his actions will cause more harm than good.
18. The need of those who do good deeds for doing such deeds is greater than those in need [of the good deeds done in their favor], because doing good deeds entails rewards and honor and adds to one's good repute. Therefore, whenever one does a good deed, he has first done himself a good turn.
19. Righteousness is the ornament of indigence.
20. Gratitude is the ornament of power.
21. Humility is the ornament of affliction.
22. Humbleness is the ornament of stature and standing.
23. Eloquence is the ornament of speech.
24. Exact memorization is the ornament in the retelling of a tale.
25. Modesty is the ornament of knowledge.
26. Proper comportment and etiquette are the ornaments of wisdom.
27. Being of good cheer is the ornament of munificence and generosity.
28. Not begrudging one anything is the ornament of good behavior and clemency.
29. Paying attention and being fully present is the ornament of prayer and one's daily acts of ritual devotion.

30. Leaving off the doing of that which is frivolous and useless is the ornament of righteousness and piety.
31. Anyone who believes in God ﷻ and trusts in Him will be saved by God ﷻ from any and all wickedness and sin, and will be kept secure by God ﷻ from any enemy.
32. Religion engenders honor and pride.
33. Knowledge is a treasure, and silence is light.
34. Nothing destroys [the truth of] religion as do reprehensible innovations (*bid'a'*).
35. Nothing corrupts [the souls of] men like avarice and greed.
36. People are reformed when they are presided over by worthy and righteous leaders.
37. Afflictions and trials are averted by supplication to God ﷻ.
38. Patience and forbearance in the face of a calamity that has afflicted someone is [itself] a calamity for an enemy who is looking to point the finger of blame and reproach.
39. How is it possible for [the life of] one whose Lord of Providence is Almighty God ﷻ to be wasted?
40. How is it possible for one who is being pursued by God ﷻ to escape from His clutches?
41. Someone asked the Imam ﷺ to give him some advice in a short sentence. The Imam ﷺ said, "Keep yourself [away] from deeds which will cause you ignominy in this world and punishment in the next."

Imam Ali ibn Muhammad al-Hādī

1 Birth

Imam Abul-Hasan Ali ibn Muhammad al-Hādī an-Naqī ؈ (212 – 254 AH/ 827 – 868 CE), the tenth Imam of the Shī'a, was born on the fifteenth day of Dhī-Hijja in the year 212 AH in the vicinity of Medina in a district known as Siryā. His father was Imam Jawād ؈ and his mother, Lady Samāna, was a pious and virtuous lady who was peerless among the women of her era in her dedication to her devotions, to the point that it has been related that she was constantly in a state of ritual fasting, and there was none like her in her attaining to the higher spiritual states. Imam Hādī ؈ has stated concerning his mother: "On my authority, my mother is one who has attained to a [high] spiritual station (*ārif*). She is one of the People of Heaven. The rebel Satan cannot approach her; and she is immune to the deceptions of the oppressors and the enemies [of God], and God ؈ is her protector and guardian."

The most well-known of the titles of the Tenth Imam ﷺ are an-Naqī (the Immaculate, the Pure) and al-Hādī (the Guide). His patronymic (*kunya*) is Abul-Hasan ath-Thālith (the Third 'Father of Hasan').[67]

Imam Hādī ﷺ attained to the office of the imamate[68] after his father was martyred in the year 220 AH, at which point he was eight years of age. His tenure of the office lasted 33 years. His blessed and bountiful life lasted 42 years, after which he attainted to martyrdom in the year 254 AH.

Those who have seen the Imam have stated that he was of medium height, was fair-skinned with a ruddy hue, had large eyes with generous eyebrows, and a pleasant and cheerful countenance.

The life of the Imam coincided with the reign of seven Abbāsid caliphs. Prior to his attaining to the office of the imamate, it coincided with the caliphate of al-Ma'mūn and al- Mu'tasim, the former's brother; and his imamate coincided with the continuation of the caliphate of al-Mu'tasim, as well as with the caliphates of al-Wāthiq, al- Mu'tasim's son; al-Mutawakkil, al-Wāthiq's brother; al-Muntasir, who was al-Mutawakkil's son; al-Musta'īn, the son of al- Muntasir's uncle (Muntasir's cousin on his paternal side, in other words); and al-Mu'taz, another one of al-Mutawakkil's sons. Imam Hādī ﷺ attained to martyrdom during the reign of al- Mu'taz.

---

[67] In the usage of Shī'a narrators of hadīth and historians, the First 'Father of Hasan' is the Seventh Imam, Imam Mūsā al-Kāżim ﷺ, and the Second 'Father of Hasan' is the Eighth Imam, Imam Ali b. Mūsā ar-Ridā ﷺ.

[68] Imamate - The religio-political leadership of the community. In the Shī'a conception of the leadership of the community, the functions of statesmanship, the discovery, interpretation and implementation of the sacred or revealed law, and the spiritual guidance of the community is integrated and vested in one person: the Imām; whereas in the Sunni conception these functions were trifurcated and vested, respectively, in the caliph (and later the sultans), the *fuqahā* (the juris-doctors), and the heads of the Sufi orders.

The Imam 🕊 was summoned by the tyrant al-Mutawakkil from Medina to Sāmarrā (which at that time was the capital of the Abbāsids), where he lived out the rest of his life in forced exile from his hometown and his [larger] family. Imam Hādī 🕊 and his son, Imam Hasan al-Askari 🕊 both lived under house arrest in Sāmarrā [which was then known as al-Askari (or "the Garrison" town)], and are thus both known as *al-askariān* (the Two [of the] Garrison [Town]).

Imam Ali an-Naqī 🕊 left behind four sons and one daughter. After his passing, his honorable son Imam Hasan al-Askari 🕊 attained to the office of the imamate and to the leadership of the community by specific divine designation (*nass*) by way of the Prophet 🕊 and by way of the designation of the Imams 🕊 before him.

2 The Imam's Character Traits

The Immaculate[69] Imams 🕊 had a special connection with God 🕊 and with the domains of reality which are beyond the ken of ordinary human perception (*al-ghayb*) on account of their immaculacy and their being far removed from the pollution of sin. As a consequence of this special connection, like the prophets, the Imams 🕊 were granted miracles and impossible wonders (*karāmāt*) which acted as proofs of the legitimacy of their claims to be divinely appointed to the office of the imamate and of their special relationship with God 🕊. Examples of such miracles and impossible wonders (such as the Imams' supernatural knowledge) would occur by God's leave in different contexts and in accordance with the

---

[69] Immaculacy (*I'sma'* = sinlessness as well as inerrancy). The Shī'a believe the Prophet 🕊, Lady Fātima 🕊, and the Twelve Imāms 🕊 to be immaculate, meaning that they are inerrant as well as sinless. Inerrant means one who does not commit any gross error, be it intentional or unintentional. I'smat is a continual state of inerrancy as well as sinlessness in the Shī'a definition of the term (whereas Sunni Islam limits its scope to the person of the Prophet and only in his function as bringer of revelation).

demands of different situations and conditions, thereby providing proofs and the means of divinely-inspired guidance for those who had not as yet attained to faith in their imamate, and providing occasions in which those who had attained to faith would be reassured therein and have their knowledge [of the reality of the domains of reality which are beyond the ken of ordinary human perception (*al-ghayb*)] increased by this means.

Numerous miracles and impossible wonders have been witnessed to emanate from Imam Hādī ﷺ, all of which have been duly recorded in the books of hadīth and in historical chronicles. Relating the stories of all such occasions would require a separate book in its own right; we shall therefore confine ourselves here to providing a few samples of stories which speak to the Imam's character traits and his relationship with the people, with his devoted followers, and with the rulers of his day.

As was stated earlier, Imam Hādī ﷺ attained to the office of the imamate after the death of his father when he was a child of eight years of age. The fact that he was able successfully to carry out the functions of this office at such an age is one of the clearest examples of the miracles that he was granted by Almighty God ﷻ. This is because the ability to shoulder the heavy burden of such an office – which is an onerous responsibility that can only be carried out by one designated for the purpose by Almighty God ﷻ – is something that is beyond the ability of not only children who have as yet to reach the age of majority, but of intelligent adults as well.

In light of the fact that the scholars of the religious sciences and of the science of hadīth scripture in particular would refer their questions to the next Imam upon the martyrdom and death of a given Imam. They would at times even put the divinely-commissioned successor Imams to the test; and taking into account also the fact that the nobles and dignitaries of that era, including those from the House of the Prophet ﷺ

of Islam, and from among the Ālids, the Abbāsids and all of the courtesans and military commanders associated with the Abbāsid court, all of whom were adults and were at the peak of their mental faculties, and who had relations and social interactions with the House of the Imams ﷺ – taking all of this into consideration, it defies logic and is inconceivable, therefore, to believe that a mere child would be able successfully to maintain his position as the officeholder of the imamate and as the leader of the community. Unless such a commission was one that was decided upon by the will of God, and unless the tenure to this office of such a minor was affirmed by God ﷻ by way of His granting its officeholder immaculacy and supernatural knowledge and powers. It is only through such means that a child would be able correctly and comprehensively to respond to any and all questions which would have been posed to him, and to lead the community authoritatively through its trials and tribulations. It is obvious that even ordinary people, let alone the scholars and dignitaries and notables of society, are capable of distinguishing between an ordinary child and one who is capable of carrying out the functions of the leadership of the Islamic community.

This is the kind of situation that Imam Jawād ﷺ was in as well. In the previous chapter, we explained why the office of the imamate is and must necessarily be one whose officeholder, like that of the office of prophethood, is selected and appointed by God, and why, therefore, the officeholder's age has nothing to do with the question and does not enter into the equation. Thus, we will take that issue as having been addressed and will here limit ourselves to a presentation of the historical evidence of the impossible wonders (*kirāmāt*) and miracles attributed to Imam Hādī ﷺ by way of the affirmation of the legitimacy of his claim to the office of the imamate.

Khayrān al-Asbāti reports: I travelled from Iraq to Medina and had the honor of being at the service of Imam Hādī ﷺ. His Excellency asked me, "How is Wāthiq?"

I said, "Would that I were sacrificed for your cause,[70] he is doing well and is in good health. My knowledge concerning him is greater than that of anyone else's [here present in Medina at this juncture in time] as I am close to him and furthermore, am a recent arrival here."

The Imam ﷺ said, "People say that he has died."

When the Imam ﷺ uttered these words, I understood that what he meant by "people" was the Imam himself. The Imam then said, "How was Ja'far [al-Mutawakkil, who was to become the next Abbāsid caliph]?"

I said, "He is in the worst state of wretchedness in prison."

The Imam ﷺ said, "He shall become the caliph."

He then asked, "What is [the vizier or prime minister] Ibn Zayyāt up to?"

I replied, "The people are behind him and his word carries the day."

To which the Imam ﷺ replied, "[The prospect of] his remaining in a position of ascendancy are inauspicious."

His Eminence ﷺ then fell silent for a while, then continued, "There is no escape from God's fate. O Khayrān! Know that Wāthiq has died, that Ja'far al-Mutawakkil has succeeded him to his throne, and that Ibn Zayyāt has been slain."

I asked, "Would that I were sacrificed for your cause, when did all this take place?"

He replied, "Six days after you left Iraq."

No more than a few days passed before al-Mutawakkil's messenger reached Medina with the news of the events that had transpired exactly as Imam Hādī ﷺ has stated.

---

[70] A formal form of address; the English equivalent would be something like "Your honor, …" or "My liege, …"

Abū-Hāshim al-Jaʿfarī reports: I was in Medina when Buqā, Wātheq's military chief of staff, was passing through medina in pursuit of Arab tribes [who had not submitted to Wāthiq's rule]. Imam Hādī ﷺ said that we should go and inspect this Turk's materiel and equipment. And so we left and stopped at a juncture where Buqā's troop was expected to pass through. His well-equipped detachment passed before us, after which the Turkish general also arrived. The Imam ﷺ spoke a few words with him in Turkish, after which the general dismounted and kissed the foot of the Imam's mount.

I later made my way to the Turkish general and beseeched him to tell me the story of what took place between him and the Imam ﷺ that day. At first he asked, "Is this man a prophet?"

I replied, "No."

He said, "He called me by a name which I used to be called as a child in my native land of the Turks; a name which no one else was aware of."

Shaykh Sulaymān al-Balkhī al-Qundūzī, a Sunni scholar, writes in his book, *Yanābiʿ al-Mawidda*: Masʿūdī, the great historian and geographer, has related that al-Mutawakkil ordered three predatory beasts to be brought to his palace. He then invited Imam Ali an-Naqī ﷺ to come to his palace, and when that nobleman entered the palace grounds, he ordered that the gates be closed behind him so that he would be left alone with three hungry predators.

The predators approached the Imam ﷺ slowly, and while they circled the Imam ﷺ, they displayed signs of their subservience and submission to him. The Imam ﷺ in turn stroked and petted them with the sleeve of his gown.

The beasts left the Imam ﷺ, who approached a structure which was placed in the middle of the grounds. He climbed the steps and saw al-

Mutawakkil there. He spoke to the tyrant for a while, then returned to the palatial grounds. The animals approached the Imam 🕊 again and paid their respects, accompanying him to the outer gate through which the Imam 🕊 left. For his part, al-Mutawakkil, who had become humiliated and felt ashamed, sent a large sum of money as a gift to the Imam 🕊.

[His courtesans] told al-Mutawakkil, "Your cousin [Imam Hādī 🕊] dealt with the predators in a way which we all witnessed. Now you do the same!"

Al-Mutawakkil replied, "Are you intent on killing me?!"

He then swore them to strict secrecy concerning what had happened so that the [miraculous] virtues of the Imam 🕊 would remain hidden from the people.

It is reported from Ashtar al-Alawi: When I was a child, I was in the court of the oppressive Abbāsid tyrant al-Mutawakkil together with my father. In a certain gathering, there were dignitaries present from among the House of Abū-Tālib [Imam Ali's 🕊 father], from the House of Abbās [the eponymous progenitor of the Abbāsids and Abū-Tālib's brother], and from the descendants of Ja'far [another son of Abū-Tālib's beside Imam Ali 🕊].[71] At some point, Imam Hādī 🕊 entered. All of those present outside al-Mutawakkil's palace dismounted as a sign of respect and deference for His Eminence the Imam 🕊 and paid their respects. The Imam then entered the palace. After the Imam 🕊 entered the palace, some among the nobility who had dismounted in a show of respect said to themselves, "Why do we dismount in a show of respect and deference to this youth? Neither is he senior to us in terms of his age, nor is his lineage

---

[71] All three were sons (and grandsons, in the case of Ja'far) of Abdul-Muttalib, who in addition to Abbās and Abū-Tālib, had two other sons: Hamza and Abdullāh, the latter of whom was the father of the Prophet Muhammad 🕊.

nobler than ours. Upon our oath to Allāh, we will no longer dismount before him!"

Abū-Hāshim the Ja'farite who was present among the nobility replied, "Upon my oath to Allāh, when you see His Excellency ﷺ, you will [indeed] dismount from your rides as a show of respect."

Not long had passed before the Imam exited al-Mutawakkil's palace. When people saw the Imam ﷺ, they dismounted and offered their respects, and the Imam ﷺ passed by them as they were [in a] standing [position, as a posture of respect].

Abū-Hāshim then asked, "Did you not say that you would no longer dismount as a show of respect for him? So what happened?!"

They said, "Upon our oaths to Allāh, we were not able to refrain ourselves, and dismounted involuntarily!"

At a time when the majority of the people of Esfahān were followers of the Sunni rites, there lived among them a Shī'a Muslim by the name of Abd ar-Rahmān. One day he was asked, "How did it come about that you accepted the Shī'a rite and turned away from your Sunni rite?"

He replied, "The reason for my change of allegiance is the miracle I witnessed from Imam Hādī ﷺ. The story is that I was poor and destitute. But because I had an eloquent and bold tongue, the people of Esfahān decided to send me along with the great dignitaries of the city to the court of the caliph al-Mutawakkil in order to [lodge a complaint and] demand justice and equity [in a certain case]. One day [after having arrived at the capital Baghdad], I was standing outside of al-Mutawakkil's palace when I heard that the caliph had summoned Ibn ar-Ridā ﷺ to his presence.

I asked people around me, "Who is this man whom the caliph has summoned to his presence?"

They said, "This man is an Ālid[72], and the Rāfiḍīs[73] consider him to be their Imam and leader. It is possible that the caliph has summoned him in order to pronounce his death sentence to him."

I told myself, "I won't move from where I am standing until this man of the Ālid clan comes and I can see him for myself." A while later I saw a man mounted on a horse approaching al-Mutawakkil's palace. The people made way in deference to him and stood to either side in two rows and all eyes were upon him. When my eyes fell upon him, he found his special place in my heart and the light of hope shone within it. I prayed God that He keep him safe from any mischief or evil that al-Mutawakkil might have in mind for him. His Eminence's gaze was downward toward his horse's mane and he was looking to his left and to his right. When he got to where I was standing, he looked at me and said, "God answered your prayer and granted you an extended lifespan and increased you in your wealth and offspring."

Hearing these words sent shivers up and down my spine and it was not long before I lost consciousness. When I came to, my companions asked me what had happened.

I said, "It is [all] for the good."

I did not tell them anything else concerning this matter. The Imam returned unharmed from the caliphal court. Almighty God gave me a great amount of wealth, such that what I have in my possession here in my house exceeds the sum of one million Dirhams, and I have much besides this outside of my residence. Almighty God has granted me the blessing of having ten children, and my age has exceeded seventy. In truth, I believe in the leadership (imamate) of that man who was aware of the secrets of my heart and mind and whose prayers in my favor were answered.

---

[72] A member of the House of Imam Ali.

[73] A pejorative way in which some of our Sunni brothers refer to the Shī'a.

Yūnus an-Naqqāsh was Imam Hādī's ﷺ neighbor in Sāmarrā and had the continual honor of being at the Imam's service and of serving His Eminence ﷺ. One day he came to the Imam ﷺ while he was shivering from fear and while his face had become as white as chalk.

The Imam ﷺ asked, "What is the matter?"

He said, "I have prepared myself for death!"

The Imam ﷺ allowed a little smile to come over his face and asked, "But why?"

Yūnus an-Naqqāsh said, "Mūsa ibn Baghā – one of the powerful courtiers and chamberlains of the Abbāsids – gave me a gemstone and commissioned me to inscribe a pattern upon it, but the problem is that it is a fake and has no intrinsic value. When I went to inscribe the pattern, the stone broke in two. And tomorrow is the day that was appointed for me to return the stone to him. If Mūsā sees the broken stone he will either give me a thousand lashings of his whip or he will kill me!"

The Imam ﷺ said, "Don't worry. Go back home and know that nothing but good will come of the events of the morrow."

First thing the next day, Yūnus came to the Imam's ﷺ house and while trembling with fear, he said, "Mūsa ibn Baghā's messenger has arrived. What am I to do??"

His Eminence ﷺ said, "Go to him in person and know that nothing but good will come of this affair."

Yūnus said, "My lord! What should I tell him?"

The Imam ﷺ said, with a smile on his face, "Go to him and listen to what he has to say to you. You will see that nothing but good will come of this."

Yūnus left and a little while later returned with a big smile on his face and said, "My lord! When I got there, he said that his two little girls have been fighting over the gemstone, so it would seem that if it is possible, it is best to split it in two so that there are two stones; in this way, they will both be happy. He then promised me a great reward for this work."

The Imam ﷺ thanked God ﷻ and said, "What did you tell him?"

Yūnus said, "I asked him for time to think over how I can accomplish this task."

The Imam 🌿 said, "You spoke well!"

Abū-Hāshim al-Ja'farī reports: It was a time when I had been stricken with severe poverty. I had the honor of visiting Imam Hādī 🌿. I asked permission to enter; he gave it and I entered and seated myself. The Imam 🌿 said, "O Abā Hāshim! Which of the blessings which God 🌿 has given you can you recall?"

Because I did not know what to say, I remained silent. Then the Imam 🌿 himself said, "God 🌿 granted you faith, by means of which he saved your soul from the fire of eternal damnation. God 🌿 granted you good health and aided you in your obedience to Him. And God 🌿 granted you contentment, protecting your honor therewith."

The Imam 🌿 then said, "O Abā Hāshim! I said these things because I believe you want to complain to me concerning He who has given you all of these things. I have instructed my people to give you one hundred Dirhams (gold coins). Please accept this [gift] from me."

Kāfūr al-Khādim[74] reports: I used to set aside a pail of water each night so that when the Imam 🌿 awoke in the middle of the night to offer his night devotions he would have water at the ready for making his ritual ablutions. One day the Imam 🌿 asked me to fill a pail for this purpose, and then sent me on an errand. When I returned from my errand, I forgot to fill the pail with water. It so happened that the weather was very cold that night, and

---

[74] *Khādim* means servant in Arabic.

there was a nasty bite to the wind. I suddenly woke up in the middle of the night remembering that I had forgotten to prepare a pail of water for His Eminence ﷺ. I thought that the beloved man would be angry with me for my having neglected to fulfill his request, and so I hid myself in a corner out of his sight.

Suddenly I heard the Imam ﷺ calling me. I feared his reproach. I kept thinking about what I would say if he asked me why I had neglected my duty. But I had no choice but to respond to his call, so I went forward toward him.

His Eminence ﷺ said, "Why, do you not know that I never use warm water to make my ablutions? So why have you filled the pail with warm water?"

I said, "Upon my word to Allāh, it was not me who warmed the water and set the pail of water there."

The Imam ﷺ smiled and said, "Reproach is God's province. I swear upon my oath to Allāh, I shall not turn down His gift. Praise be to God ﷻ who placed us among the [select] number of those who serve him. Verily, the Prophet ﷺ said, 'God ﷻ saves His wrath for those who reject His guidance'."

It is related that one day one of the enemies of Imam Hādī ﷺ asked the Abbāsid tyrant al-Mutawakkil, "Why do you trouble yourself concerning Ali ibn Muhammad [al-Hādī] ﷺ?" Whenever he enters into your palace, everyone present pays him their respects and treats him with honor and behaves as if they are at his beck and call, to the point that they will not allow him even to draw a curtain aside or to open a door. If news of this kind of treatment reaches the ears of the common folk, they will lose trust in you and think to themselves that the caliph must indeed know the high spiritual station of the Imam ﷺ for him to treat him with such respect and honor."

The caliph asked, "So what is to be done then?"

The man replied, "Every time he comes to pay you a visit, let him draw the curtain aside himself and let him open the door for himself, [and generally treat him like you would any other ordinary person] so that any hardship that befalls others likewise befalls him."

The caliph al-Mutawakkil instructed his staff and courtesans, saying that no one is allowed to wait on the Imam ﷺ and to serve him, and ordered his spies to be on the lookout for any who violates his instructions and to report such a case to him.

One day al-Mutawakkil invited the Imam ﷺ to his palace. His spies reported to him that when the Imam ﷺ was to make his entry, a gust of wind set the curtains aside and opened the door for him so that he was not burdened with the trifling onus of having to open the curtain and door himself. Al-Mutawakkil told them to be sure to monitor the Imam's ﷺ egress and to report back to him on this. The spies reported that when the Imam ﷺ made his exit, a gust of wind arose again; and again, the curtains were set aside and the door was opened for him so that he was not burdened with having to open the curtain or door himself on his exit either!

The caliph became concerned that news of the Imam's ﷺ supernatural powers would reach the people, thereby strengthening their faith in his leadership. He thus instructed his staff to do as they did before and set the curtain aside and to open the door for him.

Quṭb ar-Rāwandī has reported: The Abbāsid caliph ordered the Turkish contingent among his troops (which were ninety thousand in number) to fill their horses' saddlebags with clay and to empty them in a designated place in the desert. When the troops had finished carrying out his command, a large mound of ruddy clay had been made. The caliph then instructed them to compact and level the large mound and to place his throne upon it. He then seated himself upon his throne and summoned Imam Hādī ﷺ to his presence. When the Imam ﷺ joined him, he ordered his troops to march before them in full army gear and regalia, wanting to impress his authority and power upon the Imam ﷺ in order to intimidate him and to rid the Imam ﷺ of any thoughts of insurrection against the caliph that he or any of the other Ālids might be entertaining.

After the demonstration was concluded the Imam ﷺ told the caliph, "Would you like me to also show you my legion now?"

The caliph answered in the affirmative. His Eminence ﷺ then raised his hands up in supplication to Almighty God, and then turned to the caliph and said, "Take a look!"

The caliph looked and saw the entire field of his vision from east to west and from the earth to the heavens filled with angels armed with weapons and armaments, ready for battle.

Having seen this sight, the caliph fainted and fell from his throne to the ground!

Ishāq ibn Abdullāh al-'Alawi reports: A difference of opinion arose between my father and my uncles concerning the days of the year in which supererogatory ritual fasting was recommended. Consequently, they decided to seek the help of Imam Hādī ﷺ to make a ruling so that the truth would be settled between them.

At this time, the Imam ﷺ resided in Suryā, and had not as yet been summoned to Sāmarrā. As soon as they entered into the presence of the Imam ﷺ, because the Imam ﷺ was aware of the nature of their difference by virtue of his supernatural knowledge, he did not wait for them to mention their question and said, "Are you ready to put your question to me concerning the recommended days of the year for the supererogatory ritual fasts?"

They replied, "Verily, O son of the Apostle of God!"

His Eminence said, "Those days consist of

- the 17th of Rabi' al-Awwal, which is the day when the Most Noble Prophet was born;
- the 27th of Rajab, which is the day when the Most Noble Prophet was commissioned to his prophethood;
- the 25th of Dhī-Qa'da, which is the day when the Earth was created; and
- the 18th of Dhī-Hajja, which is the day of [the Sermon of] Ghadīr [Khumm],⁷⁵ when the Commander of the Faithful [Ali ibn Abī-Tālib] was appointed by the Prophet as the successor to his ministry and to the leadership of his community."

Abū-Hāshim al-Ja'farī reports: Because of the great love I had for Imam Hādī, one day I told His Eminence, "O son of the Apostle of God! Whenever I take my leave from your presence in Sāmarrā and return to Baghdad, the passion of wanting to visit you again does not let me eat or sleep [properly], and I become restless, and alas, I do not have a swift horse on which I can ride to make pilgrimage to your presence continually. I have a donkey who is old and weak and who no longer has the power to

---

⁷⁵ Ghadīr Khumm is the name of the pond at which the Prophet stopped his caravan on the way back from his final pilgrimage, at which he appointed Imam Ali as his immediate successor, and at which he appointed the People of his House as his successors more generally.

be my mount. Pray supplicate to almighty God ﷻ on my behalf to grant me the power to make pilgrimage to your presence on a continual basis."

The Imam then ؑ prayed for me. After his supplication, my donkey and I were granted such a tremendous amount of energy that I would make my morning ritual devotions in Baghdad, mount my ride and start on the long journey[76] to Sāmarrā, and would reach it before the day was done, and would call upon the Imam ؑ, and if I so desired, could return to Baghdad that same evening.

One day a woman was brought to the court of the Abbāsid caliph al-Mutawakkil. She said, "I am Zaynab, the daughter of Lady Fāṭimaᵗ al-Zahrā ؑ, and the grand-daughter of the Prophet ﷺ."

Mutawakkil said, "Decades have passed from the time of Zaynab's death. How is it that you have been able to maintain your youth??"

The young woman replied, "One day, the Apostle of God ﷺ placed his hand on my head and made a prayer for me. Since then, my youth returns to me every forty years."

Mutawakkil who had become bewildered by the woman told his staff to summon the leaders of the House of Abū-Ṭālib, the House of Abbās, and various dignitaries from the tribe of Quraysh more generally. When they had been gathered, the woman repeated her claim. Those present said, "This woman lies. Zaynab ؑ died a few years after the event of Āshūrā."

The young woman replied, "It is you who lie! From that day to the present, I have been hidden from view by God's will, and no one was aware of my condition, and today I have reappeared by God's will."

---

[76] Sāmarrā stands on the east bank of the Tigris in the Saladin Governorate, 125 kilometers (78 miles) north of Baghdad.

Mutawakkil asked the dignitaries, "Do you have a rational and firm reason for refuting her claim?"

Everyone was tongue-tied and no one gave any response until someone spoke up and said, "Only one person can engage this woman in argument and prove the falsity of her claim, and that person is His Eminence the Imam al-Hādī ﷺ."

Mutawakkil ordered the Imam ﷺ to be brought to him, by force if necessary. When His Eminence ﷺ made his appearance, Mutawakkil related the story of the woman to him.

His Eminence the Imam ﷺ said, "This woman is lying. Zaynab ﷺ died in such and such a year."

Mutawakkil said, "Others have said the same thing. But do you have a reason to prove your claim?"

Imām Hādī ﷺ replied, "My evidence is the fact that the flesh of the children of Lady Fātima ﷺ is forbidden to beast of prey. Send her among hungry lions; if she is telling the truth, they will not harm her."

When Mutawakkil told the woman of Imam Hādī's response to her claim, she replied, "He wants to kill me with this ruse!"

In reply, the Imam ﷺ said, "There are several offspring of Lady Fātima ﷺ here present. Choose any one of them that you will to test the truth of my claim."

The faces of everyone present became white as chalk [from fear of being chosen as the subject of the test by the young woman], and they each were searching for a solution [to get them out of their bind]. They said, "Why don't you go to the lions yourself instead of telling others to do so?" Mutawakkil who was delighted with this retort said, "O Abul-Hasan, why don't you go to the lions yourself?"

The Imam ﷺ said, "If that is your desire, I shall certainly do so."

Mutawakkil then said, "I beg you then to put an end to this affair personally."

At al-Mutawakkil's behest, a ladder was lowered into a great pit where several wild lions were kept, and His Eminence Imam Hādī ﷺ used it to lower himself into the pit. The sharp-toothed predators circled around the Imam ﷺ, and the Imam ﷺ went into a seated position in the middle of the circle that the lions had made. The great beasts would come to the Imam ﷺ and rub their heads to the ground before him in a sign of their submission to him, and the Imam ﷺ would stroke their heads and pet them. Eventually the Imam ﷺ ordered the lions to make way, and the wild predators each made their way meekly to a corner.

At this point one of the enemies of the Imam ﷺ told Mutawakkil, "Bring him out of that pit at once, for if the people see him in there with the lions, they will turn to him [as their leader]."

Mutawakkil asked the Imam ﷺ to come out of the pit. When the Imam ﷺ was making his way to the ladder and up it, the lions came to him and rubbed their heads against his clothes. But the Imam ﷺ ordered them to return to where they were, and the lions duly complied.

His Eminence the Imam ﷺ came out of the pit and said, "Anyone who claims to be the progeny of Lady Fātima ﷺ can make their way into the pit and take his or her seat beside the beasts of prey."

The woman who had burst into tears from the freight of the prospect said, "I lied and made a false claim. This was because I was an indigent and wretched girl, and I wanted to earn my fortune by this ruse."

Mutawakkil ordered her to be thrown among the lions, but presently al-Mutawakkil's mother came out and interceded on behalf of the young woman. The caliph then forgave the woman and set her free.

Īsā ibn Ahmad was a Shī'a Muslim and a companion of Imam Hādī ﷺ. He reports: One day it happened that I was honored to be in the presence of Imam Ali an-Naqī ﷺ. I told him, "O son of the Apostle of God! It is some time since I have become the subject of al-Mutawakkil's wrath. He has cut off my stipend and distanced himself from me, and this has caused me much suffering and hardship because I suspect that he has discovered my allegiance to Your Eminence, and that I am honored to make frequent pilgrimages to your presence. However, as the caliph holds you in great respect and would not turn down any request of yours, I beseech you to intercede on my behalf so that I can return to my work and resume my normal life again."

The Imam ﷺ replied, "Your case will be resolved, God ﷻ willing."

I was elated and took my leave from the presence of the Imam ﷺ and headed back home. At night several people came to my door and asked for me by name with raised voices. I opened the door and asked them what their business was. They said that the caliph had summoned me on an urgent matter. I left the house in a state of anxiety intermingled with hope and made my way to al-Mutawakkil's palace in the accompaniment of his soldiers. When I reached the door of the caliph's chambers, I found Fath ibn Khāqān standing there. When he saw me, he came forward and said, "Where have you been? The caliph has been looking for you for some time, and we have expended much effort searching for you!"

When I entered the caliphal chambers al-Mutawakkil was seated on his bed. When he saw me, he smiled and said, "O Abū-Mūsā! I had neglected you for a while as I have been very busy with pressing matters; but why did you also forget us and not remind us of your rights and stipend? So now tell me what I owe you so that I can pay it forthwith!"

I stated what credits I had, and the caliph instructed his accountant to pay me double what I had mentioned. I then asked permission to leave and left the chamber.

Fath ibn Khāqān was still standing outside the door. I asked him, "Did Imam Hādī ﷺ pay a visit here today?"

"No," he said.

"Did the Imam ﷺ send a letter to the caliph today in which I was recommended to the caliph by him?"

The answer was negative again.

While I was still amazed and dumb-founded by what had just taken place, I had just left the palace grounds when I saw that Fath ibn Khāqān was running after me at speed. I stopped to let him catch up to me and asked, "Did you need me for something?"

He said, "I have no doubt that Imam Hādī ﷺ has made a prayer for you. Ask His Eminence ﷺ to pray for me too!"

I was honored to be in the presence of the Imam ﷺ on the morrow of the following day. On seeing me the Imam ﷺ asked me, "Is everything to your satisfaction now?"

I said, "Yes, O my master! I attained to my satisfaction thanks to your good graces. But when I asked around, I was told that you had not been to visit the caliph, and neither had you sent a missive to him. So how were you able to set my affairs in order?"

The Imam ﷺ said, "In important matters, we resort only to Almighty God, and rely on none other than Him in our times of hardship and trials. And whenever we supplicate God ﷻ for something, our prayers are [invariably] answered. And if we turn away from God, He too will turn away from us."

I said, "Fath ibn Khāqān asked that you make a supplication to God ﷻ on his behalf and to teach him a prayer."

The Imam ﷺ replied, "He pretends to befriend us on the outside, but on the inside, he keeps his distance from us. Therefore, prayer will be of no avail for him, because prayers are answered only for those who are sincere in their obedience to God, and who confess to and have certainty in the *wilāyat*[77] of the Prophet ﷺ and of us, the Ahl al-Bayt ﷺ; so that

---

[77] *Wilāyaʾ*: dominion, sovereignty, proxy sovereignty or regency, authority, guardianship, jurisdiction, reign, command, and by no means least, religious solidarity among the community of those who have attained to faith based on propinquity or spiritual proximity to God. *Wilāyaʾ* means spiritual proximity to God ﷻ but in most Shīʿa contexts also refers to the regency or guardianship-type sovereign authority which is vested in the Fourteen Immaculates as a result of that

the prayers of one who does not meet these conditions is not answered.

Habbat-Allāh ibn Abī-Mansūr reports: There lived in the region known as Rabī'a a Christian man by the name of Yūsuf ibn Ya'qūb ﷺ (Joseph ﷺ, the son of Jacob ﷺ) who was a longtime tried and trusted friend of my father's. One day Yūsuf ﷺ came to our home in a state of fear and agitation and went to my father and said, "al-Mutawakkil has summoned me!"

My father asked him, "What business does the caliph have with you??"

He said, "I do not know, but I fear that he might want to punish me in some way, or worse. In any event, I have vowed [to give] one hundred gold coins [in charity if I survive this trial], and I will take these with me so that if I escape with my life, I will be able to give them to the Imam of the Shī'a, Ibn ar-Ridā ﷺ.

My father said, "This is the best decision you could have made, as you have insured yourself against the caliph in this way."

The Christian went on his journey and came straight to our house upon his return, cheerful as a cricket. My father told him, "Tell me everything that happened."

The Christian related, "I entered Sāmarrā, the caliphal capital, with fear and hope in my heart. This was the first time I set foot in that

---

proximity. *Walāya'* refers to a special type of sovereignty that is the central pillar of the Shī'a conception of the imāmate or the Islamic vision of the way in which the polity of the community is to be structured, with the *imām* or leader of the community having *walīyic* or guardianship-type sovereignty over his adherents, and to whom a pledge of allegiance is due and which affirms the Imams's ﷺ regency over the affairs of the community.

city and I did not know anyone there, nor did I have any idea about the layout of the city and where things were to be found; and no one knew me there either, or anything about what my business was. I thought to myself that I should deliver the gold coins to the Imam of the Shī'a before calling upon the caliph. But I had heard that the caliph was a tyrant and that he kept a close watch on the comings and goings about the house of the Imam ؈ and does not allow him to leave his residence. I feared that if I asked where the Imam's house was, news of my inquiry might reach the caliph's spies, who would in turn report their findings to Mutawakkil, stoking his wrath towards me even further. I dwelled on this problem for an hour or so, and finally decided upon a plan. I told myself, 'I will ride a donkey and let its reins loose so that it can go in whatever direction it chooses. Maybe as I am wandering around aimlessly, I will hear tale of the Imam's residence among the people in the streets and in the bazaar and be able to reach my goal without having made a single inquiry.' I left the caravanserai together with my manservant and the gold coins, and I let loose the donkey's reins. The animal started to move on his own volition. It went through the bazaar and through several streets and neighborhoods and eventually came to rest near a house. I understood that the house was the residence of the leader of the Shī'a from how people were talking in its environs. I was startled and very pleased that I had found my objective effortlessly, and thought to myself, "This is the first sign."

As this thought was crossing my mind, a black-skinned servant came out of the house and beckoned to me. When I went to him he asked, "Are you Yūsuf ؈, the son of Ya'qūb ؈?"

I said, "Yes."

At his behest I entered into the vestibule and corridor of the house, after which he left me to myself. I thought to myself, "This is the second sign."

After a while the manservant returned and said, "Imam Hādī ؈ says that you should give me the pouch of gold."

I took out the pouch from my waistband and gave it to him and thought to myself, "This is the third sign. My Lord, how does the leader of the Shī'a have knowledge of everything and how is he able to facilitate things as he does??"

The servant returned and said, "His Eminence ﷺ has given you permission to enter. Come this way please."

I entered the room and saw the great man seated alone in his chamber. After exchanging greetings, he said to me, "O Yūsuf! Has the time not come for you to be guided [aright]?"

I replied, "My lord! I have been witness to strange happenings today which have increased my certainty in you."

The Imam ﷺ said, "Far from it! You shall not attain to faith in and enter into Islam, but your son so and so will become a Shī'a and one of our devoted followers."

The Imam ﷺ continued, "A group of people believe that our *wilāya*⁷⁸ and friendship has no benefit for you Christians. But upon my oath to Allāh, they speak not the truth. Verily, our *wilāya* and friendship benefits the likes of you. Go forth and see to the business for which you have come, and know that things will turn out to your liking."

The Christian man continued his tale: "I went to the court of the caliph with complete peace of mind and a contented heart, and without a trace of fear or anxiety, and left the caliph whole and contented."

Yūsuf ibn Ya'qūb passed away a few years later. I happened to come across one of his sons one day. He told me that he was a companion and follower of Imam Hādī ﷺ, and he told me that his father died as a Christian. Yūsuf's son was proud of the fact that he was guided to the right path by the guidance of his master Imam Ali an-Naqī ﷺ.

---

⁷⁸ See footnote #78.

Sa'īd ibn Sahl reports: Ja'far ibn Qāsim al-Hāshimi did not believe in the imamate of Imam Hādī. I was together with him on a journey when we happened to come across His Eminence Imam Hādī. His Eminence told him, "How much longer do you intend to remain in your state of slumber? Has the time not arrived for you to wake up?"

A few days passed. One of the caliph's offspring had a child and invited us to the celebration banquet. We went to the feast and after a while, Imam Hādī also joined the gathering and sat down. Everyone became quiet in a show of deference and respect for the great man. But a youth started laughing and goofing around and showing disrespect to the Imam.

His Eminence turned to the youth and said, "You fill your mouth with laughter and have become heedless of God, even though you will be in your grave in three days' time?"

The youth's smile froze on his lips, he fell silent and stopped his rowdiness. I told Ja'far ibn Qāsim, "These words of the Imam's can be grounds for proving or refuting the legitimacy of the Imam's claim to the imamate. Let us wait the three days and see what transpires."

We ate the dinner and left the banquet. The following day, the youth fell ill and passed away at the dawn of the third day. He was buried on the evening of the same day.

When we became aware of what had happened, Ja'far said, "I swear [upon my oath] to Allāh, I now believe in the leadership (*imama'*) of that honorable man!"

It is related that one day a man came to the presence of the Imam while weeping and trembling with fear. When the Imam inquired as to the reason for his tears the man replied, "They have arrested my son on account of his devotion to you, the People of the House of the Prophet

ﷺ (the *ahl al-bayt* ﷺ), and for following the way of life of the Commander of the Faithful (Ali ibn Abī-Tālib ﷺ), and they plan to throw him down from the top of a hill. They have even dug a pit at the bottom of the hill so that they can bury him there after he dies from the fall."

His Eminence ﷺ asked, "What is it that you want?"

The man said, "I want that which every mother and father wants: the health and safety of their children."

The Imam ﷺ said, "Have no fear on account of your son. Return to your home with peace of mind. Your son will come to you on the morrow."

The man thanked the Imam ﷺ, offered his respects and took his leave and returned home with peace of mind. He did not sleep a wink that night, being in wait for his son's return. At the dawning of the sun, there was a knock at the house's door. The man rushed to the door and opened it. His son entered and took his father into his arms. The father's eyes became wet with tears of joy. They entered into the living room and the father asked his son to relate the tale of what had happened to him. The son said, "They tied my hands behind my back and walked me to the top of the hill. At the bottom of the hill the mouth of the pit that they had dug for my burial was agape and beckoned me towards it. I had lost all hope of surviving this ordeal, and so I pronounced my *shahādatayn*[79] and awaited my death with tears in my eyes. Then ten men who were strangers to me came forward and asked me why I was weeping.

---

[79] The *shahādatayn* is the declaration of the testament of faith - i.e. "I bear witness that there is no deity other than God (Allāh) ﷻ and I bear witness that Muhammad is His bondsman and apostle." These words are uttered by those who know that they will be meeting their Maker soon, as an affirmation of their faith in Him and in His messenger.

I replied, "I have been arrested for the crime of befriending the People of the House of the Prophet ﷺ and for accepting their *wilāyat* [80], and they intend to put me to death for this crime."

They replied, "Would you like to see this hangman meet his death in your stead and be thrown down this hill?"

I said, "Yes, for he is a sworn enemy of the *ahl al-bayt* ﷺ, the People of the House of the Prophet ﷺ, and is the executioner of countless Shī'a Muslims."

"Very well. But this deed has a condition."

"What is the condition?"

"The condition is that you leave town under cover immediately and go to Medina and spend the rest of your days beside the sacred shrine of the Apostle of God ﷺ. Do you accept this condition?"

"Yes, I accept."

The ten strangers then took the executioner and threw him down the hill in such a way that no one heard his cries. They then threw his body into the pit and covered it with soil. Presently no one knows that the person who is in the grave is not me and that the bloodthirsty hangman has gone to his perdition. The ten strangers are outside the house waiting for me so that they can send me on my way to Medina, and I have come here to say my last farewells."

After these words, the father and son again embraced each other, and the son said his farewells and left the house, never to return.

A few days later the father went to the Imam ﷺ and related the tale to him.

From that time on, the talk on the street was about that youth. People would say, "Did you hear about so and so, and how they threw him to his death from the top of that hill and buried him in a pit at the bottom of that same hill? …"

---

[80] *Walāyat*: See *footnote #78*.

When the Imam ﷺ would hear such talk, a smile would come to his face and he would say, "People do not know that which we know."

Abū-Hāshim al-Ja'farī reports: The bloodthirsty Abbāsid caliph al-Mutawakkil had made a house out of adobe bricks in a modular fashion such that the sun's rays would always shine into its chambers wheresoever it turned on the horizon. He had placed many birdcages in this house and had imprisoned a large number of birds within them. When the birds broke out in their lament, the din was so loud that it was as if the ears of Heaven itself would be pierced. Mutawakkil took pleasure in the melancholy hubbub and ruckus of the birds and enjoyed seeing the people being ill at ease and tormented [by this condition].

On certain occasions the caliph would sojourn in that house and accept company there. People would go to him in that house to pay their respects and would say things in that loud ruckus which the caliph could not hear, and he would say things which were not fully comprehensible to his interlocutors, who would nod their head nonetheless out of politeness or by way of standing on ceremony, and would affirm what the caliph was saying, as he smiled at them with pleasure.
But whenever the People of the House of the Prophet ﷺ invited Imam Ali an-Naqī ﷺ to that house, all the birds would cease their chatter and song immediately upon the Imam's ﷺ entry into the house. The partridges would stop bantering with each other and the other birds would not move an inch, and it would be as if they were frozen in place. Mutawakkil would speak to the Imam ﷺ and the Imam ﷺ would listen to him in the complete silence which reigned over the house and respond to him, and the people there gathered would be stunned at the silence that prevailed while the Imam ﷺ was present in the house. Once the Imam's ﷺ business was finished and he would take his leave and exit the house, the partridges

would resume their debates, the blue-jays would pick up where they left off in their arguments, and the birds would generally start their chatter and banter and raise a deplorable din once more!

Mutawakkil's guards and spies were charged with securing the Imam's ﷺ whereabouts in Medina and monitoring his comings and goings and reporting to the caliph's governor in Medina, who would in turn report back to the caliph himself.

The governor of Medina was an evil and villainous man who constantly plotted against the Imam ﷺ and strove to make life difficult for him. Such was the Imam's ﷺ living conditions in Medina when the caliph decided to summon him to Sāmarrā where he had his garrison and which served as his capital, and where he could keep the Imam ﷺ under house arrest and keep a much closer eye on him. To this purpose the caliph instructed Yaḥyā ibn Harthama to march on Medina with his contingent and bring the Imam ﷺ to Sāmarrā.

Yaḥyā ibn Harthama reports: The news had already reached the people of Medina that the caliph had an evil intention or some wicked plan with respect to Imam Ali an-Naqī ﷺ, to the point that when I entered Medina, the people there surrounded me and my platoon and started pleading, moaning and wailing, begging me not to harm the Imam ﷺ.

I placated them by telling them I had not come to kill or molest the Imam ﷺ, and that rather, my assignment was to honorably escort the Imam ﷺ to Sāmarrā.

I then went to the Imam's ﷺ house and searched it, but found nothing but the Quran and books of prayer. The Imam's ﷺ behavior toward me was nothing if not kind and respectful, such that he found a special place in my heart and I was impressed by the awe and grandeur of the great man.

I gave the caliph's letter to the Imam ﷺ who, having read it, instructed his family to pack their belongings and prepare for the journey to Sāmarrā.

The Imam ﷺ and his entourage left Medina while the people of Medina had closed their shops and had come out to bid the Imam ﷺ farewell and to escort him to the edge of the city. My troops and I had surrounded the Imam ﷺ and I had given strict orders to my troops to be sure to treat the Imam ﷺ with respect and to obey his instructions and demands, and to make sure that no disrespect or offense arose on our part.

In one of the days that we spent on the journey, I saw His Eminence ﷺ mount his horse having donned rain clothes and having tied his horse's tail in a knot. I was taken aback because the sky was clear and not a single cloud could be seen on the horizon and the sun shone in the fullness of its intensity.

But it was not long before the weather changed. Clouds rushed forward and hid the sun behind them. Thunder and lightning filled the sky and a flood-like torrent began to rain down, and it rained so hard that it put me and my troops to quite some trouble.

A while later the rain stopped and the sky cleared. The Imam ﷺ called me and said, "I know you were surprised at what I did and doubted [the wisdom of] my [actions] in your heart. Because I have lived in the desert, I can recognize winds which are followed by rain and can smell the rain on them. There was a morning breeze today and I smelled the rain on it, which is why I prepared for it."

In time we reached Baghdad. I went to the house of Ishāq ibn Ibrāhīm, the Governor, for my quarters. When Ishāq saw me, he said to me with a worried tone in his voice, "Man alive! The person you have brought with you is the son of the Prophet ﷺ! You know al-Mutawakkil well, and well do you know also the enmity and rancor which he holds in his heart toward the House and Family of the Prophet ﷺ . Thus, if you say anything to the caliph which will cause him to want to murder the

Imam ﷺ, you will have bought yourself the enmity of the Prophet ﷺ and his blessed and purified House. Beware lest you do such a thing!"

I said, "I swear [upon my oath] to Allāh, I have not seen any untoward deed from His Eminence ﷺ, nor have I heard anything against al-Mutawakkil being uttered by him. Everything that I have seen during my time with him has been honorable and nothing short of exemplary."

A few days later we left Baghdad for Sāmarrā. When we arrived at Sāmarrā, I went directly to Wasayf al-Turkī. He was the general of al-Mutawakkil's army, and I served directly under his command. After I gave him the report of my assignment, he said, "O Yahyā! I swear [upon my oath] to Allāh, if even a single hair is diminished from the head of this nobleman, you will have to answer to me!"

I gave him all the assurances that I could think of on the spur of the moment and took my leave and headed for the court of the caliph; but I was bewildered at the words of caution of the Governor of Baghdad and the Chief of Staff of the Caliph's army, and could not make head or tail of the reason for such counsels no matter how I tried. When I entered the palace, permission to enter the caliphal chambers was granted at once. I entered and gave the report of my assignment to the caliph and related each and every detail of what I had witnessed of the Imam ﷺ during the journey. Mutawakkil asked to see the Imam ﷺ and honored him and presented him with a very valuable gift which was befitting the Imam's ﷺ station, and did not hold back in any way in honoring the Imam ﷺ and in paying him due tribute.

[The great historian and geographer] al-Mas'ūdī reports: One day al-Mutawakkil summoned Imam Ali an-Naqī ﷺ to his palace. When the Imam ﷺ entered the palace, he stood facing the qibla (i.e. the direction of prayer facing the Great Mosque of the Ka'ba in Mecca) and began praying to his Lord and Maker. Presently one of the Imam's ﷺ enemies arrived also, and seeing the Imam ﷺ busy with his devotions, went and stood in front of him and shouted, "How long do you intend to put up this pretense [of religiosity]??"

The man's shouting turned everyone's attention to the Imam ﷺ who quickly brought his devotions to a close and greeted the gathering. He then turned to that man and said, "If you slandered me with the accusation of duplicity and hypocrisy which you levelled against me, may God ﷻ utterly destroy you."

The Imam's ﷺ words had not yet finished ringing in the room when that man fell to the floor and his heart stopped beating. People gathered round him in haste, only to see that he had died and it was as if it had been ages since his spirit had departed his body.

The news of this occurrence spread through al-Mutawakkil's palace and then throughout the town like wildfire and became a further cause for the caliph's enmity and rancor towards Imam Hādī ﷺ, and for the people's becoming further acquainted with the spiritual station of the great man.

Ahmad ibn Isrāīl reports: I was Mu'tazz ibn al-Mutawakkil's scribe. I was at his service wherever he went and would write down what he said. One day I went with Mu'tazz to the palace of his father Mutawakkil, the Abbāsid caliph. Mutawakkil was seated on his throne and Fath ibn Khāqān, his vizier or prime minister was standing beside him. Mu'tazz greeted the caliph and remained standing, and I stood behind him. The custom was such that whenever Mu'tazz entered the caliphal chambers, [being the heir-apparent], the caliph would honor him formally, engage him in discussions [concerning matters of state] and give him some instructions to carry out. But it so happened that on this particular day the caliph was so angry and incensed that he did not notice his son's entry and did not hear or acknowledge his greeting. Mutawakkil was extremely angry and was speaking to Fath ibn Khāqān while he was red in the face, saying, "The person whom you are defending has done such and such…"

For his part, Fath ibn Khāqān was trying to douse the flames of the caliph's anger by way of making placatory statements such as, "These things which you say about Ibn ar-Ridā [Imam Hādī ﷺ] are lies which people have falsely attributed to him, and he himself is not aware of these things…"

But al-Mutawakkil was not to be placated, and shouted, "I shall kill this duplicitous scoundrel who carries out a pretense of religiosity, all the while undermining the government and the public order!"

He then ordered four newly captured slaves to be prepared. They were from the Turkic tribe of Khaz and did not speak Arabic and the caliph spoke to them through a translator. Mutawakkil gave them each a sword and said, "After that man enters and I give you the sign, all of you should attack him in unison and kill him."

And then, while he was still trembling with anger, he said, "I swear [upon my oath] to Allāh ﷻ that after killing him, I shall burn his body in a great fire! He then ordered his aides to summon Imam Hādī ﷺ to the palace.

About an hour had passed when the Imam ﷺ entered, moving slowly and with deliberation and quite at peace, with no trace of fear or anxiety on his face. When al-Mutawakkil saw the Imam ﷺ, he stood up at haste from his throne, approached the Imam ﷺ, embraced him, kissed his forehead and hands and greeted him with the greatest possible respect, while he still held a sword in his hand. He then said, "My lord! O son of the Apostle of God ﷺ! O he who is the best of creation! My dear cousin! My lord and master! For what reason have you troubled yourself at this time of day and honored us with your presence?"

The Imam ﷺ replied, "Your messenger came and summoned me here."

Mutawakkil said, "That imbecile has lied! My lord and master, pray return to your home!"

He then turned to Mu'tazz and Fath ibn Khāqān and said, "Escort your lord and my master to his home!"

When the Imam ﷺ was taking his leave from the chamber, the four Khaz bondsmen threw their drawn swords onto the ground and having become taken by the great Imam's ﷺ awe and grandeur and sacrality, kneeled before His Eminence ﷺ and paid their respects to him.

After the Imam was on his way back to his house, the caliph said to the translator, "Ask them why they did not obey my order and why they did not carry out their duty?"

The bondsmen replied, "That nobleman had such a tremendous awe and grandeur and sacred spiritual quality about his person that by being in his presence we were no longer ourselves and lost all volition and were unable to act in any other way [than to show him the respect that was due him]."

[The great Shī'a scholar of the science of hadīth] Sayyid Ibn Tāwūs reports: One day, al-Mutawakkil, who was constantly looking for ways in which to harass and pester Imam Hādī ﷺ, hatched a plan. That day, which was a very hot day, he and his vizier Fath ibn Khāqān mounted their horses and started forward at high noon. Before doing so the caliph had instructed all of the nobility and the dignitaries and notables of the city to follow them on foot. One of the people who was supposed to follow them was Imam Ali an-Naqī ﷺ.

Zarrāfi, who was al-Mutawakkil's chamberlain, says, "In those days, I saw Imam Hādī ﷺ who was walking in tandem with the dignitaries and notables of the city. I went up to him and said, 'O son of the Apostle of God 🌼, why have you troubled yourself [to join this procession in this heat]'?"

The Imam 🌼 replied, "Their intention is to humble and humiliate me, whereas my standing in God's eyes is not less than that of Sāleh's 🌼 camel[81]."

Zarrāfi reports: When I returned home, I related the story to the teacher of my children, because I suspected that he was a Shī'a Muslim and I wanted to test him. When I finished telling him the story, he abjured me against uttering any falsehood and asked, "Did you [really] hear these words from Imam Hādī 🌼 [personally]?"

I swore that I was telling the truth and that I had indeed heard the words from Imam Hādī 🌼 himself. The teacher said, "Then look out for your interests, for the caliph will be killed in three days' time. Be sure you do not get entangled in this affair, for otherwise you will come to harm also."

I asked, "How is it possible for you to make this prophecy?"
He said, "Because the Imam 🌼 never lies. According to the text of the Quran, after the people to whom the prophet Sālih 🌼 has been sent had slew the she-camel, Almighty God 🌼 destroyed them after three days."

When I heard these words, I became certain that he is a Muslim of the Shī'a rite, so I grew angry at him, cursed him and shouted at him, and threw him out of my house. But then I got to thinking, "What if he was telling the truth, and that there is a pregnant danger that is hanging over me?" And so, I decided to take precautions. I stayed at home for three days and gathered my family and wealth around me, and prepared myself and my family for any unexpected event. And I avoided going to the court of the caliph so as not to become entangled in any intrigues, if any were afoot.

---

[81] This is a Quranic reference. See 7:73 – 7:79, as well as 11:61 – 11:68.

On the third day, al-Muntasir, al-Mutawakkil's son, attacked al-Mutawakkil's court with his faithful bondsmen and killed him and his vizier Fath ibn Khāqān, ripping them to shreds.

After this incident, I attained to faith in the *wilāya*[t 82] and imamate of Imam Hādī ﷺ. Later on, I was honored to be in the presence of the Imam ﷺ and related the story of what had taken place between myself and the teacher of my children.

The Imam ﷺ said, "That teacher had spoken the truth. That day, I cursed al-Mutawakkil and Almighty God ﷻ answered my prayer."

Hasan ibn Mas'ūd, a companion of Imam Hādī's ﷺ reports: I had said some controversial things in a mixed crowd and our enemies had torn my robe apart [in the scuffle that ensued] and had injured one of my fingers. I was putting some distance between myself and the place where the scuffle took place when a rider rode into me by accident and sprained my shoulder! After this, I was honored to be at the service of Imam Ali an-Naqī ﷺ and told him, "What an ill-fated day! May Almighty God ﷻ remove the evil of this day from my person!"

Imam Hādī ﷺ said, "O Hasan! [It is surprising to hear] you, who are well acquainted with our ways, to place the blame of your own sin on someone else's shoulders!"

I realized I had said something in error, and so I said, "My lord, I have hope to be forgiven; I shouldn't have said what I did."

The Imam ﷺ said, "Indeed. How is it the day's fault? People are themselves to be blamed for their indiscretions and their failure to take adequate precautions. They do not know when to say something and when not to say something, and then, when they are requited for their deeds,

---

[82] *Walāya*[t]: See footnote #78.

they consider the day or the night to be ill-omened; and this actually borders on shirk[83], because it is not as if the day or the night are independent agents who have powers over one's destiny."

I said, "I turn in repentance to the court of the Lord. Thus have I repented. I did not intend to approach the borderline of *shirk*; I was upset and made a mistake."

The Imam ﷺ repeated, "Being upset is itself a touchstone and criterion for one to understand his powers of self-control and his strengths and weaknesses therein."

Someone fell ill and made a sacred vow (*nadhr*) that he would donate a large amount of money to charity if he were to regain his health. He soon got better and the fulfillment of his vow became religiously incumbent on him. But he did not know how much he needed to donate in order to fulfill his religious obligation under the vow that he had undertaken and in order for him to avoid committing a sin of omission. He put his question to a group of his acquaintances and received different answers, none of which were convincing.

One day he was honored to be in the presence of Imam Hādī ﷺ. After exchanging greetings and having shown the appropriate protocols of respect, the man laid out his problem before the Imam ﷺ. The Imam ﷺ replied, "If you pay out eighty Dirhams in charity, you will have fulfilled

---

[83] *Shirk*: 1. assigning partners alongside or as co-equals to God; idolatry; polytheism; 2. paying obeisance to anything other than God; 3. fidelity (*tawhīd*) and Infidelity (*shirk*) to the Exclusivity of God's Providential Lordship in the Social Order; 4. Believing that there are other factors that have any affect or impact on one's fate other than one's actions or the actions of other elements which God's will allows for various reasons to have a part in one's individual and collective providence.

your obligation under your vow; and if you pay more, that is up to you and your reward will be with God ﷻ."

The man asked, "May I ask Your Eminence the reason for this [specific quantity]?"

The Imam ؑ said, "Almighty God ﷻ told His Prophet ﷺ in the Quran, '[9:25] *Indeed, God ﷻ has succored you on many occasions.*' This verse concerns the battles of the Prophet Muhammad ﷺ, who triumphed on eighty occasions in such battles. Almighty God ﷻ considered this number to be "many". Now [the standard for] money is considered to be minted coins [of gold], and a Dirham is the name given to such coins of gold. Thus, eighty Dirhams is the minimum number which can rightly be considered to be "many" [which is the amount that you had vowed to give]."

The man thanked the Imam ؑ and left his presence in a state of contentment and satisfaction, and went on to pay his obligation to charity with peace of mind.

Yahyā ibn Aktham was the Chief Justice of Baghdad, the caliphal capital, from the reign of al-Ma'mūn to the reign of al-Mutawakkil, who succeeded him. Yahyā ibn Aktham was a morally corrupt debauchee who was envious of the high level of scholarship and learning which Imam Jawad ؑ and Imam Hādī ؑ enjoyed. Thus, he wanted very much and even craved for an opportunity where he could supposedly catch one of the Imams ؑ in an error concerning a juridical ruling or concerning a fine point in theology, for example, so that he could use the occasion to bring about their ignominy and shame before specialists and the masses of the people alike.

He had of course tried on many occasions to succeed in such endeavors, all of which were to no avail; but he would not learn his lesson and persisted in his perversion. Thus, he always had a retinue of complex questions on matters of jurisprudence and theology up his sleeve so that he could catch out the companions of the Imams ﷺ on some pretext or another when an occasion presented itself, thereby satisfying his itch for mischief against the Imams ﷺ.

One such occasion was when Yaḥyā ibn Aktham wrote a letter to Mūsā al-Mubarqaʿ, Imam Hādī's ﷺ brother, putting a few technical questions to him and asking for a written response.

Mūsā took the letter to his honorable brother, Imam Ali an-Naqī ﷺ and said, "This son of Aktham [i.e. Yaḥyā] has written me again, putting certain questions to me and asking me for my authoritative legal opinions (*fatwas*) on the matters presented."

The Imam ﷺ asked, "Have you provided him with any *fatwas* yet?"

Mūsā al- Mubarqaʿ replied, "No. I have come to ask your opinion so that I can provide the proper response to the questions."

The Imam ﷺ asked, "What are the questions?"

Mūsā al- Mubarqaʿ replied, "He has asked me the following:

1. Almighty God ﷻ states in the Quran:

قَالَ عِفْرِيتٌ مِّنَ الْجِنِّ أَنَا آتِيكَ بِهِ قَبْلَ أَن تَقُومَ مِن مَّقَامِكَ ۖ وَإِنِّي عَلَيْهِ لَقَوِيٌّ أَمِينٌ ﴿٣٩﴾ قَالَ الَّذِي عِندَهُ عِلْمٌ مِّنَ الْكِتَابِ أَنَا آتِيكَ بِهِ قَبْلَ أَن يَرْتَدَّ إِلَيْكَ طَرْفُكَ ۚ فَلَمَّا رَآهُ مُسْتَقِرًّا عِندَهُ قَالَ هَٰذَا مِن فَضْلِ رَبِّي لِيَبْلُوَنِي أَأَشْكُرُ أَمْ أَكْفُرُ ۖ وَمَن شَكَرَ فَإِنَّمَا يَشْكُرُ لِنَفْسِهِ ۖ وَمَن كَفَرَ فَإِنَّ رَبِّي غَنِيٌّ كَرِيمٌ ﴿٤٠﴾

[27:39] Said a bold one of the invisible beings [subject to Solomon ﷺ]: "I shall bring it to thee ere thou rise from thy council-seat - for, behold, I am powerful enough to do it, [and] worthy of trust!" [27:40] Answered he who was illumined by revelation: "[Nay,] as for me - I shall bring it to thee ere the twinkling of thy eye ceases!"

[The question is:] Was not Solomon himself capable of carrying out this task? In which case, why did he have to rely on the supernatural knowledge and powers of Āsif to do so?

2. Almighty God ﷻ states in the Quran:

$$وَرَفَعَ أَبَوَيْهِ عَلَى الْعَرْشِ وَخَرُّوا لَهُ سُجَّدًا ۖ وَقَالَ يَا أَبَتِ هَٰذَا تَأْوِيلُ رُؤْيَايَ مِن قَبْلُ قَدْ جَعَلَهَا رَبِّي حَقًّا ۖ وَقَدْ أَحْسَنَ بِي إِذْ أَخْرَجَنِي مِنَ السِّجْنِ وَجَاءَ بِكُم مِّنَ الْبَدْوِ مِن بَعْدِ أَن نَّزَغَ الشَّيْطَانُ بَيْنِي وَبَيْنَ إِخْوَتِي ۚ إِنَّ رَبِّي لَطِيفٌ لِّمَا يَشَاءُ ۚ إِنَّهُ هُوَ الْعَلِيمُ الْحَكِيمُ$$

[12:100] And he [Joseph ﷺ] raised his parents to the highest place of honor; and they [all] fell down before Him, prostrating themselves in adoration. O my father! this is the significance of my vision of old; my Lord has indeed made it to be true; and He was indeed kind to me when He brought me forth from the prison and brought you from the desert after the Shaitan had sown dissensions between me and my brothers, surely my Lord is benignant to whom He pleases; surely He is the Knowing, the Wise.

How is it that Jacob ﷺ, who was himself a Prophet ﷺ, "fell down before Joseph ﷺ, prostrating himself in adoration."?

3. Almighty God ﷻ states in the Quran:

$$\text{فَإِن كُنتَ فِي شَكٍّ مِّمَّا أَنزَلْنَا إِلَيْكَ فَاسْأَلِ الَّذِينَ يَقْرَءُونَ الْكِتَابَ مِن قَبْلِكَ ۚ لَقَدْ جَاءَكَ الْحَقُّ مِن رَّبِّكَ فَلَا تَكُونَنَّ مِنَ الْمُمْتَرِينَ ﴿٩٤﴾}$$

[10:94] And so, [O Prophet ﷺ,] if thou art in doubt about [the truth of] what We have [now] bestowed upon thee from on high, ask those who read the divine writ [revealed] before thy time: [and thou wilt find that,] surely, the truth has now come unto thee from thy Lord of Providence.

If the person to whom this verse is addressed is the Prophet ﷺ, then why was he in doubt about that which God ﷻ had revealed? And if the verse is addressed to someone other than the Prophet ﷺ, then who is it who is being addressed?

4. On what authority did Ali ibn Abī-Tālib ﷺ order the injured among the enemy troops to be killed in the Battle of Siffin, while his army was in a state of advancing on the enemy as well as when it was in a state of retreat; whereas in the Battle of the Camel he instructed his army not to slay those who were fleeing from the battle or those who had been injured, saying, "Anyone who lays down his arms and returns to his house will be given sanctuary." In short, why did His Eminence Imam Ali ﷺ issue two different rulings in two situations which were similar?

[Mūsā al-Mubarqa' continued,] "And Yahyā mentions nine other questions as well." Imam Hādī ﷺ said, "Respond to him as per the following:"

In the Name of God, the Compassionate, the Merciful.

Your letter, may God 🌺 guide you to the path of righteousness, reached us. Your intention in writing such a letter was to test us and harass and annoy us, so that if the response would perhaps be incorrect, you would have a means by which to find fault [with us]. God 🌺 will recompense you in accordance with [the purity of] your intentions [or lack thereof]. We shall respond to and explain the questions which you have raised, so pay attention and stay focused on the fact that [by so doing] the argument [in the case that is being prepared] against you [for use on the Day of Judgement] has been completed (*i'timām-e hujjat*). That is all.

1. You asked about God's words concerning one who was illumined by revelation (i.e. Āsif ibn Barkhīā). It was not the case that Solomon 🌺 knew not what Āsif ibn Barkhīā knew; rather, he wanted to make it known to the people that Āsif ibn Barkhīā was to be Solomon's 🌺 *wasī* (inheritor, legatee, executor, and successor) after him, so that they would not fall into a dispute concerning his succession after his passing. And this was similarly the case during the prophet David's 🌺 time, when Solomon's 🌺 legateeship was determined and made manifest for all to see in a similar manner.

2. Concerning the prostration of Jacob 🌺 and his progeny to Joseph 🌺, this was done in obedience to God's command and as a demonstration of how much they loved and adored Him. This was similarly the case when the angels were commanded by God 🌺 to prostrate themselves before Adam 🌺, which was not a sign of their having worshipped Adam 🌺 but was a prostration for and on behalf of God 🌺, at God's command.

3. Concerning God's ﷻ words about doubt with respect to that which had been revealed, the person to whom the verse is addressing is the Apostle ﷺ of God ﷻ, but the subjects of the doubt in question are the ignorant people who would say, "Why did God ﷻ not commission an angel to act as a prophet for us, for there is no difference between us and the Most Noble Prophet ﷺ in so far as we both eat and sleep and put on clothes and walk through the markets."

Almighty God ﷻ is telling the Prophet ﷺ: "Ask those who have read the divine writ [revealed] hitherto, in front of those who ask such ignorant questions, whether thy Lord of Providence has commissioned any prophets before thy time other than any who eat and sleep and put on clothes and walk through the markets. And that you, O Prophet ﷺ, are no different than them. And the fact that Almighty God ﷻ says "…if you are in doubt…" is simply a case of the observation of fairness in one's speech, which anyone with a knowledge of rhetoric well understands."[84]

4. And finally, concerning the difference in the ruling and behavior of the commander of the faithful in the Battles of Siffin and the Battle of the Camel was on account of the fact that in the Battle of the Camel, Talha, one of the leaders of the enemy

---

[84] In other words, the Imam ﷺ is saying that Almighty God ﷻ is assuming for the sake of argument that if the Prophet were to be in doubt like the doubters who he is confronted with in his ministry, which of course he is not, then he together with them together can ask the people to whom earlier revelations were revealed concerning the nature of the prophets who were sent to them (and whether they were men of flesh and bones like the prophet before them, or whether they were angels). This rhetorical custom wherein one lowers oneself to the level of one's interlocutors' understanding is done as a courtesy to them and as a show of empathy in order that they understand that one knows where they are coming from, so that they can then see all the better the point to which you are guiding them to.

faction, was killed, and Zubayr, their other leader, fled and was killed while fleeing from the field of battle; and consequently, the adversary's army no longer had a leader to whom to return and around whom to rally and take up arms anew. They thus gave up the fight and returned to their homes, and were no longer intent on rebellion, but rather, were ready and willing to be disarmed. The [correct] ruling in their case, therefore, was that they should be disarmed and that no further harm should befall them, because they were not seeking to continue the battle.

But the soldiers of the foe at the Battle of Siffin were returning to an army that was powerful and at the ready, and which was being led, moreover, by a leader who was wily and cunning and who was able to resupply them with swords and spears and shields and armor [and everything else they needed to rejoin the fray and resume the fight]. He would see to their needs and visit the injured and provide them with the medical attention they needed [to ensure a speedy recovery] and provide anyone who had lost their mount with fresh cavalry, and [in short], would [do everything in his power to] return them to the field of battle.

Therefore, His Eminence Imam Ali ﷺ did not have the same ruling for these two groups [whose conditions were very different]. Rather, he would explain to both that whosoever turns away from the [path of] truth and justice will either have to turn back in repentance or be killed."

The Imam ﷺ provided similar crushing and irrefutable responses for the other nine questions, all of which made Yaḥyā ibn Aktham think twice before posing questions whose sole purpose was to seek fault.

Abul-Hasan was a Fatimid descendant of the Prophet ﷺ whose ancestry went back with a few removes to Imam Sādiq ؏. He lived in Qom. He was a drinker and lived a life of poverty and indigence.

During that time, Imam Hādī's ؏ representative Ahmad ibn Ishāq also lived in Qom. One day, some business came by Abul-Hasan's way for which he needed help. And so, it was on account of this business that he went to Ahmad's house. But because Ahmad knew that Abul-Hasan drank, he did not let him into his house and turned him back.

Sometime later, Ahmad traveled to Sāmarrā in order to meet with Imam Hādī ؏, but the Imam ؏ did not accept him into his presence. Ahmad composed a message to the Imam ؏ saying, "Allow me to have the honor of seeing you so that I will come to know where I have erred."

After many such entreaties, the Imam ؏ relented and gave him permission to enter. When Ahmad asked about his mistake, the Imam ؏ said, "My cousin came to you [for help] but you turned him away."

Ahmad said, "I did so because he is a drinker of wine."

The Imam ؏ said, "You should have taken his familial bond into consideration and respected his standing, as he could have shown regret and turned in repentance."

A while passed and Ahmad returned to Qom. When Abul-Hasan went to see him, Ahmad stood up fully erect [as a show of respect] before him, honored him by placing him at the head of the gathering, and paid him much attention.

When the sitting was over, Abul-Hasan asked Ahmad, "What came over you? Before you would not let me into your house and turned me away, whereas now that you have returned from Sāmarrā, you treat me with such honor and respect?"

Ahmad said, "I am acting under the strict orders of the Imam ؏."

He then told Abul-Hasan his story. When Ahmad finished telling the tale, Abul-Hasan said, "Woe unto me and would that I was dust for having polluted myself with this wicked sin!"

He repented from drink at that very moment and never again went back to drinking wine. And so, he was guided aright by the attention that the Imam ﷺ paid to him.

3 The Imam and his Relations with the Caliphs

The continued struggle of the Members of the House of the Prophet ﷺ of Islam and their sustained conflict with the usurping and oppressive caliphs is one of the glorious if bloody chapters of the history of Shī'a Islam. Our noble Imams ﷺ were constantly the subject of the ire of the caliphs and their tyrannical governors and generals thanks to their refusal to capitulate to oppression and injustice and their insistance that justice be served. The usurper caliphs knew that the Imams ﷺ of the Shī'a would not miss a single opportunity that presented itself for the guidance of the people or for establishing justice or for standing up for the rights of the oppressed or for fighting against unbelief, oppression and corruption. Thus they constantly saw themselves as being threatened by the uninterrupted chain of guidance and means of resistance which the Imams of the Ahl al-Bayt ﷺ provided the people.

The Abbāsid caliphs who had taken the place of the Umayyad tyrants by the use of chicanery and deception and who ruled over the masses in the name of their supposed vice-regency of God ﷻ and of the Prophet ﷺ of Islam, like the Umayyad usurpers before them, did not refrain from using any means whatsoever that was at their disposal to slander and ultimately to stamp out the House of the Apostle of God ﷺ whose right to the leadership of the community they had stolen and were intent on keeping to themselves. They wanted to use any means possible to distort the luminous and brilliant face of the true leaders of Islam and to show them in a bad light, to crush their honor and dignity and respect, and to prevent them from being able act as mentors and guides of the people by various schemes and machinations whose ultimate purpose was to neutralize the love that the people naturally felt toward the august family of their noble Prophet ﷺ.

None of the various plots and machinations which the Abbāsid caliph al-Ma'mūn employed in order to achieve his malevolent objective of showing his own rein in a legitimate light and in order to legitimate his covering up of the light of the true imamate – none of this can remain hidden from anyone who is familiar with the history of the interaction of the Imams ؏ with the caliphs whose stock in trade is oppression and tyranny. Some of this history was reviewed by us in the other books in this series having to do with the lives of the Imams ar-Riḍā ؏ and al-Jawād ؏.

After al-Ma'mūn, al-Mu'tasim continued those same plans against the Ahl al-Bayt ؏, which was the reason he summoned Imam Jawād ؏ from Medina to Baghdad so that he could keep a closer eye on him and have much stricter control over the Imam's ؏ affairs and, ultimately, to martyr him. He also imprisoned many of the dignitaries from among the Ālids on the pretext that they did not wear black clothing (which was the color of the Abbāsid's formal attire), and all of these great men from among the progeny of Imam Ali ؏ either died their natural death in the Abbāsid dungeons or were murdered there.

al-Mu'tasim died in Sāmarrā in the year 227 AH and was succeeded by his son al-Wāthiq, who continued the same policy of enmity toward the Ahl al-Bayt ؏ which his father al- al-Mu'tasim and his uncle al-Ma'mūn pursued before him. Like the rest of the caliphs who pretended to be defenders of the bounds of Islam, al-Wāthiq was a debauchee and a habitual drinker and it can be said that he even went to extremes in the pursuits of the pleasures of the flesh and the stomach. He had turned to taking special drugs in order to enhance his promiscuous pleasures and it was these drugs that were his eventual undoing, causing his death in Sāmarrā in the year 232 AH.

Unlike his predecessors, al-Wāthiq's treatment of the Ālids was not harsh and violent, which is why the Ālids were able to gather around their Imam ﷺ in Sāmarrā during his reign and enjoyed relatively more leeway. But his successor, al-Mutawakkil, put an end to their freedom of movement and disbanded them, placing the Imam ﷺ under strict house arrest.

Al-Wāthiq's successor al-Mutawakkil was one of the most vile and criminal caliphs among the Abbāsid dynasty, and it was al-Mutawakkil's rein more than any other of the Abbāsid caliphs which corresponded with Imam Hādī's ﷺ imamate, and this overlap lasted more than fourteen years. The years of this decade and a half were the hardest years for Imam Hādī ﷺ and his followers because al-Mutawakkil was the most heretical and wicked of scoundrels and had a heart full of rancor for the Commander of the Faithful Ali ibn Abī-Tālib ﷺ and his progeny and their devoted followers. During al-Mutawakkil's reign, a large number of Ālids were either executed, poisoned or were forced underground.

Al-Mutawakkil used to dream up fantasies about the Shāfi'ī scholar Muhammad ibn Idrīs (who was no longer alive during his reign) and encourage the Muslim community to follow his rulings and rite. This was one of the ways in which he tried to dissuade people from being drawn to and following the teachings of the Imams ﷺ who were sent by God ﷺ to guide mankind. Another one of his reactionary measures occurred in the year 236 AH when he ordered the shrine of Imam Husaiin ﷺ and the buildings in its environs to be razed to the ground and to till the ground of the shrine so as to preclude pilgrimage to that sacred soil.

Al-Mutawakkil feared that Imam Husain's ﷺ shrine and its environs would be turned into a base of activity against his regime, and that the struggle for justice and the martyrdom of the great Imam ﷺ would become an inspirational model of behavior for the people's insurrections for establishing a just government in lieu of the criminal and oppressive reign of the caliphal court. But the Shī'a and the devotees of the Lord of the Martyrs[85] ﷺ never once gave up their efforts at making pilgrimage to

---

[85] A title of Imam Husain's ﷺ.

the pure and hallowed soil of his grave under any condition. It is even related that the shrine was rebuilt and rebuilt again and that al-Mutawakkil destroyed it no less than seventeen times and threatened the pilgrims with arrest and placed two guard stations in the environs of the shrine but was ultimately unable to prevent the people from making pilgrimage to the grave of the Lord of the Martyrs ﷺ.

The pilgrims suffered untold bodily harm and all sorts of inhuman tortures at the hands of al-Mutawakkil's henchmen, but they would yet again return to Karbalā and make pilgrimage to the shrine of their lord and master, Imam Husain ﷺ. After al-Mutawakkil's death, the Shī'a rebuilt Imam Husain's ﷺ shrine in cooperation with the House of Imam Ali ﷺ.

The destruction of the grave of the beloved grandson of the Prophet ﷺ raised the ire of the people. The people of Baghdad wrote slogans against al-Mutawakkil on the walls of the city and in the mosques and the poets lampooned him with their verse. The poem that follows is an example of the poetry that has been composed to revile that tyrant:

> I swear [upon my oath] to Allāh that if the Umayyads unjustly murdered the son of the daughter of the Prophet ﷺ ,
> We are now witness to those who are from the family[86] of the Prophet ﷺ commit a crime[87] that is tantamount to the crime committed by the Umayyads.[88]
>
> This is the grave of Husain ﷺ that has been desecrated!

---

[86] The Banī Abbās or Abbāsids go back to Abbās who like the Prophet's father Abdullāh, was a son of Abdul-Mottaleb. Thus, the Abbāsids are paternal cousins of the Prophet ﷺ.
[87] Reference to the razing of the shrine of Imam Husain ﷺ.
[88] Reference to the murder of Imam Husain in Karbalā at the hands of Yazīd the accursed Umayyad caliph.

It seems that the Banī Abbās regret the fact that they did not have a share in Imam Husain's ﷺ murder!

So now, by demolishing that sacred shrine and desecrating and profaning that sacred soil, they are following in the footsteps of the Umayyads and affirming their support for the action of their predecessors.

Indeed, in those days when ordinary people did not have access to media and means of mass communication, and the mosques and pulpits and sermons and public gathering places were under the control of those who were on the payroll of the Abbāsids, they would give expression to their grievances by means such as the poetry cited above.

Poets who were bound to the principles of Islam and felt a sense of responsibility to protect its tenets and values would apply their rhetorical skills to composing effective poetry against al-Mutawakkil and to raising people's awareness about the crimes of the Abbāsids. Likewise, al-Mutawakkil stopped short of no crime, no matter how vile and lowly, to silence any and all voices of descent, and cracked down harshly on the scholars and poets and the leadership of groups who refused to cooperate with his usurper regime, killing many of them in the most outrageous manner imaginable.

The renowned Shī'a poet Ibn Sikkīt who is called the "Imam" of the Arab poets, was the mentor of al-Mutawakkil's children. The caliph's spies had informed him that his children's mentor was a devotee of the Ahl al-Bayt ﷺ and a follower of the path of the House of the Prophet ﷺ ; and so, the caliph was biding his time and waiting for an opportunity to put his loyalty to the test.

One day, al-Mutawakkil pointed to his two children al-Mu'tazz and al-Mu'ayyad and asked Ibn Sikkīt, "Which are dearer to you, these two boys or [Imam] Hasan ﷺ and [Imam] Husain ﷺ?"

Ibn Sikkīt who realized it was no longer possible to remain silent concerning his loyalties, answered bravely, "The grave of the servant of the

Commander of the Faithful Ali ibn Abī-Tālib ﷺ is better than you and your children!"

Al-Mutawakkil rose up in anger like an injured bear and ordered his men to remove the Shīʿa poet's tongue from the back of his mouth. Thus it was that this symbol of nobility, honor and courage was martyred at the age of fifty-eight. (May the blessings of God ﷻ and the angels and the righteous among men be sent unto his soul. Amen.)

Like the other caliphs before him, al-Mutawakkil was a profligate spendthrift when it came to wasting the wealth of the public treasury. As has been written in the chronicles of his life, he built himself several extravagant palaces, spending one million and seven hundred thousand gold Dinars for the construction of the "Mutawakkil Tower" alone, a structure which is still standing in Sāmarrā today.

What is painful to consider is that while all this profligacy and wasting away of the public's wealth was taking place in Baghdad and Sāmarrā, the family of the Prophet ﷺ was in such dire financial straits that a number of the noble family's womenfolk in Medina did not even have a single set of proper clothes with which to offer their ritual devotions to their Maker in and were obliged to take turns wearing the single set of attire that was worthy of offering devotions to the Lord in when it came time for them to make their ritual devotions. And these women who were the progeny of the Prophet ﷺ of Islam were obliged to make ends meet by spinning wool into yarn and were in this state of dire poverty until al-Mutawakkil finally went to his bottomless perdition after which their condition was slightly improved.

Mutawakkil's enmity and malice toward the Commander of the Faithful Ali ibn Abī-Tālib ﷺ drove him to unbelievable depths of depravity. He would keep the company of the *nawāsib*[89] and had ordered

---

[89] *Nawāsib* is the plural of *nasabi* which is a word used to describe anyone who is an enemy of the Family of the Prophet of Islam and of the People of his august

a clown to make fun of the Commander of the Faithful ﷺ by means of some unspeakably hideous acts which he would witness and laugh at in order to please his dark heart and filthy mind; he would drink to this clown's obscene antics and let out loud peals of laughter that can only come out of the mouth of a drunkard.

Such horrible behavior is not surprising in any given individual and certainly not in a wonton debauchee and degenerate of the likes of al-Mutawakkil. What is more astonishing and disheartening is the mindset of those among the community of Muslims who considered and still consider such a reprobate degenerate to be the caliph and successor to the Most Noble Prophet ﷺ and to be the legitimate sovereign (*walī al-amr*) of the Muslim nation, pledging their allegiance to him and obeying him and turning their backs to the true Islam offered to them by the Household of prophecy and immaculacy. Pity man for the depths to which his ignorance and waywardness drive him, and pity him and woe unto him for the extent to which Satan the Accursed has sway and mastery over his words and deeds!

Verily, al-Mutawakkil's criminal abuse of the Imams ﷺ and their followers reached such a depth that he admitted to it himself. The story is as follows:

One day, Fath ibn Khāqān, al-Mutawakkil's vizier, saw the caliph deep in thought. He asked him fawningly, "Why are you so deep in thought? By Allāh, no one on the face of the earth lives as good a life as you do!"

The tyrant replied, "Better than my life is the life of a man who has a large house, a worthy wife, financial security, and does not have me [as his sovereign] to persecute and torment and humiliate him."

Al-Mutawakkil's persecution of the purified Household of the Prophet ﷺ reached a point where he would arrest and torture people for

---

Household, the Ahl al-Bayt ﷺ; and of the Shīʿa or their devoted followers more generally.

the crime of being a follower of the noble Imams ﷺ, and this made things very difficult for the Imams of the Ahl al-Bayt ﷺ.

Al-Mutawakkil appointed Omar ibn Farah as the governor of Mecca and Medina. That man prevented the people from associating with the House of the Ālids and pursued this ungodly aim with diligence, to the point that people refrained from having any interactions with the Household of the Prophet ﷺ for fear of their lives. Mecca had once again reverted to the Days of pre-Islamic Ignorance where the ruler of the city forbade any interaction with the Family of the Prophet ﷺ and imposed a general boycott on them; and these conditions made life very hard for the Ahl al-Bayt ﷺ in both Mecca and Madina.

It goes without saying that given the fear that the usurping Abbāsid tyrants had of the spiritual influence of the Imams of the Ahl al-Bayt ﷺ on society at large and given the love of the masses for their Imams, they felt that they could not cease their persecution of them and leave them in peace. In the case of al-Mutawakkil, in addition to this general fear which all of the caliphs had of the Ahl al-Bayt ﷺ due to the ultimate illegitimacy of their regime, there was his personal enmity and rancor toward the Commander of the Faithful Ali ibn Abī-Tālib ﷺ which added grist to the mill of his persecution and torment of the Imams ﷺ. And so, all of these factors decided him to summon Imam Hādī ﷺ from his domicile in Medina to the caliphal capital in Sāmarrā, so that he could keep him under close surveillance and under house arrest and have strict control over who was allowed to visit the Imam ﷺ and who was not.

And it came to pass that in the year 243 AH, al-Mutawakkil summoned Imam Hādī ﷺ from Medina to Sāmarrā, where he was to spend the rest of his days, i.e. until the year 254 AH. The summon took the form of a respectful invitation, but it was understood that there was no choice in the matter, and that what was being imposed on the Imam and his family was no less than a form of interior exile in a house next to his garrison in Sāmarrā. That bloodthirsty despot kept Imam Hādī ﷺ under strict supervision and control, and the other caliphs that succeeded him continued this same policy of persecution and oppression until the great Imam was martyred in the year 254 AH.

The story of the exile of the Imam ﷺ is as follows. During al-Mutawakkil's reign, there was a man by the name of Abdullāh ibn Muhammad who was in charge of military affairs as well as the communal prayer service in Madina. He would persecute Imam Hādī ﷺ and slander him and talk behind his back to al-Mutawakkil.

Imam Hādī ﷺ became aware of the slander and wrote a letter to al-Mutawakkil informing him of Abdullāh ibn Muhammad's lies and enmity toward him. Mutawakkil ordered his scribe to respond to the Imam's ﷺ letter and to respectfully invite him to Sāmarrā. The text of the caliph's response is as follows:

> In the Name of God, the Compassionate, the Merciful.
> ... But to move on to the business at hand (*ammā ba'd*). Verily, the sovereign (*amīr*) recognizes your station and takes your ties of kinship [to the Prophet ﷺ] into consideration, and believes it to be necessary [to observe and respect] your rights [to the full extent of propriety] ... The Amīr has dismissed Abdullāh ibn Muhammad from his office on account of his ignorance of your rights, his failure to show due respect to you, and because of the [false] charges that he has levelled against you. The Amīr knows that you are innocent of these charges, and that you have [nothing but] sincerity of intention in [the entirety of] your righteous words and deeds. He also knows that you had not prepared to carry out the actions which you were accused of [by Abdullāh ibn Muhammad]. The Amīr has appointed Muhammad ibn Faḍl in [Abdullāh ibn Muhammad's] stead and has instructed him to respect and honor you and to follow your lead and to obey your commands.

But the Amīr is eager to see you and would like to renew his covenant with you; thus, if you would like to see him and would like to stay with him, kindly pay us a visit at your convenience and at a time that is opportune, bringing with you whosoever you will of your family, companions and attendants. We leave the choice of the timing of the journey and the decisions as to where and when to sojourn along the way to Your Excellency; and if you so desire, Yaḥyā ibn Harthama who is a friend of the Amīr's, and his troops can be at your service on your journey, if you deem this to be expedient. We have instructed him to obey your commands. Thus, beseech Allāh to grant you of his blessings until you meet the Amīr. No one from among the Amīr's brothers and children and those who are close to him and from among his kin is dearer to him that Your Excellency.

May peace be with you.

There is no doubt that the Imam ؑ was well aware of al-Mutawakkil's ill will and evil intentions; but he had no choice but to go to Sāmarrā because the act of turning down the caliph's invitation would become a tool in the hands of the Imam's enemies and slanderers who would then agitate al-Mutawakkil all the more and provide him with more occasions and pretexts to continue his unabated persecution. And the proof for the fact that the Imam ؑ was well aware of the true nature of al-Mutawakkil's intensions is that the Imam ؑ himself later stated, "They brought me from Medina to Sāmarrā under duress."

In any event, the Imam ؑ received the letter and headed for Sāmarrā, accompanied by Yaḥyā ibn Harthama and his troops. When the party reached Sāmarrā, al-Mutawakkil did not allow the Imam ؑ to enter the city that same day, ordering him to be taken to an abandoned and run-down caravanserai that was used by the homeless and was entirely unsuitable for the station, stature and standing of the Imam ؑ and his family. The Imam ؑ and his entourage stayed there that night, after which the caliph appointed a more appropriate residence for him to which they were transferred. Thereafter, the caliph treated the Imam ﷺ with all due respect and honor in all outward appearances, whereas the reality of the situation was that he was intent on defaming him and destroying his reputation and standing within the community.

Sālih ibn Sa'īd reports: I was honored to be at the service of His Eminence ﷺ on the day he entered the dilapidated caravanserai, and I said to him, "Would that I were sacrificed for your cause,[90] these wicked oppressors want to put out your light in every possible way and not to fulfill your rights, even to the point that they have stationed you in this dilapidated caravanserai which is where the indigent and wretched reside!"

The honorable Imam ﷺ pointed in a certain direction and said, "Look over there, O Sa'īd."

I looked over to where the Imam ﷺ was pointing and was amazed to see meticulously arranged lush gardens with all manner of fruit trees beneath which were running streams that sparkled with alacrity. I was astonished and aghast.

The Imam ﷺ said, "Wherever we are, this is our [lot], O son of Sa'īd! We are not in the caravanserai of the destitute."

During his stay in Sāmarrā, Imam Ali an-Naqī ﷺ suffered many afflictions. He was the subject of much torment and intimidation, especially from al-Mutawakkil, from whose quarters arose many hazards that threatened him.

The examples to which we shall now refer are emblematic of the delicate and dangerous condition which our dear Imam ﷺ found himself in the Abbāsid garrison town of Sāmarrā and are proofs of the forbearance

---

[90] A formal form of address. See footnote #71.

and endurance and fortitude of that Proof of God ﷻ (*hujjatallāh*)⁹¹ in the face of the imposter illegitimate power (*tāghūt*).⁹²

Saqr ibn Abī-Dalf reports: When Imam Hādī ﷺ was brought to Sāmarrā, I went [to Sāmarrā] to inquire as to his health and well-being. Zarrāfī, al-Mutawakkil's chamberlain, saw me and gave me permission to enter. When I entered, he asked, "What business brings you here?"

I said, "It is all for the good…"

He said, "Be seated."

I sat, but fear overcame me and I went deep in my own thoughts and thought to myself that I had made a mistake [to have engaged in as dangerous a venture such as to want to see the Imam ﷺ].

Zarrāfī dismissed the people who were present and when we were alone, he said, "State your business."

I answered, "I have come for the purpose of doing a good deed."

He said, "It would seem you have come to inquire as to the status of your master."

I said, "Who is my master? My master is the caliph!"

He replied, "Be quiet! Your master is in the right. Fear not, for I am with you and consider him to be my Imam."

I praised God ﷻ. He then added, "Do you want to see him?"

When I answered in the affirmative, he said, "Wait for a while until the messenger leaves."

---

⁹¹ *Hujjat*: see footnotes #6 and #7 for an explanation of this key word.

⁹² *Tāghūt*: the false or illegitimate authority of anything or anyone other than God; the social orders established by illegitimate powers; forms of idolatry and heathenism; hegemonic powers and the forces of idolatry; imposter powers who are pretenders to the throne of legitimate sovereignty supposedly sanctioned by God.

When the messenger left, Zarrāfī told his attendant, "Take this man to the cell where the Ālid is being kept and leave him there and come back."

When I got there, I saw the nobleman seated on some hessian matting, in front of which a grave had been dug. After we exchanged greetings, the Imam ﷺ said, "Be seated."

When I sat down, His Eminence ﷺ asked, "What brings you here?"

I said, "I came to see how you were doing."

As I said this, my gaze fell onto the grave and tears began to stream down my cheeks involuntarily.

The Imam ﷺ said, "Do not weep, for no harm will come to me at this time."

I thanked God, and then asked about the meaning of a hadīth report[93] which the Imam ﷺ provided, after which he said, "You should leave me to myself now and return, as it is not safe for you to be in my presence, and I am concerned that some harm might come to you from the authorities."

The Sunni scholar Ibn Jawzī reports: One day charges of conspiracy to revolt were brought against Imam Hādī ﷺ to al-Mutawakkil, telling him that documents and weapons and other paraphernalia having to do with an armed revolt had reached him from his followers in the city of Qom (in north-central Iran), and that he was preparing to rebel against the regime.

Al-Mutawakkil mustered a squad of soldiers who raided the Imam's ﷺ house by night but failed to come up with any evidence of a conspiracy. What they found instead was the Imam ﷺ alone in a room,

---

[93] *Hadīth*: See footnote #5.

having closed the door on himself, seated on a dirt floor in a robe of coarse wool, engaged in reciting the Quran and offering his ritual devotions to God ﷻ.

The soldiers arrested the Imam ﷺ and took him to the caliph in that same attire. When they presented the Imam ﷺ to the caliph, they said, "We found nothing in his house, and he was seated facing the qibla (the direction of prayer) reciting the Quran."

When al-Mutawakkil saw him, the Imam's ﷺ grandeur and majesty overtook him and he was filled with awe. He involuntarily paid him his respects and seated him next to himself; but impudently offered him the goblet of wine that he was holding in his hand.

The Imam ﷺ turned down the offer and attested that his flesh and blood have never been polluted with such ignominy and asked the despot to be excused from partaking in such things. The caliph did not insist but asked the Imam ﷺ to recite some verses of poetry [instead].

The Imam said, "I do not know many poems by heart."

But the caliph exceeded all bounds of persistence, saying, "But you must."

With a celestial yet doleful voice, the Imam ﷺ began to recite the following verses:

> They passed their nights and days on the summit of mountains,
> Guarded by powerful men,
> But the mountain peaks failed to save them from the [looming] threat of death.

> After having been ensconced in places of honor and security,
> They were dragged from the heights and placed in the pits [of their graves].
> What an unpleasant abode the grave is!

> After they were buried, a crier cried out,

"Where are those bracelets and crowns and glamorous clothes [now]?
"Where are those pampered faces in whose honor veils[94] were erected?"

The grave replied to the crier,
"Those visages are now crawling with worms."

The effect of the forceful words of the Imam ﷺ were such that al-Mutawakkil involuntarily began to weep bitter tears, to the point where his beard became wet, and the others present also started to weep profusely. Al-Mutawakkil ordered the wine to be collected and thrown away, and gave a gift of four thousand Dirhams to the Imam ﷺ and returned the nobleman to his home with an escort of honor.

But it should not be imagined that the slander and machinations of the enemies of the Imam ﷺ or the malice and rancor of the caliph toward him came to an end. To the contrary, they were like injured snakes who were looking for an opportunity to sink their venom into the flesh of His Eminence the Imam ﷺ and bring about the conditions of his martyrdom. But they were heedless of the fact that Almighty God ﷻ will perfect His will and expose the wily plots of the deceitful.

In time a canker appeared in al-Mutawakkil's body and it began to fester to the point where his physicians were unable to cure it, and none had the courage to perform an operation. His condition deteriorated by the day, and it seemed as if he was at death's door. The caliph's mother was originally a bondmaiden from Khārazm[95] and was a person who

---

[94] Reference to those who enjoyed courts and private chambers secured by guards and chamberlains.

[95] Khārazm or Transoxiana, known in Arabic and Persian sources as Māwarun-Nahr, is the ancient name used for the portion of Central Asia corresponding approximately with modern-day Uzbekistan, Tajikistan, southern Kyrgyzstan and

believed in God ﷻ. She made a sacred vow (*nadhr*) that if her son recovered, she would make a donation of a large sum of money to Imam Ali an-Naqī ؏, and bade the caliph's vizier, Fath ibn Khāqān, to consult with the Imam ؏ concerning the caliph's cure. Fath ibn Khāqān told the caliph, "By your leave, I intend to send word to this Ālid sage; perhaps he will know of a remedy for your illness."

The caliph said, "There is no harm in it."

A contingent went to the Imam ؏ and described his condition. His Eminence ؏ named a very common drug [to be the cure]. When this news reached the court, a number of courtesans laughed and made fun of the whole venture. But Fath ibn Khāqān said, "No harm can come from giving this drug a try."

When a poultice was prepared with the drug and placed on the wound, it began to heal quickly.

Al-Mutawakkil's mother placed ten thousand gold Dinārs in a sack in fulfillment of her vow and waxed and sealed the sack and sent it anonymously to Imam Hādī ؏. The caliph also sent a gift of five hundred gold Dinārs to the Imam ؏.

After al-Mutawakkil recovered from his illness and was no longer bed-ridden, his spies said to him, "What are you waiting for? Imam Hādī's ؏ supporters have sent him arms and sacks of gold and he and his followers are preparing to take up arms and wage war against you!"

The caliph became fearful and asked for Sa'īd the Chamberlain and told him, "Get ready to make a night raid on the house of Imam Hādī ؏ and to bring back to me all of the weapons and gold that you find there, together with the Imam ؏ himself."

Sa'īd the Chamberlain then reports: At midnight I took a ladder and entered the Imam's ؏ house through his roof and saw His Eminence busy at prayer on some hessian matting. After offering him my salaams, I

---

southwest Kazakhstan. Geographically, it is the region between the Āmū Daryā and Sīr Daryā rivers.

told him the nature of my assignment. He said, "Go and make your search and take whatever you find."

We went and searched every nook and cranny and did not find anything other than a sack of gold which had the caliph's mother's seal upon it and another sack of gold which the caliph had sent to the Imam ﷺ. I then found a sword at the side of the Imam's prayer rug which was sheathed in a wooden sheath. I took it together with the sealed sacks of gold and together we made our way to the caliph's palace. When the caliph saw his mother's seal, he sent for her and asked her about it. His mother said, "I had made a *nadhr* (sacred vow) during the time of your illness, and this is the sack of gold which I sent [in fulfillment of my vow], and no one has broken its seal yet."

The other sack contained the gold that the caliph had sent himself.

Now that the caliph had realized his mistake and that he had yet again fallen for the slander of the enemies of the Imam ﷺ, he added one more sack of gold to the other ones and said, "O Saʿīd! Take these to His Eminence ﷺ and beg his pardon."

Saʿīd says, "I went to the Imam ﷺ and said, "O noble son of the Prophet ﷺ! Forgive us our trespasses, for we have sinned against you. But what choice did we have, for we were acting on information that told us there were people secreted in your residence who were fanning the flames of rebellion."

The honorable Imam ﷺ quoted the following verse of the Quran in reply: "It will not be long before the oppressors realize to Whom is their return."[96]

---

[96] The reference was not provided in the original text and we were not able to locate it independently.

The ignominious reign of the caliph al-Mutawakkil finally came to an end when he and his vizier Fath ibn Khāqān were murdered while drinking and engaging in all manner of debauchery by a group of Turkish guards at Muntasir's behest, who was al-Mutawakkil's son; ridding the world of their vile existence.

Al- Muntasir took to the helm of the ship of state the following morning and ordered some of his father's palaces be destroyed. Al-Muntasir did not persecute the Shī'a like his father, showing kindness and endearment to Imam Hādī ﷺ and his followers. He gave permission to the people to make pilgrimage to the grave of the Lord of the Martyrs, Imam Husain ﷺ, and generally did right by the Shī'a and treated them with benevolence. He also ordered that the Fadak[97] property be returned to the progeny of Imam Hasan ﷺ and Imam Husain ﷺ, and returned to the Ālids control of the religious endowments which were in their hands before Al- Muntasir's predecessors expropriated them.

Al- Muntasir's reign was short-lived; he died under mysterious circumstances in the year 248 AH. He was succeeded by his cousin al-Musta'īn, a grandson of al- Muntasir. Al- Musta'īn took after the rest of the Abbāsids in terms of his policy of persecuting the Shī'a. During his reign, a group of Ālids rose up in insurrection against him and were killed.

Al- Musta'īn was unable to overcome the revolt which arose from within the ranks of his own Turkish guards, who released al-Mu'tazz from his prison cell and pledged allegiance to him. Al- Mu'tazz overcame al-Musta'īn, who eventually came to terms with him. But while al- Mu'tazz outwardly made peace with al- Musta'īn, he summoned him to Sāmarrā and had him murdered on his way there.

Al- Musta'īn had enabled some of his close aides and the heads of his Turkish guards to have unencumbered access to the funds of the public

---

[97] Fadak: Land that was the inheritance of Lady Fātima ﷺ but which was denied to her by the caliphs.

treasury, which they proceeded to waste with their profligate ways. He also treated our Immaculate Imams ﷺ outrageously; according to some hadīth reports, he became the subject of a curse of Imam Hasan al-Askarī ﷺ and was consequently murdered.

Al-Mustaʿīn was succeeded by al-Muʿtazz, al-Mutawakkil's son and al-Muntasir's brother. His treatment of the Ālids was also very bad, and several Ālid leaders were executed or poisoned during his reign.

Imam Ali an-Naqī ﷺ also attained to martyrdom during the reign of this despot.

Al-Muʿtazz was eventually overthrown by a rebellion of his Turkish guards who consigned him to an underground dungeon where he eventually met his death.

Refer to the chart at the beginning of the book for a listing of the Abbāsid caliphs up to the period of our discussion.

4 Imamology in the Words of the Imam

Our Twelve Imams – may the peace and blessings of God ﷻ always be with their sacred light – were not only the leaders of the community of the faithful and the expositors of the sacred ordinances of the Quran, but in addition to that, were immaculate models of Shīʿa culture, reflections of the light of the Divine on Earth, God's perfect proofs (*hujjat*)[98] for all of humanity, and the central axis of the universe and the intermediary through which the grace of the Creator reaches His creatures. They are the luminous mirrors in which God's attributes are reflected and are the highest peaks of human virtues and perfection. They are the epiphanic manifestations of God's sublimely exalted Knowledge and Power and are perfect examples of immaculate beings, being free not only from sin, but from any and all gross errors, be they intentional or unintentional. They are connected to the Heavens, to the domains of reality which are beyond

---

[98] *Hujjat*: see footnotes #6 and #7 for an explanation of this key word.

the ken of ordinary human perception (*al-ghayb*), and to the celestial beings (angels) which occupy these domains, and are fully aware of all that has occurred in the world of the past, and of all that is to come in the world that is to be. They are the depositories of all of the Divine Mysteries and are the inheritors of all of the perfections of the prophets.

The existence of his Eminence the Prophet Muhammad ﷺ and of his Purified and Immaculate Family ﷺ is the central axis around which the compass of being revolves. The aegis of their august regency and dominion transcends that of the other prophets commissioned by God ﷻ. Theirs is a station that is unavailable to any but themselves; by God's leave, it is a high rank and station that is exclusive to his Eminence the Prophet ﷺ Muhammad and to his Purified and Immaculate Family ﷺ, and no quarter is given by God ﷻ to any who would covet it.

The foregoing descriptions of the actual rank and spiritual stations of the Imams ﷺ is naught but a sampling of all that is established for them by way of scripture, both Quranic and by way of authoritative hadīth reports of the Prophet ﷺ and of the Imams ﷺ themselves, all of which have been recorded and analyzed at length in various books of the great Shī'a theologians and chroniclers of hadith; books to which the gentle reader is referred for further information and confirmation, as we do not have the space to delve into further detail in this book.

Our honorable lord and master, the tenth shining star in the firmament of the Imāmate, Imam Hādī ﷺ has honored and blessed us with his deep and prodigious words in a *ziārat*[99] known as the Ziārat-e Jāmi'a taken from the

---

[99] *Ziārat*: 1. The act of making pilgrimage to a pilgrimage site, usually a shrine of a prophet, imam or *imamzāda* (the progeny of an imam); 2. A liturgical form of supplication or ritual prayer recited specifically during one's pilgrimage to a sacred shrine or location. (The second meaning is the one that is intended here.)

depths of the oceans of his knowledge. [In this *ziārat*] the Imam ﷺ has displayed to our incomplete minds, which are unworthy of comprehending the entirety of the realities of the station of the imamate, a sampling of the blooms of the Garden of the Divine. May our souls be sacrificed for the cause for which he was martyred and for the pure earth of the grave in which he is buried, for he informed us earthlings of the magnitude of the grandeur of the Heavens and of the beauty of the Divine with the blazing rays of his luminous words and guided those of us who thirst for divine guidance to God's paradisal wellspring al-Kawthar.[100]

His Eminence Imam Hādī ﷺ taught a prayer to one of his devotees who had asked him what to recite when making pilgrimage to the shrines of the Immaculate Imams ﷺ which we thought it would be a pity not to include ﷺ part of this short biography of the Imam's ﷺ life, as it is a treasure trove of information by means of which knowledge of the Imams ﷺ and the Imamate (imāmology) can be gleaned.

Some of the greatest minds within Shī'a scholarship consider this *ziārat* to be the greatest of the *jāmi'a ziārāt*, and great scholars have included it in their books, including Shaykh Sadūq (d. 381 AH), who has included it in his highly authoritative *Man lā Yahḍuruh' al-Faqīh* (which is one of the four "canonical" texts of Hadīth scripture within Shī'a Islam), as well as including it in his *Uyūn Akhbār ar-Riḍā*. In the beginning of the aforementioned book Shaykh Sadūq writes, "I include material in this book on the basis of which I make my *fatāwā* (authoritative juridical rulings) and consider these sources as definitive sacred proofs (*hujjat ash-shar'ī*) between my Maker and myself."

Shaykh Tūsī (d. 460 AH) has also included it in his book *Tahdhīb al-Ahkām* (which is also another one of the four "canonical" Shī'a texts). Allāma Majlisī has stated concerning this *ziārat*: "In terms of its

---

[100] al-Kawthar: 1. The name of the 108th Sura of the Quran; 2. A spring located in Heaven; 3. A title of Lady Fātima ﷺ (based on the attribution of the Surat al-Kawthar to Her Eminence, per Shī'a hadith reports and Quranic exegesis).

provenance title (*sanad*), the *ziārat-e jāmi'a* is one of the most sound and reliable of the *ziārāt*; and in terms of its content, rhetorical style and eloquence, it is the best among them."

Majlisī the First (Allāma Muhammad Bāqir Majlisī's father) has written: "In an apocalypse (*mukāshifa*; unveiling) that occurred to me in the shrine of His Eminence the Commander of the Faithful (Ali ibn Abī-Tālib ﷺ), I entered into the presence of His Eminence the Mahdī (may God ﷻ hasten the advent of his noble person) and recited the Ziārat-e Jāmi'a in a loud voice. When the recital was done, His Eminence said, "It is a good *ziārat*."

Majlisī the First continues: "In most cases I rely on this *ziārat* and there is no doubt that its composer is Imam Hādī ﷺ and that it has been presented to [and its authenticity ratified by] the Lord of the Age (*imām az-zamān*) ﷺ and that its text is the most perfected and best of the *ziārāt*."

Muhaddith an-Nūrī states, "During his Hajj pilgrimage, Sayyid Ahmad Dashtī was privileged to be in the presence of the Lord of the Age, His Eminence the Mahdī (may God ﷻ hasten the advent of his noble person) of the House of the Prophet ﷺ who recommended him to the recitation of supererogatory supplications, and to the *ziārat* of Āshūrā and Jāmi'a, saying, "Why do you [plural] not recite the supererogatory supplications (*nāfila*)? [And he repeated the word three times:] *nāfila, nāfila, nāfila*! Why do you [plural] not recite the [*ziārat* of] Āshūrā? Āshūrā, Āshūrā, Āshūrā! Why do you [plural] not recite the [*ziārat* of] Jāmi'a? Jāmi'a, Jāmi'a, Jāmi'a!"

The eloquence of the style and the weight of the content in terms of the wisdom and purport that can be felt emanating from it speak, in themselves, to the authenticity of the *ziārat* and commend its expressive and exalted knowledge to the reader. And now, by starting with the sending of blessings of peace unto the noble spirit of Imam Hādī ﷺ, we shall proceed to present the *ziārat* and its translation for the mental and emotional and spiritual edification of the gentle reader.

5 The Ziārat-e Jāmi'a Kabīra

This *ziārat*[101] is attributed to the Tenth Imam, Imam Ali an-Naqī ﷺ who taught it to Mūsā ibn Abdullāh an-Nakh'ī at his request to teach him a comprehensive way of paying homage to any of the Immaculate Imams ﷺ when making pilgrimage to their shrines or from afar.

Mūsā ibn Abdullāh an-Nakh'ī reports: I said to Imam Hādī ﷺ, "O son of the Prophet ﷺ of God, teach me an eloquent and perfected *ziārat* so that I can recite it whenever I make pilgrimage to any one of you." His Eminence the Imam al-Hādī ﷺ said, "You must have [already] made your major ablution (*ghusl*). When you reach the threshold of the shrine, stand still and recite the *shahādatayn*.[102] Then, having entered the sanctuary [of the shrine] (*haram*), repeat the *takbīr*[103] one hundred times, then say:"

أَشْهَدُ أَنْ لاَ إِلَهَ إِلاَّ اللهُ

I bear witness that there is no deity save Allāh ﷻ

وَحْدَهُ لاَ شَرِيكَ لَهُ

Alone without having any associate

وَأَشْهَدُ أَنَّ مُحَمَّداً صَلَّى اللهُ عَلَيْهِ وَآلِهِ عَبْدُهُ وَرَسُولُهُ

And I bear witness that Muhammad—blessings of Allāh be upon him—is His servant and Messenger

الله أكبر

When you enter and catch sight of the tomb, you should halt again and repeat saying *Allāhu Akbar* (Allāh is the Greatest) —thirty times. 'Very serene and venerable, you should walk a few yards with slow steps and then

---

[101] We have not been able to ascertain the identity of the translator of this *ziārat*.
[102] See footnote #80.
[103] *Takbīr*: The chanting of the words *allāhu akbar* (God ﷻ is great or God ﷻ is greater) [than any other power]; the proclamation of the greatness and utter transcendence of God.

halt anew and repeating saying *Allāhu Akbar* thirty times. As you come within reach of the tomb, you should repeat saying *Allāhu Akbar* forty times so that you would have said it one hundred times. After that, you should recite the following:

Peace be on you O the family of the Prophet	اَلسَّلَامُ عَلَيْكُمْ يَا أَهْلَ بَيْتِ النُّبُوَّةِ
You are the seat of the Divine mission	وَ مَوْضِعَ الرِّسَالَةِ
Unto you the Angels turn	وَمُخْتَلَفَ الْمَلَائِكَةِ
You are the destination of the Divine revelation	وَمَهْبِطَ الْوَحْيِ
the originating source of mercy	وَمَعْدِنَ الرَّحْمَةِ
the treasures of knowledge	وَخُزَّانَ الْعِلْمِ
the ultimate in forbearance	وَمُنْتَهَى الْحِلْمِ
the foundation of generosity	وَأُصُولَ الْكَرَمِ
the leaders of all nations	وَقَادَةَ الْأُمَمِ
You administer and distribute the bounties	وَأَوْلِيَاءَ النِّعَمِ
You are the elements of virtues	وَعَنَاصِرَ الْأَبْرَارِ
the pillars of goodness	وَدَعَائِمَ الْأَخْيَارِ
You direct and guide mankind	وَسَاسَةَ الْعِبَادِ
You protect and support lands	وَأَرْكَانَ الْبِلَادِ
The doors to faith	وَأَبْوَابَ الْإِيمَانِ
the trustees of the All-beneficent Allāh	وَأُمَنَاءَ الرَّحْمَنِ

Imam Ali ibn Muhammad al-Hādī

The distinguished descendants of the Prophets	وَسُلَالَةِ النَّبِيِّينَ
The choice descendants of the Messengers	وَصَفْوَةِ الْمُرْسَلِينَ
The Household of the best Individual in the estimation of the Lord of the worlds	وَعِتْرَةِ خِيَرَةِ رَبِّ الْعَالَمِينَ
And upon you be the mercy and blessings of Allāh	وَرَحْمَةُ اللَّهِ وَبَرَكَاتُهُ
Peace be on the Guides imams to the Right Path	السَّلَامُ عَلَى أَئِمَّةِ الْهُدَى
The lanterns in darkness	وَمَصَابِيحِ الدُّجَى
The patterns of piety	وَأَعْلَامِ التُّقَى
The actual ones endued with understanding	وَذَوِي النُّهَى
The ones of thought	وَأُولِي الْحِجَى
The shelters for people	وَكَهْفِ الْوَرَى
The inheritors of the Prophets	وَوَرَثَةِ الْأَنْبِيَاءِ
The perfect specimen	وَالْمَثَلِ الْأَعْلَى
The most excellent calling unto the good	وَالدَّعْوَةِ الْحُسْنَى
The decisive arguments of Allāh against the inhabitants of the world, the Hereafter and the former	وَحُجَجِ اللَّهِ عَلَى أَهْلِ الدُّنْيَا وَالْآخِرَةِ وَالْأُولَى
And upon you be the mercy and blessings of Allāh	وَرَحْمَةُ اللَّهِ وَبَرَكَاتُهُ
Peace be on the exponents of the views and beliefs which acquaint with the awareness of Allāh	السَّلَامُ عَلَى مَحَالِّ مَعْرِفَةِ اللَّهِ
wherever you are there are blessings of Allāh	وَمَسَاكِنِ بَرَكَةِ اللَّهِ

The Unknown Imams

وَمَعَادِنِ حِكْمَةِ اللهِ
the wisdom of Allāh is deposited with you

وَحَفَظَةِ سِرِّ اللهِ
the secrets of Allāh have been put in your safekeeping

وَحَمَلَةِ كِتَابِ اللهِ
you know the Book of Allāh by heart

وَأَوْصِيَاءِ نَبِيِّ اللهِ
you are the successors of the Prophet ﷺ of Allāh

وَذُرِّيَّةَ رَسُولِ اللهِ صَلَّى اللهُ عَلَيْهِ وَآلِهِ
the children of the Messenger of Allāh

وَرَحْمَةُ اللهِ وَبَرَكَاتُهُ
And upon you be the mercy and blessings of Allāh

السَّلَامُ عَلَى الدُّعَاةِ إِلَى اللهِ
Peace be on you who invite people unto Allāh

وَالْأَدِلَّاءِ عَلَى مَرْضَاةِ اللهِ
guide with clear arguments unto that which win Allāh's pleasure

وَالْمُسْتَقِرِّينَ فِي أَمْرِ اللهِ
abide by the laws of Allāh

الثَّامِّينَ فِي مَحَبَّةِ اللهِ
love Allāh from the bottom of the heart

وَالْمُخْلِصِينَ فِي تَوْحِيدِ اللهِ
sincerely believe in the One and Only Allāh

وَالْمُظْهِرِينَ لِأَمْرِ اللهِ وَنَهْيِهِ
make clear that which is made lawful and that which is made unlawful by Allāh

وَعِبَادِهِ الْمُكْرَمِينَ
you are the honored bondmen

الَّذِينَ لَا يَسْبِقُونَهُ بِالْقَوْلِ وَهُمْ بِأَمْرِهِ يَعْمَلُونَ
who speak not until He has spoken
and act by His command

وَرَحْمَةُ اللهِ وَبَرَكَاتُهُ
And upon you be the mercy and blessings of Allāh

السَّلَامُ عَلَى الْأَئِمَّةِ الدُّعَاةِ
Peace be on the Guides Imams who give a calling

وَالْقَادَةِ الْهُدَاةِ
and lead unto guidance

Imam Ali ibn Muhammad al-Hādī

you are the loving guardians

the protecting defenders

the followers people of the remembrance the Holy Quran

those who are in authority

that good which Allāh has left with people

His choicest and His group

The store of His Knowledge

His argument, His path

His light, His proof

And upon you be the mercy and blessings of Allāh

I bear witness that there is no God ﷻ save Allāh

the One and there is no partner with Him

just as Allāh Himself testifies to His own Oneness

and His Angels also testify for His Oneness

And also his creatures who know the truth also testify

there is no God ﷻ save He; the Almighty the All-wise

I bear witness that Muhammad is His elected bondsman

His approved Messenger

He sent him with the guidance and the Religion of truth

وَالسَّادَةِ الْوُلَاةِ

وَالذَّادَةِ الْحُمَاةِ

وَأَهْلِ الذِّكْرِ

وَأُولِي الْأَمْرِ

وَبَقِيَّةِ اللَّهِ

وَخِيَرَتِهِ وَحِزْبِهِ

وَعَيْبَةِ عِلْمِهِ

وَحُجَّتِهِ وَصِرَاطِهِ

وَنُورِهِ وَبُرْهَانِهِ

وَرَحْمَةُ اللَّهِ وَبَرَكَاتُهُ

أَشْهَدُ أَنْ لَا إِلَهَ إِلَّا اللَّهُ

وَحْدَهُ لَا شَرِيكَ لَهُ

كَمَا شَهِدَ اللَّهُ لِنَفْسِهِ

وَشَهِدَتْ لَهُ مَلَائِكَتُهُ

وَأُولُوا الْعِلْمِ مِنْ خَلْقِهِ

لَا إِلَهَ إِلَّا هُوَ الْعَزِيزُ الْحَكِيمُ

وَأَشْهَدُ أَنَّ مُحَمَّداً عَبْدُهُ الْمُنْتَجَبُ

وَرَسُولُهُ الْمُرْتَضَى

أَرْسَلَهُ بِالْهُدَى وَدِينِ الْحَقِّ

that He may cause it to prevail over all religions	لِيُظْهِرَهُ عَلَى الدِّينِ كُلِّهِ
however much the idol-worshippers may be averse	وَلَوْ كَرِهَ الْمُشْرِكُونَ
I bear witness that all of you are the rightly guided Imams	وَأَشْهَدُ أَنَّكُمُ الْأَئِمَّةُ الرَّاشِدُونَ
The truly guided, the infallible	الْمَهْدِيُّونَ الْمَعْصُومُونَ
The highly revered, the favorite	الْمُكَرَّمُونَ الْمُقَرَّبُونَ
The pious, the truthful	الْمُتَّقُونَ الصَّادِقُونَ
The chosen, the obedient servants of Allāh	الْمُصْطَفَوْنَ الْمُطِيعُونَ لِلَّهِ
who establish the rule of God	الْقَوَّامُونَ بِأَمْرِهِ
put into practice that which He wills	الْعَامِلُونَ بِإِرَادَتِهِ
win and possess His excellence	الْفَائِزُونَ بِكَرَامَتِهِ
He elected you to have His knowledge	اصْطَفَاكُمْ بِعِلْمِهِ
He chose you to be aware of what issues forth or what comes to pass	وَارْتَضَاكُمْ لِغَيْبِهِ
placed His trust in you to let you know inside and out of His secrets	وَاخْتَارَكُمْ لِسِرِّهِ
strengthened you with His omnipotence	وَاجْتَبَاكُمْ بِقُدْرَتِهِ
equipped you with His guidance	وَأَعَزَّكُمْ بِهُدَاهُ
distinguished you with His clear proofs	وَخَصَّكُمْ بِبُرْهَانِهِ
glorified you with His Light	وَانْتَجَبَكُمْ لِنُورِهِ

Imam Ali ibn Muhammad al-Hādī

وَأَيَّدَكُمْ بِرُوحِهِ
confirmed you with His Holy spirit

وَرَضِيَكُمْ خُلَفَاءَ فِي أَرْضِهِ
made a choice of you to represent Him in His earth

وَحُجَجاً عَلَى بَرِيَّتِهِ
so that you make evident manifest and establish His truth

وَأَنْصَاراً لِدِينِهِ
give currency to His religion

وَحَفَظَةً لِسِرِّهِ
protect His confidence

وَخَزَنَةً لِعِلْمِهِ
treasure His knowledge

وَمُسْتَوْدَعاً لِحِكْمَتِهِ
store and invest His wisdom

وَتَرَاجِمَةً لِوَحْيِهِ
Interpret His revelation

وَأَرْكَاناً لِتَوْحِيدِهِ
consolidate and preserve His Oneness

وَشُهَدَاءَ عَلَى خَلْقِهِ
bear witness to the act of creation you witnessed all that has been created by Allāh

وَأَعْلَاماً لِعِبَادِهِ
you are the signs Allāh has set for His servants

وَمَنَاراً فِي بِلَادِهِ
you are the torches Allāh has lighted in His lands

وَأَدِلَّاءَ عَلَى صِرَاطِهِ
you show the direction unto His path

عَصَمَكُمُ اللهُ مِنَ الزَّلَلِ
Allāh preserved you guiltless and free from error

وَآمَنَكُمْ مِنَ الْفِتَنِ
kept you safe disorderliness

وَطَهَّرَكُمْ مِنَ الدَّنَسِ
freed you from dirt

وَأَذْهَبَ عَنْكُمُ الرِّجْسَ
from unruly removed uncleanness from you

وَطَهَّرَكُمْ تَطْهِيراً
and cleansed you with a thorough cleansing

فَعَظَّمْتُمْ جَلَالَهُ

213

So, you have glorified His majesty

وَأَكْبَرْتُمْ شَأْنَهُ

Have declared great His magnificence

وَمَجَّدْتُمْ كَرَمَهُ

Have venerated His glory

وَأَدَمْتُمْ ذِكْرَهُ

Have perpetuated mentioning Him

وَوَكَّدْتُمْ مِيثَاقَهُ

Have consolidated His covenant

وَأَحْكَمْتُمْ عَقْدَ طَاعَتِهِ

Have made firm your pledge of obedience to Him

وَنَصَحْتُمْ لَهُ فِي السِّرِّ وَالْعَلَانِيَةِ

Have advised people for His sake privately and publicly

وَدَعَوْتُمْ إِلَى سَبِيلِهِ بِالْحِكْمَةِ وَالْمَوْعِظَةِ الْحَسَنَةِ

Have called unto His way through words of wisdom and fair Admonition

وَبَذَلْتُمْ أَنْفُسَكُمْ فِي مَرْضَاتِهِ

not sparing your own lives, took pains and made efforts to do as He willed

وَصَبَرْتُمْ عَلَى مَا أَصَابَكُمْ فِي جَنْبِهِ

exercised self-control and faced untold hardships in His cause

وَأَقَمْتُمُ الصَّلَاةَ

established prayers

وَآتَيْتُمُ الزَّكَاةَ

gave prescribed alms

وَأَمَرْتُمْ بِالْمَعْرُوفِ

advised to do that which is lawful

وَنَهَيْتُمْ عَنِ الْمُنْكَرِ

warned not to do that which is unlawful

وَجَاهَدْتُمْ فِي اللهِ حَقَّ جِهَادِهِ

strived in the way of Allāh in letter and spirit

حَتَّى أَعْلَنْتُمْ دَعْوَتَهُ

until you made known every aspect of His true Message

وَبَيَّنْتُمْ فَرَائِضَهُ

rendered clear the obligations

and defined the boundaries laid down by Him	وَأَقَمْتُمْ حُدُودَهُ
communicated and propagated His constitution	وَنَشَرْتُمْ شَرَائِعَ أَحْكَامِهِ
demonstrated the rule of conduct approved by Him	وَسَنَنْتُمْ سُنَّتَهُ
and went ahead resolutely to accomplish that which is dear to Him	وَصِرْتُمْ فِي ذَلِكَ مِنْهُ إِلَى الرِّضَا
surrendered to His will	وَسَلَّمْتُمْ لَهُ الْقَضَاءَ
proved true the Messengers sent by Him before you	وَصَدَّقْتُمْ مِنْ رُسُلِهِ مَنْ مَضَى
therefore, whoso turns away from you misses the aim (and deviates from the right path)	فَالرَّاغِبُ عَنْكُمْ مَارِقٌ
whoso closely adhere to you reaches the destination	وَاللَّازِمُ لَكُمْ لَاحِقٌ
whoso fails short of that which is as it ought to be in your case compare and contrast to lower in grade destroys himself	وَالْمُقَصِّرُ فِي حَقِّكُمْ زَاهِقٌ
Verily truth is with you amid you in you and it always directs itself unto you	وَالْحَقُّ مَعَكُمْ وَفِيكُمْ وَمِنْكُمْ وَإِلَيْكُمْ
you deserve it as it stays permanently with you	وَأَنْتُمْ أَهْلُهُ وَمَعْدِنُهُ
the inheritance of Prophethood is with you	وَمِيرَاثُ النُّبُوَّةِ عِنْدَكُمْ
you are the ultimate destination to which the people will have to come back	وَإِيَابُ الْخَلْقِ إِلَيْكُمْ
to give an account of themselves before you	وَحِسَابُهُمْ عَلَيْكُمْ
	وَفَصْلُ الْخِطَابِ عِنْدَكُمْ

it is your privilege to separate evil from good
in clear words

وَآيَاتُ اللَّهِ لَدَيْكُمْ

in the light of the signs guidelines of Allāh
you are fully aware of

وَعَزَائِمُهُ فِيكُمْ

because for His unavoidable decrees
and plan He relies upon you

وَنُورُهُ وَبُرْهَانُهُ عِنْدَكُمْ

you are the true reflection of His light and Signs

وَأَمْرُهُ إِلَيْكُمْ

authority to guide has been conferred on you

مَنْ وَالَاكُمْ فَقَدْ وَالَى اللَّهَ

he who is fond of you is a friend of Allāh

وَمَنْ عَادَاكُمْ فَقَدْ عَادَى اللَّهَ

whoso turns against you comes in conflict
with Allāh

وَمَنْ أَحَبَّكُمْ فَقَدْ أَحَبَّ اللَّهَ

he who loves you is a beloved of Allāh

وَمَنْ أَبْغَضَكُمْ فَقَدْ أَبْغَضَ اللَّهَ

whoso bears a grudge against you
holds Allāh in contempt

وَمَنِ اعْتَصَمَ بِكُمْ فَقَدِ اعْتَصَمَ بِاللَّهِ

whoso takes refuge with you takes
asylum with Allāh

أَنْتُمُ الصِّرَاطُ الْأَقْوَمُ

you are the main means of approach the right way

وَالسَّبِيلُ الْأَعْظَمُ

You are the greatest path (to Allāh)

وَشُهَدَاءُ دَارِ الْفَنَاءِ

you give witness to what takes place
in this mortal world

وَشُفَعَاءُ دَارِ الْبَقَاءِ

And you are the interceders (for the believers)
on the Day of Judgement

وَالرَّحْمَةُ الْمَوْصُولَةُ

you are the mercy perpetual and progressive

وَالْآيَةُ الْمَخْزُونَةُ

The signs highly valued and treasured

وَالْأَمَانَةُ الْمَحْفُوظَةُ

mainstay well-guarded

وَالْبَابُ الْمُبْتَلَى بِهِ النَّاسُ

forum of justice wherein people
are put to test and trial

مَنْ أَتَاكُمْ نَجَا

whoso comes near you is saved assured a blissful afterlife

وَمَنْ لَمْ يَأْتِكُمْ هَلَكَ

whoso does not come near you is ruined doomed to everlasting distress

إِلَى اللَّهِ تَدْعُونَ

you invite people unto Allāh

وَعَلَيْهِ تَدُلُّونَ

show the right way leading to Him

وَبِهِ تُؤْمِنُونَ

Believe in Him

وَلَهُ تُسَلِّمُونَ

willingly surrender to Him

وَبِأَمْرِهِ تَعْمَلُونَ

act upon His law and command

وَإِلَى سَبِيلِهِ تُرْشِدُونَ

Guide to His path

وَبِقَوْلِهِ تَحْكُمُونَ

exercise authority in the name of His word

سَعِدَ مَنْ وَالَاكُمْ

happy and successful is he who stands by you

وَهَلَكَ مَنْ عَادَاكُمْ

lost and desolate is he who forsakes you

وَخَابَ مَنْ جَحَدَكُمْ

indistinct and little known is
he who knows better but denies you

وَضَلَّ مَنْ فَارَقَكُمْ

whoso separates himself from you goes astray

وَفَازَ مَنْ تَمَسَّكَ بِكُمْ

whoso clings to you attains his purpose	وَأَمِنَ مَنْ لَجَأَ إِلَيْكُمْ
whoso takes refuge with you saves himself	وَسَلِمَ مَنْ صَدَّقَكُمْ
blessed is he who becomes aware of your truthfulness	وَهُدِيَ مَنِ اعْتَصَمَ بِكُمْ
he who is watched over by you finds the right path	مَنِ اتَّبَعَكُمْ فَالْجَنَّةُ مَأْوَاهُ
whoso follows you shall dwell in the Paradise	وَمَنْ خَالَفَكُمْ فَالنَّارُ مَثْوَاهُ
whoso turns against you shall rot in Hell	وَمَنْ جَحَدَكُمْ كَافِرٌ
he who says no to you in fact renounces the faith	وَمَنْ حَارَبَكُمْ مُشْرِكٌ
he who makes war against you is as bad as a polytheist	
he who forsakes you shall find himself in the lowest tier of the burning fire	وَمَنْ رَدَّ عَلَيْكُمْ فِي أَسْفَلِ دَرْكٍ مِنَ الْجَحِيمِ
I know for sure that certainly you are like what is said above	أَشْهَدُ أَنَّ هَذَا سَابِقٌ لَكُمْ فِيمَا مَضَى
and shall continue to be so in future	وَجَارٍ لَكُمْ فِيمَا بَقِيَ
your souls, light and form are made from the same clay	وَأَنَّ أَرْوَاحَكُمْ وَنُورَكُمْ وَطِينَتَكُمْ وَاحِدَةٌ
They are thoroughly pure and infallible altogether	طَابَتْ وَطَهُرَتْ بَعْضُهَا مِنْ بَعْضٍ
Allāh created you in the form of light	خَلَقَكُمُ اللهُ أَنْوَاراً
then kept you closely attached with His Throne	فَجَعَلَكُمْ بِعَرْشِهِ مُحْدِقِينَ
until you were sent down in this	حَتَّى مَنَّ عَلَيْنَا بِكُمْ

world as a favor to us

فَجَعَلَكُمْ فِي بُيُوتٍ أَذِنَ اللهُ أَنْ تُرْفَعَ وَيُذْكَرَ فِيهَا اسْمُهُ

allowed you to pronounce and praise His name aloud in the Houses of Allāh

وَجَعَلَ صَلاَتَنَا عَلَيْكُمْ وَمَا خَصَّنَا بِهِ مِنْ وِلاَيَتِكُمْ طِيباً لِخَلْقِنَا

made our sending blessings on you and being loyal to you as signs of the legitimacy of our birth

وَطَهَارَةً لِأَنْفُسِنَا

and the purity of our souls

وَتَزْكِيَةً لَنَا

And the refinement our manners

وَكَفَّارَةً لِذُنُوبِنَا

And His forgiving our sins

فَكُنَّا عِنْدَهُ مُسَلِّمِينَ بِفَضْلِكُمْ

We thus have become among those who believe undoubtedly in your (excellent) virtues

وَمَعْرُوفِينَ بِتَصْدِيقِنَا إِيَّاكُمْ

and by becoming aware of your true status we have been distinguished

فَبَلَغَ اللهُ بِكُمْ أَشْرَفَ مَحَلِّ الْمُكَرَّمِينَ

Allāh made you reach the noblest position of glory

وَأَعْلَى مَنَازِلِ الْمُقَرَّبِينَ

the highest station nearest to Allāh

وَأَرْفَعَ دَرَجَاتِ الْمُرْسَلِينَ

and the loftiest status of the Messengers

حَيْثُ لاَ يَلْحَقُهُ لاَحِقٌ

where none can ever reach you

وَلاَ يَفُوقُهُ فَائِقٌ

nor can anyone surpass you

وَلاَ يَسْبِقُهُ سَابِقٌ

nor can anyone ever precede you

وَلاَ يَطْمَعُ فِي إِدْرَاكِهِ طَامِعٌ

No can anyone look forward to reaching your positions	حَتَّى لاَ يَبْقَى مَلَكٌ مُقَرَّبٌ
even the favorite Angels went for it	
nor the commissioned Prophets	وَلاَ نَبِيٌّ مُرْسَلٌ
nor a friend nor a martyr	وَلاَ صِدِّيقٌ وَلاَ شَهِيدٌ
nor a scholar nor an ignorant	وَلاَ عَالِمٌ وَلاَ جَاهِلٌ
nor an inferior nor a superior	وَلاَ دَنِيٌّ وَلاَ فَاضِلٌ
nor a pious faithful	وَلاَ مُؤْمِنٌ صَالِحٌ
nor a wicked sinner	وَلاَ فَاجِرٌ طَالِحٌ
nor an obstinate tyrant	وَلاَ جَبَّارٌ عَنِيدٌ
nor a devilish rebel	وَلاَ شَيْطَانٌ مَرِيدٌ
nor any other being had ever been there	وَلاَ خَلْقٌ فِيمَا بَيْنَ ذَلِكَ شَهِيدٌ
except that Allāh informs them of the grandeur of your decisive authority	إِلاَّ عَرَّفَهُمْ جَلاَلَةَ أَمْرِكُمْ
importance of your thoughtful ideas	وَعِظَمَ خَطَرِكُمْ
power of your meaningful intelligence	وَكِبَرَ شَأْنِكُمْ
thoroughness of your enlightenment	وَتَمَامَ نُورِكُمْ
strength and goodness of your essence	وَصِدْقَ مَقَاعِدِكُمْ
proof of the durability of your office	وَثَبَاتَ مَقَامِكُمْ
distinction of your position	وَشَرَفَ مَحَلِّكُمْ

Imam Ali ibn Muhammad al-Hādī

وَمَنْزِلَتِكُمْ عِنْدَهُ

and the glory of your rank and dignity in His estimation

وَكَرَامَتَكُمْ عَلَيْهِ

your venerable grace in His perception

وَخَاصَّتَكُمْ لَدَيْهِ

your special friendship with Him

وَقُرْبَ مَنْزِلَتِكُمْ مِنْهُ

and the closest nearness you have near Him

بِأَبِي أَنْتُمْ وَأُمِّي وَأَهْلِي وَمَالِي وَأُسْرَتِي

My father, mother, family, property
and possessions are at your disposal

أَشْهِدُ اللهَ وَأُشْهِدُكُمْ أَنِّي مُؤْمِنٌ بِكُمْ وَبِمَا آمَنْتُمْ بِهِ

I beseech Allāh and you to bear witness
that I believe in you and in that in which you believe

كَافِرٌ بِعَدُوِّكُمْ وَبِمَا كَفَرْتُمْ بِهِ

I renounce your enemies and whatever you renounce

مُسْتَبْصِرٌ بِشَأْنِكُمْ

I am fully aware of your glorious purpose

وَبِضَلَالَةِ مَنْ خَالَفَكُمْ

and of the deviation of him whoever oppose you

مُوَالٍ لَكُمْ وَلِأَوْلِيَائِكُمْ

I am your friend and a friend of your friends

مُبْغِضٌ لِأَعْدَائِكُمْ وَمُعَادٍ لَهُمْ

I dislike your enemies and strive against their designs

سِلْمٌ لِمَنْ سَالَمَكُمْ

I am at peace with those who make peace with you

وَحَرْبٌ لِمَنْ حَارَبَكُمْ

I take the field against those who march against you

مُحَقِّقٌ لِمَا حَقَّقْتُمْ

I accept as true that which acknowledges your truth

مُبْطِلٌ لِمَا أَبْطَلْتُمْ

I prove false that which takes a stand against you

مُطِيعٌ لَكُمْ

I follow in your footsteps

عَارِفٌ بِحَقِّكُمْ

I am fully aware of your rights and privileges

مُقِرٌّ بِفَضْلِكُمْ	I recognize your superiority over others
مُحْتَمِلٌ لِعِلْمِكُمْ	I carry and preserve your knowledge
مُحْتَجِبٌ بِذِمَّتِكُمْ	I take refuge under your protective shelter
مُعْتَرِفٌ بِكُمْ	I respond to you
مُؤْمِنٌ بِإِيَابِكُمْ	I know for sure that you will come back
مُصَدِّقٌ بِرَجْعَتِكُمْ	I anticipate and look for your just and fair order
مُنْتَظِرٌ لأَمْرِكُمْ	I believe in your promised return
مُرْتَقِبٌ لِدَوْلَتِكُمْ	I anticipate the advent of your State
آخِذٌ بِقَوْلِكُمْ	I hold fast to that which you have said
عَامِلٌ بِأَمْرِكُمْ	I carry out your orders
مُسْتَجِيرٌ بِكُمْ	I take shelter in your neighborhood
زَائِرٌ لَكُمْ	I make a visit to do homage and praise you
لَائِذٌ عَائِذٌ بِقُبُورِكُمْ	for me your resting abodes are sanctuaries
مُسْتَشْفِعٌ إِلَى اللهِ عَزَّ وَجَلَّ بِكُمْ	in the court of the Almighty you are my advocates
وَمُتَقَرِّبٌ بِكُمْ إِلَيْهِ	I seek His nearness through you
وَمُقَدِّمُكُمْ أَمَامَ طَلِبَتِي وَحَوَائِجِي وَإِرَادَتِي	for seeking fulfillment of my wants and desire
فِي كُلِّ أَحْوَالِي وَأُمُورِي	under all circumstances I follow you to make headway
مُؤْمِنٌ بِسِرِّكُمْ وَعَلَانِيَتِكُمْ	

I believe in your invisibility, visibility Presence, absence	وَشَاهِدِكُمْ وَغَائِبِكُمْ
and in the first of you and the last of you	وَأَوَّلِكُمْ وَآخِرِكُمْ
I entrust to you the total charge of everything concerning me	وَمُفَوِّضٌ فِي ذَلِكَ كُلِّهِ إِلَيْكُمْ
I gladly consent to that which you think is good for me	وَمُسَلِّمٌ فِيهِ مَعَكُمْ
from the bottom of my heart I surrender to you	وَقَلْبِي لَكُمْ مُسَلِّمٌ
your opinion is my opinion	وَرَأْيِي لَكُمْ تَبَعٌ
I am prepared and ready to stand up for you	وَنُصْرَتِي لَكُمْ مُعَدَّةٌ
till Allāh the Supreme gives a new life to His Religion through you	حَتَّى يُحْيِيَ اللهُ تَعَالَى دِينَهُ بِكُمْ
brings you back again in His 'Days'	وَيَرُدَّكُمْ فِي أَيَّامِهِ
Manifest you to set up His fair and just rule	وَيُظْهِرَكُمْ لِعَدْلِهِ
you take root in and take possession of His earth the world	وَيُمَكِّنَكُمْ فِي أَرْضِهِ
so I am with you, with you, not other than you	فَمَعَكُمْ مَعَكُمْ لَا مَعَ غَيْرِكُمْ
I have full faith in you	آمَنْتُ بِكُمْ
I love and cherish the last of you just as I love and cherish the first of you	وَتَوَلَّيْتُ آخِرَكُمْ بِمَا تَوَلَّيْتُ بِهِ أَوَّلَكُمْ
I turn to the Almighty Allāh disconnecting all links with your enemies	وَبَرِئْتُ إِلَى اللهِ عَزَّ وَجَلَّ مِنْ أَعْدَائِكُمْ
	وَمِنَ الْجِبْتِ وَالطَّاغُوتِ

from Jibt and Tāghūt	وَالشَّيَاطِينِ وَحِزْبِهِمُ
and the devils and their followers	الظَّالِمِينَ لَكُمْ
who took liberties with you	وَالْجَاحِدِينَ لِحَقِّكُمْ
the renegades who suppressed your rights	وَالْمَارِقِينَ مِنْ وِلاَيَتِكُمْ
the turncoats who ran away from your guardianship	وَالْغَاصِبِينَ لِإِرْثِكُمْ
the swindlers who usurped your succession	وَالشَّاكِّينَ فِيكُمْ
the unbelievers who hesitated to accept you as true	وَالْمُنْحَرِفِينَ عَنْكُمْ
the deserters who turned against you	وَمِنْ كُلِّ وَلِيجَةٍ دُونَكُمْ
and from every affinity apart from you	وَكُلِّ مُطَاعٍ سِوَاكُمْ
every allegiance other than unto you	وَمِنَ الْأَئِمَّةِ الَّذِينَ يَدْعُونَ إِلَى النَّارِ
from the leadership which directs to the Fire	فَثَبِّتَنِي اللهُ أَبَداً مَا حَيِيتُ عَلَى مُوَالاَتِكُمْ
May Allāh keep intact my love and attachment with you for ever so far I am alive	وَمَحَبَّتِكُمْ وَدِينِكُمْ
and make me adhere to your creed	وَوَفَّقَنِي لِطَاعَتِكُمْ
find obedience unto you convenient	وَرَزَقَنِي شَفَاعَتَكُمْ
obtain your intercession	وَجَعَلَنِي مِنْ خِيَارِ مَوَالِيكُمْ
be among your fortunate disciples	التَّابِعِينَ لِمَا دَعَوْتُمْ إِلَيْهِ
Who hold fast to your traditions	وَجَعَلَنِي مِمَّنْ يَقْتَصُّ آثَارَكُمْ
And make me follow in your footsteps	وَيَسْلُكُ سَبِيلَكُمْ

Imam Ali ibn Muḥammad al-Hādī

And track your Path	وَيَهْتَدِي بِهُدَاكُمْ
abide by your guidance	
to be raised in your group on the Day of Judgement	وَيُحْشَرَ فِي زُمْرَتِكُمْ
brought back during your reappearance	وَيَكِرَّ فِي رَجْعَتِكُمْ
called upon to help you in your administration	وَيُمَلَّكَ فِي دَوْلَتِكُمْ
honored to live in your safe and sound supervision	وَيُشَرَّفَ فِي عَافِيَتِكُمْ
right there in the middle of your 'days'	وَيُمَكَّنَ فِي أَيَّامِكُمْ
delighted and thrilled by seeing you in person	وَتَقَرَّ عَيْنُهُ غَداً بِرُؤْيَتِكُمْ
My father, mother, children, possessions and myself are at your disposal	بِأَبِي أَنْتُمْ وَأُمِّي وَنَفْسِي وَأَهْلِي وَمَالِي
whoso desires nearness to Allāh in fact makes a beginning with you	مَنْ أَرَادَ اللهَ بَدَأَ بِكُمْ
whoso professes the Unity of God ﷻ in fact takes after you	وَمَنْ وَحَّدَهُ قَبِلَ عَنْكُمْ
whoso moves towards Him has to turn to you	وَمَنْ قَصَدَهُ تَوَجَّهَ بِكُمْ
O my masters I cannot count and mention your merits	مَوَالِيَّ لاَ أُحْصِي ثَنَاءَكُمْ
I am unable to come up to the height where your true appreciation can be enjoyed and your real class can be determined	وَلاَ أَبْلُغُ مِنَ الْمَدْحِ كُنْهَكُمْ وَمِنَ الْوَصْفِ قَدْرَكُمْ
You are the light of the virtuous	وَأَنْتُمْ نُورُ الْأَخْيَارِ
	وَهُدَاةُ الْأَبْرَارِ

225

The guides of the pious ones	وَحُجَجُ الْجَبَّارِ
The claims of the Omnipotent (Lord)	
Allāh had created you in the first place	بِكُمْ فَتَحَ اللَّهُ
and then disclosed to you His plan of creation	وَبِكُمْ يَخْتِمُ اللَّهُ
on account of you He sent down abundant and far-spread rain	وَبِكُمْ يُنَزِّلُ الْغَيْثَ
because of you the sky prevents itself from falling down over the earth unless He permits	وَبِكُمْ يُمْسِكُ السَّمَاءَ أَنْ تَقَعَ عَلَى الْأَرْضِ إِلَّا بِإِذْنِهِ
due to you He drives away troubles and dismisses hardships	وَبِكُمْ يُنَفِّسُ الْهَمَّ وَيَكْشِفُ الضُّرَّ
with you is that with which His Messengers came down	وَعِنْدَكُمْ مَا نَزَلَتْ بِهِ رُسُلُهُ
And with which His Angels descended	وَهَبَطَتْ بِهِ مَلَائِكَتُهُ
and to your forefather,	وَإِلَى جَدِّكُمْ
Note: If it is the tomb of Imam Ali ibn Abi Talib is the visited, you should say instead, "And to your cousin"	وَإِلَى ابْنِ عَمِّكَ
the Truthful Spirit was sent	بُعِثَ الرُّوحُ الْأَمِينُ
Allāh has given you that which He has not given to anyone in the whole universe	آتَاكُمُ اللَّهُ مَا لَمْ يُؤْتِ أَحَداً مِنَ الْعَالَمِينَ
all the highborn hang their heads before your noble lineage	طَأْطَأَ كُلُّ شَرِيفٍ لِشَرَفِكُمْ

Imam Ali ibn Muhammad al-Hādī

وَبَخَعَ كُلُّ مُتَكَبِّرٍ لِطَاعَتِكُمْ

every valiant lord submits to you
in your obedience

وَخَضَعَ كُلُّ جَبَّارٍ لِفَضْلِكُمْ

every type of heroism is dwarfed before
your completeness and perfection

وَذَلَّ كُلُّ شَيْءٍ لَكُمْ

everything humbles itself in front of you

وَأَشْرَقَتِ الْأَرْضُ بِنُورِكُمْ

your light lights up the earth

وَفَازَ الْفَائِزُونَ بِوِلَايَتِكُمْ

those who love and cherish you attain their end

بِكُمْ يُسْلَكُ إِلَى الرِّضْوَانِ

and conduct themselves to the Paradise

وَعَلَى مَنْ جَحَدَ وِلَايَتَكُمْ غَضَبُ الرَّحْمَنِ

and those who forsake your friendship
earn displeasure of the All-compassionate

بِأَبِي أَنْتُمْ وَأُمِّي وَنَفْسِي وَأَهْلِي وَمَالِي

My father, mother, myself, my children
and possessions are at your disposal

ذِكْرُكُمْ فِي الذَّاكِرِينَ

Although people make mention of you

وَأَسْمَاؤُكُمْ فِي الْأَسْمَاءِ

your names are called along with other names

وَأَجْسَادُكُمْ فِي الْأَجْسَادِ

your figures appeared among other humans

وَأَرْوَاحُكُمْ فِي الْأَرْوَاحِ

your souls rest with other souls

وَأَنْفُسُكُمْ فِي النُّفُوسِ

your beings existed side by side with other beings

وَآثَارُكُمْ فِي الْآثَارِ

your traditions are cited with other traditions

وَقُبُورُكُمْ فِي الْقُبُورِ

your resting places are seen amidst others

فَمَا أَحْلَى أَسْمَاءَكُمْ

but most gracious are your names

وَأَكْرَمَ أَنْفُسَكُمْ

most generous and merciful are your lives	وَأَعْظَمَ شَأْنَكُمْ
superlative is your nature and disposition	وَأَجَلَّ خَطَرَكُمْ
befitting is your station	وَأَوْفَى عَهْدَكُمْ
dependable is your covenant	وَأَصْدَقَ وَعْدَكُمْ
true is your promise	كَلَامُكُمْ نُورٌ
your words give light	وَأَمْرُكُمْ رُشْدٌ
your administration is just and fair	وَوَصِيَّتُكُمُ التَّقْوَى
Piety is your will	وَفِعْلُكُمُ الْخَيْرُ
your deeds are good	وَعَادَتُكُمُ الْإِحْسَانُ
doing good is your manner of living	وَسَجِيَّتُكُمُ الْكَرَمُ
generosity is your habit	وَشَأْنُكُمُ الْحَقُّ وَالصِّدْقُ وَالرِّفْقُ
fair dealing, conformity to reality and helping others are in your nature	
your words are final and decisive	وَقَوْلُكُمْ حُكْمٌ وَحَتْمٌ
your opinion is based upon knowledge, temperance and forethought	وَرَأْيُكُمْ عِلْمٌ وَحِلْمٌ وَحَزْمٌ
if goodness is mentioned, you are its beginning	إِنْ ذُكِرَ الْخَيْرُ كُنْتُمْ أَوَّلَهُ
And its origin and branch and core	وَأَصْلَهُ وَفَرْعَهُ وَمَعْدِنَهُ
And its resting place and its ultimate	وَمَأْوَاهُ وَمُنْتَهَاهُ
My father, mother and I are at your disposal	بِأَبِي أَنْتُمْ وَأُمِّي وَنَفْسِي

Imam Ali ibn Muḥammad al-Hādī

كَيْفَ أَصِفُ حُسْنَ ثَنَائِكُمْ

How shall I describe the beauty and goodness of your merits?

وَأُحْصِي جَمِيلَ بَلَائِكُمْ

How shall I define the grace and decorum you displayed in the hour of test and trial?

وَبِكُمْ أَخْرَجَنَا اللهُ مِنَ الذُّلِّ

It is on account of you that Allāh pulls us out of the depth of degradation

وَفَرَّجَ عَنَّا غَمَرَاتِ الْكُرُوبِ

sets us free from the clutches of hardships

وَأَنْقَذَنَا مِنْ شَفَا جُرُفِ الْهَلَكَاتِ وَمِنَ النَّارِ

takes us to safety from the precipice of annihilation and from failing down into the Hell

بِأَبِي أَنْتُمْ وَأُمِّي وَنَفْسِي

My father, mother and I are at your disposal

بِمُوَالَاتِكُمْ عَلَّمَنَا اللهُ مَعَالِمَ دِينِنَا

Because of our friendship with you Allāh taught us the laws of our religion

وَأَصْلَحَ مَا كَانَ فَسَدَ مِنْ دُنْيَانَا

put in order that which had been spoiled and corrupted in our world

وَبِمُوَالَاتِكُمْ تَمَّتِ الْكَلِمَةُ

by being loyal to you the Word has been completed

وَعَظُمَتِ النِّعْمَةُ

and the Grace has become great

وَائْتَلَفَتِ الْفُرْقَةُ

And the discord has turned into togetherness

وَبِمُوَالَاتِكُمْ تُقْبَلُ الطَّاعَةُ الْمُفْتَرَضَةُ

And only is by our loyalty to you the obligatory obedience (to Allāh) accepted

وَلَكُمُ الْمَوَدَّةُ الْوَاجِبَةُ

And only is the obligatory adoration yours

وَالدَّرَجَاتُ الرَّفِيعَةُ

And so are the highest ranks

وَالْمَقَامُ الْمَحْمُودُ

And so is the Praised Standing

And so is the renowned station in Almighty Allāh's view

وَالْمَكَانُ الْمَعْلُومُ عِنْدَ اللَّهِ عَزَّ وَجَلَّ

And topmost office

وَالْجَاهُ الْعَظِيمُ

And the supreme rank

وَالشَّأْنُ الْكَبِيرُ

And the admitted intercession

وَالشَّفَاعَةُ الْمَقْبُولَةُ

O our Lord, we believe in that which
Thou has sent down and follow the Messenger;
so write our names among those who bear witness

رَبَّنَا آمَنَّا بِمَا أَنْزَلْتَ وَاتَّبَعْنَا الرَّسُولَ فَاكْتُبْنَا مَعَ الشَّاهِدِينَ

Our Lord! Cause not our hearts to
stray after Thou hast guided us, and bestow upon us
mercy from Thy Presence. Lo! Thou, only Thou, art the Bestower.

رَبَّنَا لاَ تُزِغْ قُلُوبَنَا بَعْدَ إِذْ هَدَيْتَنَا وَهَبْ لَنَا مِنْ لَدُنْكَ رَحْمَةً إِنَّكَ أَنْتَ الْوَهَّابُ

Glory be to our Lord for in fact the
promise of our Lord immediately takes effect

سُبْحَانَ رَبِّنَا إِنْ كَانَ وَعْدُ رَبِّنَا لَمَفْعُولاً

O trusted representative of Allāh

يَا وَلِيَّ اللَّهِ

the barriers of wrongdoings separating me
from Allāh cannot be removed save by
attaining your satisfaction

إِنَّ بَيْنِي وَبَيْنَ اللَّهِ عَزَّ وَجَلَّ ذُنُوباً لاَ يَأْتِي عَلَيْهَا إِلاَّ رِضَاكُمْ

therefore in the name of the divine authority
 delegated to you

فَبِحَقِّ مَنِ ائْتَمَنَكُمْ عَلَى سِرِّهِ وَاسْتَرْعَاكُمْ أَمْرَ خَلْقِهِ

the administration of the human society entrusted to you

وَقَرَنَ طَاعَتَكُمْ بِطَاعَتِهِ

and joining obedience to Him to the obedience to you

لَمَّا اسْتَوْهَبْتُمْ ذُنُوبِي

I implore to you to pardon my sins

وَكُنْتُمْ شُفَعَائِي

And to intercede for me

فَإِنِّي لَكُمْ مُطِيعٌ

For I obey you

مَنْ أَطَاعَكُمْ فَقَدْ أَطَاعَ اللَّهَ

He who obeys you in fact obeys Allāh

وَمَنْ عَصَاكُمْ فَقَدْ عَصَى اللَّهَ

he who disobeys you in fact disobeys Allāh

وَمَنْ أَحَبَّكُمْ فَقَدْ أَحَبَّ اللَّهَ

he who loves you in fact loves Allāh

وَمَنْ أَبْغَضَكُمْ فَقَدْ أَبْغَضَ اللَّهَ

he who hates you in fact hates Allāh

اللَّهُمَّ إِنِّي لَوْ وَجَدْتُ شُفَعَاءَ أَقْرَبَ إِلَيْكَ مِنْ مُحَمَّدٍ وَأَهْلِ بَيْتِهِ الْأَخْيَارِ الْأَئِمَّةِ الْأَبْرَارِ لَجَعَلْتُهُمْ شُفَعَائِي

O Allāh, had I known interceders that are closer to You than Muhammad and his Household, the virtuous and pious Imams, I would have chosen to intercede for me before You

فَبِحَقِّهِمُ الَّذِي أَوْجَبْتَ لَهُمْ عَلَيْكَ

So I beseech You by their Right that You have made obligatory upon us to follow

أَسْأَلُكَ أَنْ تُدْخِلَنِي فِي جُمْلَةِ الْعَارِ فِينَ بِهِمْ وَبِحَقِّهِمْ

To include me with the group of those

231

who recognize their Right and them

وَفِي زُمْرَةِ الْمَرْحُومِينَ بِشَفَاعَتِهِمْ

And with the assembly of those on whom You will have mercy on account of their (Muhammad and his Household) intercession

إِنَّكَ أَرْحَمُ الرَّاحِمِينَ

Verily, You are the All-merciful

وَصَلَّى اللهُ عَلَى مُحَمَّدٍ وَآلِهِ الطَّاهِرِينَ

Blessings of Allāh be upon Muhammad and his infallible Household.

وَسَلَّمَ تَسْلِيماً كَثِيراً

And His thorough peace be upon them

وَحَسْبُنَا اللهُ وَنِعْمَ الْوَكِيلُ

Allāh is Sufficient for us! Most Excellent is He in Whom we trust!

6 The Imam's Students

Even though the atmosphere of repression and the political climate generally limited the people's access to the Imam and the possibility of their benefiting from his wisdom and teachings, nonetheless, a certain number of those who were passionate about the teachings of the Quran and the school of the Ahl al-Bayt ﷺ were able to partake of the blessings of the Imam ﷺ to the extent of the limits of their individual capacities, and to attain to exalted stations of faith and understanding. Shaykh Ṭūsī mentions the names of 185 people who have related hadith reports on the authority of Imam Hādī ﷺ among whom there are many brilliant personalities, some of whom we shall provide brief introductions to.

1. His Eminence Abdul-Aẓīm al-Husainī

Abdul-Aẓīm al-Husainī was preeminent among the historians and scholars of the science of hadith and had attained to a high station in terms of his piety and self-denial of the lower pleasures of the world. He had personally met several of the great companions of the sixth, seventh and eighth Imams ﷺ, and was himself considered to be one of the great companions and students and hadith transmitters (*rāwī*) of Imam Jawād ﷺ and Imam Hādī ﷺ.

The great Shīʿa scholar Sāhib ibn Ubbād writes: "Abdul-Aẓīm al-Husainī was fully aware of [all] matters relating to [the creedal beliefs of our] religion and to those which related to the ordinances of the Quran."

Abū-Himād ar-Rāzī states: I had the honor of being in the company of Imam Hadi ﷺ and asked him some questions. When I was taking my leave the Imam ﷺ said, "Whenever a problem [concerning the teachings and ordinances of the religion] arise for you, address your question to Abdul-Aẓīm al-Husainī, and send him my regards."

His Eminence Abdul-Aẓīm al-Husainī had attained to such a degree of fidelity and wisdom that Imam Hādī ﷺ once told him, "You are [one of the people who are counted] among [those who are] our true friends."

On one occasion Abdul-Aẓīm al-Husainī presented his beliefs to the Imam, and Imam Hādī ﷺ affirmed his understanding of the creed. As Abdul-Aẓīm al-Husainī himself relates: I had the honor of being in the presence of my lord and master Imam Hādī ﷺ, and when his gaze fell upon me, he said, "My complements to you, O Abul-Qāsim. You are a true friend of ours."

I said, "O son of the Apostle of God, I would like to present [what I believe] my religion [to be] to you [for your evaluation], so that if my presentation meets with your approval, I will have been confirmed in my faith, [and shall keep it unaltered, God ﷻ willing,] until I meet my Lord the Sublimely Exalted."

The Imam ﷺ said, "Proceed."

[A Shī'a Creed]

I said, "I believe that Almighty God ﷻ is One and that there is nothing like Him, and that He is neither [in the station of] agnosticism to the point of nihilism (*ibtāl*) nor is He [in the station of] anthropomorphism (*tashbīh*). God ﷻ the Sublimely Exalted is neither a body (*jism*), nor a form (*sūra'*), and neither is he an attribute (*araḍ*) or an essence (*jawhar*); rather, He is the creator of bodies and forms and essences and attributes, and He is the Creator and Owner and Commissioner of all things. And I believe that Muhammad is His servant and messenger and the last of the divinely-appointed prophets, and that no other Prophet ﷺ shall be commissioned until the Day of Resurrection, and that his sacred law (*sharī'a'*) and religion (*dīn*) are the ultimate sacred law and religion, and that no other sacred law or religion will be revealed after it [even unto Judgment Day].

"And I believe the leader (*Imam*) and successor and guardian after the Most Noble Prophet ﷺ to be the Commander of the Faithful Ali ibn Abī-Tālib ﷺ, after whom it was Imam Hasan ﷺ, and then Imam al-Husayn ﷺ, Imam Ali ibn al-Husayn ﷺ, Imam Muhammad ibn Ali ﷺ, Imam Ja'far ibn Muhammad ﷺ, Imam Mūsā ibn Ja'far ﷺ, Imam Ali ibn

Mūsā, Imam Muhammad ibn Ali ﷺ, after which you are my lord and master."

The Imam ﷺ said, "After me, my son Hasan [b. Muhammad al-Askari ﷺ] shall be the Imam. Therefore, how do you see [the position of] the people with respect to his son[104]?"

I said, "Why, my lord, how is he [different]?"

The Imam ﷺ said, "It is on account of the fact that he will not be seen until such a time that he rises up in resurrection and fills the world with equity and justice, just as it had been filed with iniquity and injustice prior to his uprising."

I then said, "I confess that those who befriend the Ahl al-Bayt ﷺ are the friends of God ﷻ, and those who have enmity toward them are the enemies of God; and that obeying them is the same as obeying God ﷻ, and disobeying them is the same as disobeying God ﷻ.

"And I believe in the Night Journey (*mi'rāj*) of the Prophet ﷺ, in the Questioning in the Grave, in Heaven and Hell, in the Sirāt [Bridge], and in the Scales [of Justice]; that all of these are true and real, and that the coming of the Day of Resurrection is something that is certain and in which there can be no doubt, and that Almighty God ﷻ shall raise [all of] the dead [on that day to answer for their deeds].

"And I believe that the religiously obligatory duties after [belief in and allegiance to the] *wilāya'* (regency and dominion) [of the Imam of the Age] are: the performance of the ritual devotions (*salā'*, Persian: *namāz*), paying the purifying due (*zakā'*), making the ritual fast (*sawm*, Persian: *rūzeh*), Making the Hajj pilgrimage, the sacred struggle [against one's inner enemies and against the outer enemies of God] (*jihād*), and

---

[104] Imam Hasan al-Askari's ﷺ son is the Twelfth Imam and the Mahdi ﷺ, the Universal Savior of humanity who went into a state of occultation (or disappearance from the physical plane shortly after he was born – probably at age 5, but accounts vary) and will return to the physical plane to establish a reign of truth and justice before the end of time and the resurrection.

enjoining the doing of that which is right, and forbidding the doing of that which is wrong (*amr bi ma'rūf wa nahy min al-munkar*)."

The Imam ﷺ said, "O Abul-Qāsim, upon my oath to Allāh, this is the same religion which He has chosen for His devotees. Be steadfast upon its path. May God ﷻ keep you steadfast in this world and in the hereafter in your [righteous] words [and deeds]."

From what has reached us in the historical chronicles, His Eminence Abdul-Aẓīm al-Husainī was sought by the authorities and travelled to Iran in order to escape their clutches, seeking refuge in the town of Rey (just south of present-day Tehran).

It is written in the chronicles of his life, "His Eminence Abdul-Aẓīm al-Husainī came to Rey while he was a refugee from the Sultan of the day, and resided in the cellar of a man from among the Shī'a by the name of Sikkat al-Mawālī, where he preoccupied himself in prayer and the ritual devotions. He spent his days in supplication to his Lord, and his nights in prayer and supererogatory devotions. Occasionally he would leave the cellar and make pilgrimage to the grave that is next to where he is now buried, which is known as the grave of Imamzādeh Hamza, and would say, "He [Hamza] is a son of Imam Mūsā ibn Ja'far ﷺ."

He continued living in hiding in Rey until the news of his whereabouts gradually made it back to the members of the House of the Prophet ﷺ, so that most of them came to know him. Sometime later, a believer from among the Shī'a saw the Prophet ﷺ in a dream who told him, "They will bring [the body of] a man from among my progeny from Sikkat al-Mawālī and will bury him next to an apple tree in the garden of Abdul-Jabbār ibn Abdul-Wahhāb." In this dream, the Prophet ﷺ pointed to the same spot where Abdul-Aẓīm al-Husainī is now buried.

When the man who had the dream went to buy the apple tree and the land surrounding it from its owner, the owner asked him, "For what purpose do you want [to own] the tree and its land?"

The buyer related the tale of his dream to the owner, after which the owner said, "I too have seen a dream similar to yours."

The owner then made a religious endowment of the tree and of the whole apple orchard to His Eminence Abdul-Aẓīm al-Husainī and to the Shī'a of the Ahl al-Bayt ﷺ to be used as a cemetery for the believers.

After a while, His Eminence Abdul-Aẓīm al-Husainī fell ill and passed away from this world. When they were performing the ritual washing of his body in preparation for the burial (*ghusl*), a scroll was found in his trouser pocket in which his genealogy [back to his forefather Imam Husain ﷺ] was inscribed.

The death of His Eminence Abdul-Aẓīm al-Husainī occurred during the imamate of Imam Hādī ﷺ and the height of his august and divine character must be sought in a hadith report that has been related by Muhammad ibn Yahyā al-Attār, who reports:

Imam Hādī ﷺ asked someone who had the honor of being in his company, "Where have you been?"

The man said, "I made a pilgrimage to the grave of Imam Husain ﷺ."

The Imam ﷺ replied, "Know that if you had made a pilgrimage to the shrine of Abdul-Aẓīm which is in your town, you would be as one who has made pilgrimage to the grave of Imam Husain ﷺ."

His Eminence Abdul-Aẓīm al-Husainī is considered to be one of the most reliable (*muwaththaq*) narrators of hadith reports who lived during the period of the presence of the Imams ﷺ. This nobleman was also a scholar of the Quranic sciences, and mention is made of two of his books [which are no longer extant]: a book of commentary on the sermons of the Commander of the Faithful Ali ibn Abī-Ṭālib ﷺ, and another book with the title *Yawm al-Wilīya*.

2. Husain ibn Sa'īd al-Ahvāzī

Husain ibn Sa'īd al-Ahvāzī was a companion and devotee of Imam Riḍā ﷺ, Imam Jawād ﷺ, and Imam Hādī ﷺ, and has related hadith reports from all three Imams ﷺ. He was originally from Kūfa, but was transferred to Ahvāz (in south-west Iran) together with his brother, after which he moved to Qom, where he lived out the rest of his days.

Husain ibn Sa'īd is the author of thirty books on the subjects of theology and religious jurisprudence (*fiqh*), the proper mode of spiritual comportment and courtesy (*adab*), and the proper mode of ethical conduct (*akhlāq*). His books are famous among Shī'a scholarship. Majlisī the First writes concerning him, "A consensus [among our scholars] is discernible concerning his reliability as a transmitter of hadith reports as well as about his acting on [the precepts and tenets contained within] such reports."

The late Allāma [Muhammad Bāqir] Majlisī writes concerning Husain ibn Sa'īd: "He is reliable and trustworthy [as a transmitter of hadīth reports], and is among the grandees of [Shī'a] scholarship; he was a man who had attained to a high [scholarly and spiritual] station."

The late Shaykh Tūsī writes: "In addition to Husain ibn Sa'īd's exalted scholarly standing, he was active in the guidance of the people. As a consequence [of his proselytizing activity], he introduced Ishāq ibn Ibrāhīm al-Hadīnī and Ali ibn Rayyān to Imam Ridā ﷺ, thereby becoming the cause of their acquaintance with Shī'a Islam and the true rite [within Islam]. These gentlemen would listen to hadith reports [of the Prophet ﷺ] and would learn the teachings of Islam as a consequence of serving him [Imam Ridā ﷺ]. Husain ibn Sa'īd also introduced Abdullāh ibn Muhammad al-Hadīnī and others to Imam Ridā ﷺ and was the catalyst for their attaining to exalted spiritual stations as a result of which they were able to make great contributions to the service of Islam.

3. Fadl ibn Shādhān an-Neyshāpūrī

He was a great scholar and a reliable and trustworthy transmitter of hadith reports, as well as being a theologian who was adept at dogmatics and apologetic arguments and proofs. He was personally witness to several of the most august companions of the Imams ﷺ such as Muhammad ibn Abī-Umayr, Safwān ibn Yahyā, etc. spending about fifty years in their company and discourse, learning from their direct relationship with the

Imams ﷺ. As he relates himself, "When Hishām ibn Hakam passed away, Yūnus ibn Abdur-Rahmān became his successor (*khalīfa*) [among the surviving Companions of the Imams], and when he passed, Sakkāk became their leader (*khalīfa*) in responding to the opponents [of the Shī'a] among the people; and presently, I am the leader [of the Shī'a] among the people."

The late Shaykh Tūsī has mentioned Fadl ibn Shādhān as being among the companions of Imam Hādī ﷺ and of Imam Hasan al-Askari ﷺ; and some of the scholars of the science of *rijāl*[105] have stated that in addition to being a companion of Imam Hādī ﷺ and of Imam Hasan al-Askari ﷺ, he was also a companion of Imam Jawād ﷺ.

Fadl ibn Shādhān has penned many books. It is said that he has written 180 books, including the book *al-Īdāh* whose subject is creedal theology (*kalām*, sometimes misleadingly referred to as speculative theology) and an exposition of the principal beliefs of the *ashāb al-hadīth*, which was published by Tehran University in 1392 (solar)/ 2013 CE.

The works of Fadl ibn Shādhān have been the subject of the interest of the great scholars, and his position with respect to the rejection or affirmation of a given transmitter of hadith reports would suffice them [in determining their own position]. The late Shaykh Kulaynī, the compiler of the great book al-Kāfi, has brought to bear some fragments of Fadl ibn Shādhān's works in this great and noble book. The author of Jāmi' ar-Riwāt writes, "Fadl ibn Shādhān is the chieftain and master of the tribe

---

[105] *Elm ar-Rijāl* (the science of *rijāl*) is a major branch within the science of hadīth. It is the science of the study and classification of the history, character, and trustworthiness of narrators of hadīth reporting. Books within this specialty compile biographical data on the narrators of *hadīth* reports and classify them in accordance with the soundness of the character of the narrators in order to ascertain and rank them in terms of the reliability of their reportage. This information is in turn used to ascertain the integrity of the chain of custody within a given provenance title (*sanad*).

of us Shī'a [scholars], and is more preeminent and venerable than one who would require an introduction."

Faḍl ibn Shādhān made a journey to visit Imam Hasan al-Askari ﷺ and was honored to be in his company. When making his exit, a book which he had written himself fell from his hand. The Imam ﷺ picked it up, studied it, and sent him blessings of mercy, saying, "I envy the people of Khorāsān for their having Faḍl ibn Shādhān among their ranks."

In another hadith report it is stated that Faḍl ibn Shādhān's book *Yawm al-Walīya* was shown to Imam Hasan al-Askari ﷺ, after which His Eminence sent him blessings of mercy three times, saying, "It is fitting that [the teachings of] this [book] be acted upon."

The great martyr, Qāḍī Nūrullāh ash-Shūshtarī writes concerning Faḍl ibn Shādhān: "He was one of the greats among the *mutikallimūn*,[106] the most learned of the Quranic exegetes and *muhaddithūn* (the scholars of the science of *hadīth*), and he ranks among the greatest dignitaries in the science of religious jurisprudence (*fiqh*). Additionally, he was a famous reciter of the Quran and was renowned for his rhetorical and oratory prowess."

Faḍl ibn Shādhān lived in Neyshāpūr. Abdullāh ibn at-Tāhir, the founder of the Tāherid dynasty, exiled him for the crime of being a Shī'a, after which he left for Beyhaqq (Sabzevār). When the Khawārij rose up in rebellion in Khorāsān, Faḍl ibn Shādhān left Khorāsān fearing for his life. He fell ill during his journey and passed away during the imamate of Imam Hasan al-Askari ﷺ and was buried in the old city of Neyshāpūr [i.e of the

---

[106] *Mutikallimūn*: These are the scholars of the science of *kalām* which is properly translated as dogmatics or dogmatic theology, and entails the study of theology, prophetology, imāmology, cosmology, Quranic anthropology and ontology, etc., for the purpose of providing rational explanations and defenses of the creedal beliefs of the faith (as opposed to speculative theology, which is something altogether different and, strictly speaking, is a branch of philosophy rather than religion).

pre-Mongol invasion]. His shrine is within one *parasang*[107] (or league) of present day Neyshāpūr and is a pilgrimage site for the Shīʿa who seek to gain *tabarruk*[108] or blessings from his shrine.

4. Abū-Hāshim al-Jaʿfarī

The lineage of Abū-Hāshim goes back to Jaʿfar ibn Abī-Tālib, Imam Ali's brother. Abū- Hāshim was a great renowned scholar and dignitary of very high standing within the Shīʿa community. He was a companion of all of the Imams from Imam Riḍā up to and including the Lord of the Age, the Imam al-Mahdī, and has related hadith reports from all of these great noblemen. Sayyid Ibn Tāwūs has considered him to be one of the General Deputies of the Lord of the Age.

Abū-Hāshim was also a poet, and has composed numerous beautiful poems in praise of the Imams.

Abū-Hāshim lived in Baghdad and died there in the year 261 AH. His shrine is a well-known pilgrimage destination for the Shīʿa faithful. He was the subject of the praise of Shīʿa and non-Shīʿa alike when it came to his piety, his fear of God (*taqwā*) [and the consequent self-control and self-discipline required meticulously to abide by His ordinances]; as well as for his knowledge and learning, and for the plethora of hadith reports which he has transmitted. His father was the governor of Yemen and was Imam Sādiq's cousin; he was preeminent in his era in terms of the nobility of his lineage among the Abū-Tālib House, and he was honored and respected by all.

---

[107] The parasang is a historical Iranian unit of itinerant distance the length of which varied according to terrain and speed of travel. The European equivalent is the league.

[108] *Tabarruk*: the property of a relic or some mundane object which has been blessed or charged in some other way with sacral properties.

7 The Imam's Martyrdom

Any researcher who looks into the life of Imam Ali an-Naqī ﷺ will realize that this great Imam lived the entirety of his life under the severest and taxing restrictions and persecution. Needless to say, this political climate of repression and persecution is not something that was unique to the time of the Imam, but was the norm – with few exceptions of very limited duration – throughout the entirety of the reign of the Umayyad as well as the Abbāsid dynasties. These usurping and oppressive tyrants and despots would ignore the general welfare of the community at large and considered the people who lived in their territories to be mere means to achieving their personal interests and ends. The atmosphere of fear was so prevalent in the absolutism of these usurper caliphs that the people dared not speak a word against these despots or to organize themselves in opposition in order to benefit from the leadership of the Immaculate Imams ﷺ.

Thus, under these political conditions, the relationship and even amount of contact allowed by the authorities between the people and the Imams ﷺ was extremely limited, and as has already been stated, the government of the day had summoned Imam Ali an-Naqī ﷺ from Medina to Sāmarrā and domiciled him and his family by force in the middle of this garrison town which doubled as the caliphal capital of the Abbāsids for a while. This migration was forced upon the Imam in order to enable the authorities to be able fully to monitor the affairs of the Imam and to have complete control over his actions.

Despite all of this pressure and the severity of the restrictions and the stark conditions in which he found himself, Imam Hādī ﷺ did not give an inch in terms of his accommodating or appeasing his oppressors. It goes without saying that the divine character of the Imam, his exalted social standing, and his policy of non-cooperation and peaceful resistance against the caliphal regime and his refusal to recognize it as legitimate was something that was a continual source of irritation, frustration and concern to the authorities. The Abbāsids were always troubled by this problem of theirs, and they eventually took what they believed was the only way open for them to deal with their problem, which was to murder the Imam.

Thus, like his honorable forefathers before him, Imam Hadi ﷺ did not leave this life by way of a natural death, but was poisoned during the reign of al-Muʿtazz and was martyred on the third of the month of Rajab in the year 254 AH, and was buried in his own house in Sāmarrā.

The shrine of the great Imam and his honorable son, Imam Hasan al-Askari ﷺ, are still extant in Sāmarrā and are pilgrimage destinations for the Shīʿa faithful.

Indeed, al-Muʿtazz and his courtiers always pretended to be the friends of the Imam, which is why they wanted to take advantage of the situation and to cover over their crimes by attending the Imam's funeral and wake. But we Shīʿa believe that the Imam who succeeds the previous Imam is the one who must say the prayers for the dead over the corpse of the Imam who has passed. This is why Imam Hasan al-Askari ﷺ, the grieving son of Imam Hādī ﷺ, said the funeral prayers for his father before his body was removed from the house by the forces of the regime for propagandistic purposes. After the Imam's corpse was removed from his home, al-Muʿtazz instructed his brother Ahmad ibn al-Mutawakkil to say the funerary prayers for the Imam ﷺ in Abī-Ahmad Street. A large crowd of people participated in the funeral proceedings of the Imam, and countless tears were shed on account of his loss, and the cries of the people were so loud that they reached the heavens. After these funeral proceedings the Imam's corpse was returned to his family home, where it was finally laid to rest.

May God's peace and blessings be unto him and unto his purified forefathers. Amen.

8 A Sampling of the Words of the Imam

In bringing this book to a close, it is fitting that we quote a few of the Imam's ﷺ aphorisms, so that we can partake of a sampling of his limitless knowledge and wisdom:

- Imam Hādī ﷺ has reported from his honorable forefathers that the Apostle of God ﷺ stated: "Faith is that which enters [fully] into one's heart and can be seen in one's deeds and is confirmed by them. And Islam is that which is current upon the tongue and by means of which marriage is made lawful."
- There will be a large number of people who are not contented with anyone who is selfish.
- Fooling around and engaging in vanities is the pastime of knaves and fools.
- Befriend and put your good will and good opinion at the disposal of anyone who befriends you and puts his good will and good opinion at your disposal.
- Do not distance yourself from [the opportunity of being of service to] one who thinks little of himself and does not value himself, on account of a concern that some evil might come [out of such a charitable service].
- The world is a market in which some profit and some lose [but judgement on which is postponed to the world to come].
- One who fears God ﷺ is respected by the people; and one who obeys God ﷺ will have his words heeded by the people; and anyone who obeys God ﷺ has no cause to be concerned about the ire of others.
- It is possible for a sinner to be forgiven his sins on account of his patience and forbearance [toward others].
- Anyone who is in the right but who acts ignorantly will put out the light of his righteousness with his ignorant behavior.

Imam Hasan ibn Ali al-Askari

1. Preface

The brilliant sun of Islam dawned like the appearance of lightning among the stormy events of history, illuminating the world of humanity which was in darkness with its radiant light, illuminating the hearts and minds of the people whom it made aware of and invited to the possibility of eternal life.

The dawn of this sun was announced by His Eminence the Prophet Muhammad ﷺ. The social conditions of his day were murky and dark. Injustice and immoral behavior had become the norm in human societies. The ignorance and wickedness of oppressors poured down on the oppressed like an angry storm. But with the dawning of the sun of Islam and the lessons of *tawhīd*[109] – which is itself the basis of all human

---

[109] *Tawhīd* is usually translated as monotheism and is the general term that covers the Islamic conception of monotheism which posits not only that there is only one God, but that He has providential lordship over all of His creation, including that of man's affairs; and that all of the orders of creation, from mineral to vegetable to animal and to man, are seamlessly integrated into God's creation and innate will which, in the case of man who has been given limited free will, is

virtues – a new spirit was born. In this way, mankind, whom resided in a state of ignorance, learned to avoid following false idols and turned to the way of the brotherhood of man. A number of people brought their capacities to bear and came to the aid of the ministry of the Prophet ﷺ of Islam and the message of the Quran, thereby laying the foundation of their felicity in this world and in the world to come.

Because the sacred ordinances of the Quran and the tenets of Islam were not revealed for a particular era or for a particular nation or tribe but were sent for the salvation of the whole of humanity in every era and for every nation, everyone turned toward Islam.

Islam – the preeminent religion from its inception to the present – opened the horizons of humanity's moral and spiritual vision, thereby manifesting humanity's true religious identity. As a consequence of the grace which is the religion of Islam, mankind is able to familiarize himself with the mystery of existence and to discover the path to his eternal voyage.

Islam arose and was uttered through the mouth of the Apostle of God ﷺ so that its lofty and beautiful facets might awaken mankind from its slumber of neglect and to guide it toward that which is right and just, and in order that mankind might be freed from his ignorance and idolatry and bondsmanship to other than God, and to learn to worship and to obey the will of the one and only God ﷻ.

In order for such an objective to obtain, Almighty God ﷻ has deemed it necessary for Imams ؑ to continue the Prophet's ministry as his divinely-appointed successors. After the passing of the Prophet ﷺ of God, twelve Imams ؑ who were the shining stars of the world of Islam continued his mission, the last of whom, the Imam al-Mahdī ؑ will appear when God ﷻ wills it and will fill the world with justice and equity.

---

exercised through God's revealed sacred laws and His providential lordship. See also footnote #37.

In this chapter, we will discuss some of the aspects of the life of the Eleventh Imam, Imam Hasan al-Askari ﷺ, who is the father of the awaited universal savior, the Imam al-Mahdī ﷺ.

2. Birth

In his farewell sermon, the Prophet ﷺ of Islam gave the following instructions with respect to the Quran and his Household:

"O ye people, I will precede you [to the next world] and you will enter into my presence at the Pond of Kawthar, a pond whose width is [equal to] the length of the distance from Basra to San'ā[110], around which are arrayed silver goblets, countless as the stars of the night sky; and [at that time], I shall ask [each of] you concerning the Two Weighty Trusts [= the two things of high value] which I left amongst you in trust. So pay attention to how you treat these two after I have departed!"

Here someone cried out, "O Prophet ﷺ of God! What are those two things of value?" And the Prophet ﷺ responded, "The first is the Book of God ﷻ one end of which is in God's hands and the other in yours. Keep it well and obey its decrees and do not allow any change to enter into it, for you will [surely] go astray [if you do]. The other is my Family (*itratī*), the Members of my House ﷺ (*ahl al-baytī*), and Almighty God ﷻ has informed me that these two shall never be parted until they enter into my presence at the Pond of Kawthar – this I have asked of my Lord. Therefore, do not surpass these two, if you are to be saved from perdition, and do not fall behind from them, for you will be annihilated. Do not [attempt to] teach them anything, as they are more knowledgeable than you."

This is the hadīth report that has become known as The Hadīth of the Two Weighty Trusts. The Sunni scholar Ahmad ibn Abdullāh,

---

[110] Towns close to present day Baghdad and Damascus respectively.

known as Abu Naʿīm[111] (974-1038 CE), relates in his book *hilyat al-awliā* (1:355) from Ibn Abbās as having reported the Prophet ﷺ to have said: "Anyone who is desirous of living like me and dying like me and [who wants] to abide [with me] in the most exalted of gardens which my Lord of Providence (*rabb*) has prepared, must be a friend to Ali and a friend to those who befriend Ali after my passing, and to defer to the Imāms [who will appear] after me, for they are of my House (*itrati*; Household, Family) and are created of my substance and given knowledge and understanding [therefrom]. Woe unto anyone from my community (*ummati*) who denies their excellence and priority and cuts off my bond with them. [Pray] God, do not allow my intercession to reach [any of] them [on Judgment Day]."

The hadīth concerning the "two weighty trusts" known as the *hadīth ath-thaqalayn* is one of the most widely accepted and authoritative of all the reports narrated from the Prophet ﷺ and it has also been recorded in the principal Sunni collections of hadīth. It possesses the highest degree of authenticity and acceptance, and one of the redactions reads as follows: "I leave among you two precious and weighty trusts, one being the Book of God ﷻ and the other my Progeny. These two legacies

---

[111] Abu Naʿīm is an early and renowned Sunnite *Hāfiż al-Quran* and *muhaddith* of the late third century. There is controversy about his being Sunni due to the numerous *ahādīth* that he reports which are full of praise for the virtues of the *ahl al-bayt* ﷺ (House) of the Prophet: some Sunni scholars deny his allegiance due to the reporting of these *ahādīth*, and some Shīʿa scholars claim him as one of our own. However, on the basis of his book *al-Imāma wa ar-radd ʿalā ar-rāfiḍa* (*The Imamate and the Rejection of the Naysayers*) it is clear that he was indeed Sunni. The title of the book includes the pejorative term of reference to the Shīʿa (*rāfiḍa*, pl. *rawāfiḍ*, 'Naysayers' or Refuseniks) and is a diatribe against the Shīʿa concept of the Imamate, with an emphasis on the priority of the right of the three caliphs over Imam Ali to rule on the basis of Sunni beliefs and political theory.

will never be separated from each other, and if you lay firm hold of them, you will never go astray."¹¹²

Certain Sunni scholars even add the following sentence at the end of the hadīth: "Ali is always with the Quran and the Quran is [always] with Ali; they too will not be separated from each other."¹¹³ Hadīth scholars attribute the transmission of this report to roughly thirty Companions of the Prophet.¹¹⁴ This means that we have a report which is *mutiwātir*¹¹⁵, establishing the profound and indissoluble link between the Quran and the House of the Prophet ﷺ, and the absolute inseparable interrelatedness of the two.

The words "Household of the Apostle of God" form an august title which has been mentioned by the Prophet ﷺ on numerous occasions. The Imams are the "Ahl al-Bayt" ﷺ of the Prophet ﷺ, meaning the members of his household, who have been purified of all defilement and sin in accordance with Sura 33:33 (the *Āyat at-Tathīr* or the Verse of Purification), who defer perfectly to the way and paradigmatic example of

---

¹¹² Muslim, *al-Sahih*, Vol. VII, p. 122; at-Tirmidhī, *Jami' al-Sahih*, Vol. II, p. 308 & 5:328 (hadīth 3874); al-Hākim, *al-Mustadrak*, Vol. III, p. 109 & 533. In his digest of the *Mustadrak*, Dhahabī has deemed this report to be *sahīh*, agreeing with al-Hākim. See also, Ahmad b. Hanbal, *al-Musnad*, Vol. III, pp. 14-17 & 5: 181-9; Nasāī's *Khasāis* p. 21; and al-Muttaqi al-Hindi's *Kanz al-A'māl* 1:44, 47-48; Dārami's *Sunan* 2:431; Ibn Sa'd, *Tabaqāt al-Kubrā*, 2:2; Ibn al-Sabbagh, *Fusul al-Muhimmah*, p. 24; al-Ganji, *Kifāyat at-Talib*, p. 130; al-Qunduzi, *Yanabi' al-Mawaddah*, pp. 17-18; al-Ya'qubi, *al-Tarikh*, Vol. II, p. 92; Fakhr al-Din al-Rādī, *al-Tafsir al-Kabir*, Vol. III, p. 18; al-Naysapuri, *Ghara'ib al-Quran*, Vol. I, p. 349.
¹¹³ al-Qunduzi, *Yanabi' al-Mawaddah*, pp. 32-40; Ibn Hajar, *as-Sawā'iq*, p. 57; al-Irbidi, *Kashf al-Ghumma'*, p.43.
¹¹⁴ al-Halabi, *as-Sīrah*, Vol. III, p. 308.
¹¹⁵ A *hadīth* which has been transmitted by so many different transmitters (and with different chains of custody) with the exact same wording as not to leave room for a shadow of a doubt as to the integrity of the chain of custody and reliability of the text.

the Prophet ﷺ and continue in his path, expounding his teachings by their words as well as by embodying them by way of example.

Imam Abu-Muhammad Hasan ibn Ali al-Askari ﷺ is the Eleventh Imam of the purified Household of the Prophet ﷺ of Islam. He was born in the 232nd year of the Islamic lunar calendar (the Hijrī calendar), which is equivalent to the year 846 of the Christian era, in Medina, the city of the Prophet ﷺ and of the receipt of revelation. His honorable father was the Tenth Imam, Imam Hādī ﷺ who passed into the next world in the year 254 AH (868 CE). His honorable mother was named Hudaytha; she is also referred to by the names Sūsan, Salīl, and Jada. According to the view of certain historians, the date of the birth of Imam Hasan ibn Ali al-Askari ﷺ is Friday the eighth day of Rabī' al-Thānī.

The Imam lived in an area of the city of Sāmarrā called Askar[116], which is why he is known as al-Askari. The Imam's name is Hasan, and his *kunya* or patronymic is Abū-Muhammad (meaning "the father of Muhammad"). His most famous titles are Zakī, Askari, and Naqī.

His Eminence Imam Abu-Muhammad Hasan ibn Ali al-Askari ﷺ was twenty-two years of age when his noble father Imam Hādī ﷺ was martyred at the hands of the Abbāsid tyrants, after which he took on the burden of responsibility for leading the world of Islam. Six years had not passed from his tenure of the office of the imamate[117] when he was martyred at the age of twenty-eight in the year 260 AH/ 873 CE. Those who had seen the Imam personally have related that he was light-

---

[116] Sāmarrā was originally a garrison town. The Imam was sent to internal exile by the Abbāsid caliphs to this garrison town which was a day's journey from their capital of Baghdad so that they could keep a close watch on him and so as to preclude his devoted followers from having access to him.

[117] The comprehensive (inclusive of political and religious) leadership of the community of the faithful.

complected, had large eyes and a handsome face, and a good physique, and that he had an august and majestic presence.

3. The Succession to his Father

None of the Immaculate Imams ﷺ relied solely on the *hadīth*[118] reports of the past (from the Prophet ﷺ as well as from past Imams ﷺ) for ensuring that there would be no misunderstanding concerning who was to succeed them to the office of the imamate; rather, they would themselves also personally name their successors publicly and explicitly in order to preclude any confusion among their ranks and close companions. It was no different in the case of Imam Hasan al-Askari ﷺ. There are numerous hadīth reports concerning the succession of His Eminence ﷺ to the imamate after the passing of his father, some of which we mention below:

1. Ali ibn Mahziār reports: I asked Imam Hādī ﷺ, "In the event something happens to you, who should we turn to for answers to our questions?" His Eminence ﷺ said, "[The office of] my succession belongs to my senior progeny, that is, al-Hasan ﷺ. Put your questions to him." This was how the Muslims became aware, through Imam Hādī's ﷺ companions, that Imam Hasan al-Askari ﷺ was to succeed Imam Hādī's ﷺ to the imamate. Therefore, a large number of people turned to him for guidance after his father's passing and pledged allegiance to him, benefitted from his knowledge, piety, and exemplary conduct; improved their moral vision and way of life; and attained to felicity in this life and in the hereafter by making Imam Hasan al-Askari ﷺ the exemplary model of their behavior.

2. Saqr ibn Abī-Dalq reports: One day I heard Imam Hādī ﷺ say, "Verily, after my son al-Hasan ﷺ, and after him, his son al-Qāim[119] shall be the

---

[118] *Hadīth*: See footnote #5.

[119] *al-Qāim*: the One who will Arise [in insurrection against the forces of tyranny] to establish justice on Earth.

Imams of this community. And the Qāim is the one who will fill the world with justice and equity at a time when it is full of injustice and oppression."

3. Nūflī reports: I was at the service of Imam Hādī ﷺ and was seated with His Eminence in the forecourt of his house. The Imam's son who was called Muhammad and who was busy at play passed in front of us. I looked at Muhammad and asked, "O Imam. Would that I were sacrificed for your cause,[120] will Muhammad be the Imam and guide of the Shī'a community after you?" The Imam looked at me and said, "No, O Nūflī! Your Imam after me is al-Hasan."

4. Yahyā ibn Yassār reports: Four months before His Eminence Imam Hādī ﷺ attained to martyrdom at the hands of the Abbāsid tyrant's henchmen, he wrote a will for his son Imam Hasan al-Askarī ﷺ in which he appointed him as his successor to the imamate, taking me and a number of other of his companions as witness to his will.

4. The Imam's Piety

The Ahl al-Bayt ﷺ of the Apostle of God ﷺ are immaculate[121] souls who have been made immune to any kind of moral impurity by God ﷺ the Sublimely Exalted. They are the leaders of the Muslim community in terms of the preeminence of their knowledge, faith, piety, asceticism, and sincerity and devotion to Almighty God ﷺ and in terms of their ethical mode of conduct. It is evident that the most significant element in the strengthening of the community is reliance on and devotion to Almighty God ﷺ.

A man by the name of Muhammad Shākirī who was in the presence of Imam Askarī ﷺ relates: At times I would see the Imam ﷺ seated in the prayer niche (*mihrāb*) entering the posture of prostration. I

---

[120] A formal and respectful way of address.
[121] Inerrant as well as sinless.

fell asleep and when I awoke, I saw that the Imam ﷺ was still in that position.

Abū-Jaʿfar al-Hāshimī reports: One day I was honored to be at the service of Imam Hasan al-Askari ﷺ. When I came into his presence the Imam ﷺ was busy writing something. When the time for the ritual devotions (*salāt*; Persian: *namāz*) arrived, the Imam ﷺ immediately stopped his writing and prepared to offer his devotions, and then went through the cycles of the ritual devotions.

The quality of the Imam's humility and piety in his devotions was such that even his detractors and adversaries would be affected by his spiritual states and would be won over and the passion for performing prayers, supplications and devotions to God ﷻ would be ignited within them.

It is related that during the time the Imam was in prison, the Abbāsid prison warden appointed two of the worst and most morally corrupt of his guards to watch over the Imam; but that even these two repented of their evil ways as a consequence of keeping the company of the Imam ﷺ and changed so completely that they attained to great spiritual states and stations in their prayers and devotions. When the other prisoners became aware of the change that had come about in these two guards, they called to them and said, "Woe unto you! What do you think about this great man, and what do you have to say about him?"

The two guards said, "What can we say about someone who spends his days in fasting and worship, and his nights in devotional prayers and supplications to his Lord? Whatever he does is an act of worship, and nothing passes his lips but litanies and prayers and supplications. O people! When His Eminence ﷺ gazes at us, our bodies begin to tremble, and our hearts begin to quiver and we feel as if we are no longer in control of our senses. It is as if we are with him [in his high spiritual state] and privy to the mysteries that he is privy to."

5. The Imam's Social and Ethical Character Traits

Like his noble father and purified ancestors before him, Imam Hasan al-Askari ﷺ shone like a beacon in the middle of the night and the pearls of wisdom that emanated from him guided the people toward God ﷻ and toward felicity. The exalted character of the Imam ﷺ as the leader of the Shī'a was not hidden from anyone in any era, and even his enemies sang his praises.

It is related that Ahmad ibn Ubaydullāh ibn Khāqān was an Abbāsid official in charge of real estate tax in the city of Qom. One day talk of the Ālid House[122] and of their beliefs came up in his office. Ahmad who had a special enmity towards the Imams of the Ahl al-Bayt ﷺ and was considered to be one of the *nawāsib*[123] said, "I have not seen or known anyone in Sāmarrā who is more preeminent that Hasan ibn Ali (Imam al-Askari) ﷺ in terms of his sobriety and equanimity, purity and nobility of character, excellence of virtues, and grandeur of character among my own clan and tribe, or among the Banī-Hāshim.[124] The people of his clan and tribe consider him to be preeminent to the dignitaries of their clan, and he is similarly thought of among the commanders of the army, being favored by the elite as well as by the masses. I have this recollection from way back that one day I was in the company of my father when the sentries announced the arrival of Abū-Muhammad ﷺ. My father said in a loud voice, "O sentries! Be sure to give him leave to enter!"

I was very surprised that the sentries referred to someone by his *kunya* or patronymic[125] and with such special reverence and respect because my father would only refer to a very few people by their *kunyas*, and these

---

[122] The House of the progeny of Imam Ali b. Abī-Tālib ﷺ.
[123] See footnote #90.
[124] The clan of the noble Prophet of Islam (which is the clan of all of the Imams ﷺ too, of course).
[125] Doing so is considered to be a sign of respect.

were people such as the close family of the caliph himself and of the caliph's heir-apparent.

I was deep in this thought when I saw a young man enter the court. He was light-complected, had a sturdy and tall physique, a handsome face, and had an august and majestic presence about him. When my father saw him, he immediately stood up and took some steps toward him in greeting him. Until that day, I had not seen my father show such respect to anyone either from the Banī-Hāshim or from anyone of the commanders of the army. Momentarily I saw my father put his hand around the man's neck and kiss his breast and face and then took him in hand toward where he had been sitting in prayer. He then sat opposite him and started to engage him in discussions on various subjects, and, in speaking to him, he repeated the formula "would that I was sacrificed for your cause"[126] on numerous occasions.

I was astonished at what I saw and could hear. Suddenly a guard entered and told my father, "[The Abbāsid caliph] al-Muwaffaq is on his way here."

The sentinels and commanders of the army would usually precede the caliph's arrival and would stand in line from the door threshold to the station where my father was situated until al-Muwaffaq entered and would remain in that position until the caliph's departure.

All the while my father's attention was on Abū-Muhammad ﷺ, with whom he was engaged in conversation in a manner which showed him the height of respect. When my father's eyes fell upon the caliph's slaves and retinue, he turned to Abū-Muhammad ﷺ and said, "Would that I was sacrificed for your cause, if you so desire, [now would be a good time to] take your leave." My father then turned to his sentries and instructed them to escort the Imam ﷺ from behind the two lines outside the court in a way such that he would not be seen by al-Muwaffaq. The Imam then arose from his seated position and my father again placed his

---

[126] A formal way of showing deference and deep respect.

hand around the Imam's neck and bade him fare well, after which the Imam ﷺ exited the chamber.

I asked my father's attendants concerning the identity of this man whom they addressed by his *kunya* and who was treated with such respect by my father. The attendants said, "He is one of the dignitaries of the Ālids who is named Hasan ibn Ali ﷺ and who is known as Ibn ar-Riḍā.[127]

This did nothing but add to my astonishment and bewilderment, and I continued to think about this issue throughout the rest of that day, which I spent in a state of uncertainty until nightfall.

My father was in the habit of reviewing the reports that had arrived during the day after having offered his ritual devotions and reporting his findings to the caliph. When he performed his devotions and began his work routine, I went to him. At this time, he did not have any company and we were alone together.

My father asked, "Ahmad, do you need me for something?"

I replied, "Yes father! If I have your permission, I will state my purpose."

He said, "Certainly, my son; pray proceed."

I said, "O father! Who was that man who I saw this morning whom you welcomed with such respect and showed such humility toward and paid such attention to, and to whom you even used the form "would that I were sacrificed for your cause" as a preface when addressing him, and sacrificed yourself and your father and mother for him?"

Ubaydollāh ibn Khāqān told his son that the man's name was [al-Imam] al-Hasan ibn Ali, known as Ibn or-Riḍā ﷺ, and after a pause which brought a brief silence to the room, continued, "O my son! If the caliphate were no longer to be in the hands of the Abbāsids, no one from the Banī-

---

[127] After the martyrdom of Imam Riḍā ﷺ, the Imams who followed in his wake, i.e. Imam Jawād ﷺ, Imam Hādī ﷺ and Imam Hasan al-Askari ﷺ were called Ibn ar-Riḍā in the court of the Abbāsid caliphs and in society at large as a sign of respect for Imam Riḍā ﷺ.

Hāshim clan would be more worthy of it other than this gentleman, and this is on account of his excellence of virtues, his [superior] knowledge [of the sacred ordinances of God's religion], his piety and asceticism and devotion to God, and the probity of his moral character and conduct. If you had seen his father, you would have witnessed an honorable and virtuous man."

In continuing the report, Ahmad relates: Hearing my father singing the praises of this man increased my concern for my father and raised my ire further. There was nothing of any importance for me to do but to look into this man's life in more detail and to carry out a thorough examination of his character and virtues and moral code of conduct.

Whosoever I asked about him would sing his praises and say what a noble and honorable man he was. If I asked any member of the Banī-Hāshim House about him, or one of the chieftains of the armed forces, or asked one of the many men of letters and noble dignitaries or justices or theologians and doctors of the law any question about him, they would all speak of him humbly and in terms of the highest possible praise, tell me about his magnanimity and nobility of character, and would remember him in terms of endearments and honor and grandeur, and talk about his sincerity and purity of heart and of his gracefulness and benevolent character.

This was how I came to learn about the dignity and majesty and popularity of His Eminence the Imam al-Askari , and from that time forward until this moment, about his exalted station and his grandeur; and I have yet to come across someone who does not remember him in any but the most honorable terms; rather, [even] his [political] adversaries and detractors held him in high esteem and had nothing but praise for him.

Allāma Majlisī has related a hadīth report narrated by Ali ibn Āsim al-Kūfī, who was one of the companions of Imam Hasan al-Askari ﷺ, which we summarize as follows.

Ali ibn Āsim reports: One day I entered into the presence of the Imam ﷺ and His Eminence showed me a floor mat upon which many prophets and apostles of God ﷻ had sat, pointing out the traces of their feet's motions on it to me.

I fell upon this sacred place and kissed it, after which I took the hand of His Eminence ﷺ and kissed it and said, "O my lord and excellency! I am powerless to help you and have nothing of any benefit to you that I can offer with my hands, save that I nurture your love and devotion in my breast, to anathemize your enemies and to send imprecations and maledictions on them in private. O my Imam! Given this, what will my fate be [on the Day of Judgment and in the hereafter]?"

His Eminence told me, "O Ali! My father related a hadīth report to me from our great ancestor, the Prophet ﷺ of God: 'Anyone who hates our enemies but is powerless in confronting them and is unable to help the Members of my Household (*ahl bayti*) but curses them in private [instead], Almighty God ﷻ will show his face to all of the angels, and he will be valued and honored by the members of my household'."

One of Imam Askari's ﷺ devotees reports: I had fallen on hard times. My father told me, "Son, let us go to see Imam Hasan al-Askari ﷺ, an Imam who is renowned for his generosity and piety."

I asked my father, "Have you ever met him?"

He said, "No my son, I have not ever had the honor of meeting that great man."

My father and I then set off. During the journey my father asked me, "My son, how many Dirhams do you think we need?" And then he said, "If His Eminence ﷺ instructs his attendants to give us five hundred Dirhams, this will suffice us, as we will be able to see to all of our needs with that sum. We would be able to buy the clothes we need with two hundred, pay off our debts with another two hundred, and the remaining hundred would be enough for our other expenses."

While my father was thinking and talking about our needs, I said to myself, "How good it would be if His Eminence ﷺ instructs his attendants that I be paid an additional three hundred Dirhams so that I can purchase a beast of burden with one hundred, keep another hundred for my future expenses, and use the rest to purchase some clothes and to pay for my expenses on a journey to the lands of Jabal[128]."

We continued our journey until we arrived at the house of the Imam ﷺ, at which point we knocked at the door and asked permission to enter. A few moments later a servant returned and announced, "Let Ali ibn Ibrāhīm and his son Muhammad enter."

When we entered into the presence of His Eminence the Imam ﷺ, we offered him our salaams and after obtaining permission, sat down. The Imam ﷺ then turned to my father and said, "O Ali! What has prevented you from coming to visit us before now?"

My father said, "O my Imam! I felt ashamed to see you in the condition that I was in."

Some time passed, and although my father's and my thirst for being in the company of our Imam could not be quenched but having received a signal from my father and having obtained permission to leave, we exited the Imam's house.

We had not taken but a few steps before the Imam's attendant came to us and gave a pouch of money to my father and said, "O Ali! In this pouch there are five hundred Dirhams, two hundred with which you can buy the clothes you need, another two hundred of which you can use

---

[128] The mountainous region in southwestern Iran, on the western flank of the Zagros mountains.

to pay off your debts, and the remaining hundred you can use for your other expenses."

The attendant then turned to me and gave me a pouch also and said, "There are three hundred Dirhams in this pouch, one hundred of which is for the purchase of a beast of burden, another hundred for your future expenses, and you can use the rest to purchase some clothes and to pay for your expenses on the journey to Sūrā[129], but do not journey to the lands of Jabal."

6. The Tale of Lady Narjis

The tale of Lady Narjis appears in the original sources of Shaykh Saddūq's *Kamāl ad-Dīn* and Shaykh Ṭūsī's *Ghaybat*. The story that follows is based on these two sources.

Bushr ibn Sulaymān was a son of Abū-Ayyūb al-Ansārī and was a close companion and neighbor of His Eminence Imam Hādī while he was domiciled in Sāmarrā. He reports the following hadīth:

One day one of the manservants of Imam Hādī who went by the name of Kāfūr came up to me and said, "The Imam has requested your presence."

When I entered into the presence of His Eminence, the Imam turned to me and said, "O Bushr ibn Sulaymān! You are a son of the Ansār. Devotion to us, the Ahl al-Bayt (the people of the House) of the Prophet has always been in the hearts of your family, as has allegiance to our sovereignty (*wilāya*).[130] This has been the case continuously since the time of the Prophet Muhammad to the present, and you have always been subject to our trust and assurance. Thus, I have chosen you for an important mission. Accomplishing this task for someone such as yourself who is a trusted companion will be a merit for you on account of which virtue you will have surpassed the other devotees and Shī'a of the Ahl al-

---

[129] A place in western Iran.
[130] *Walāya'*: See footnote #78.

Bayt ﷺ of the Prophet ﷺ of God ﷻ in your services to our guardianship and command (*wilāyaᵗ*), and will attain to a special station of honor as a consequence."

The Imam then said, "O Bushr! Presently there is a significant matter at hand; and although it has remained hidden up to now, I shall inform you of its nature. O Bushr! I now commission you and send you to a land for the mission of purchasing a bondmaiden (*kanīz*)."

The Imam then wrote a letter in his own blessed and beautiful script in letters that were foreign to me, and placed his noble seal on the folded scroll. When the letter was ready, His Eminence ﷺ brought out a pouch of money which contained 220 Sovereigns or gold coins (*ashrāfī*). He then turned to me and said, "O Bushr! Take this pouch of gold and this letter and head for Baghdad immediately. When you get there, be sure to be present at the Baghdad Bridge on the morning of such and such a day. When the ships coming from Hayrān arrive to the bank of the river, you will see a number of bondmaidens aboard those ships. You will also see there gathered a number of buyers who will be acting on behalf of the Abbāsid commanders, as well as a small number of Arab youths who will have gathered in a circle around the bondmaidens and bondsmen.

"Position yourself among that crowd and observe the proceedings from afar. It will not be long before you come across a slave-dealer by the name of Omar ibn Yazīd. Stay there and monitor that slave-dealer throughout the whole day, being sure not to neglect your observations for a single moment. The reason for the necessity of such diligence is because this man will offer to his customers a bondmaiden who fits the following description." The Imam ﷺ then proceeded to enumerate the description in detail for Bushr ibn Sulaymān: "O Bushr! That bondmaiden will be wearing two beautiful silken robes and will avoid looking at her prospective buyers; her eyes will be downcast and she will avoid looking at anyone else. You will then hear a cry from that woman in the tongue of the Byzantines (*rūmī*) on account of the hardship which she is suffering for having been placed in such a situation, and that cry will be the following: "Woe unto me! For the veil of my dignity has been rent asunder!"

Then one of the buyers will say, "I want to purchase this bondmaiden and am willing to pay 300 Sovereigns for her, as her nobility of character has made me more interested in her. The bondmaiden will then address the buyer in Arabic, saying, "O Arab! If you were to take on the countenance and form and clothes of [the prophet] Solomon ﷺ the son of David ﷺ and be a powerful king like him, enthroned and endowed with the glory and majesty of a sovereign with the whole world under your feet, I [still] would never have any inclinations toward you. Therefore, banish the thought and save your money from being wasted in this way."

The slave merchant will then turn to the bondmaiden and say, "So what am I to do, then, when you will not content yourself to any customer of mine? You tell me yourself what I am to do in order to be able to sell you [and be rid of you at a profit]!"

She will then tell the slave merchant, "Why are you in such haste to sell me? A buyer must show up toward whom my heart inclines and in whose loyalty and piety I can have trust, and whom I can consider worthy."

"You should go to her at this juncture and tell her, 'I have a letter in hand from a dignitary who has written it out of the kindness of his heart, and the letter is written in your own language in which the writer describes his munificence and generosity'."

"Then give her the letter and ask her to read it and tell her that you are my agent and that you can buy her from this slave trader if she so desires."

Bushr ibn Sulaymān says: The prophecies which Imam Ali an-Naqī ﷺ had foretold came about exactly as he had foretold, and I did as I was instructed and sat in wait at the bank of the Tigris River until the appointed time arrived and offered the letter to the bondmaiden when the opportune moment arose. When she looked at the letter and saw the Imam's handwriting, she wept profusely, then turned to Omar ibn Yazīd and said, "If you do not sell me to this man, I shall kill myself."

After this, I entered into a long haggle with the slave trader concerning the amount that was to be paid until he finally accepted the 220 Sovereigns which the Imam ﷺ had entrusted to me for the transaction. I gave the pouch of gold to him and took possession of the bondmaiden, at which transference she became very happy; and the two of us made our way toward the center of Baghdad to some quarters which I had rented.

During this journey, the bondmaiden frequently took the Imam's ﷺ letter out and kissed it and placed it on her eyes and cheeks and wept tears of joy.

I was very taken aback by this behavior of hers and said, "O madam! You kiss a letter and place it over your eyes and elate at being in possession of it, yet you have not met and do not know who the writer of the letter is.

The bondmaiden expressed surprise and bid Bushr to listen to the story of her life:

"O Bushr ibn Sulaymān! I am Malīka, the daughter of Yeshuā and the daughter of the emperor of Byzantium, and my mother is one of the daughters of Simeon ibn Hammun the Pure, the *wasī*[131] of His Eminence the prophet Jesus ﷺ.

"It so happened that one day my grandfather the emperor of Byzantium desired to wed me to his son, and at that time I was only thirteen years of age. The emperor of Byzantium was a descendant of one of the Twelve Disciples of His Eminence Jesus ﷺ and was a devout Christian theologian. He gathered three hundred prominent dignitaries and seven hundred captains of commerce and four thousand officers of the army and cavalry and tribal chieftains in his palace and ordered a throne to be made ready which had been inlaid with gems during his reign. He then placed this glorious throne on forty pillars, and had icons and crosses

---

[131] *Wasī*: ministerial inheritor, legatee, executor, and successor.

placed in prominent places, after which he placed his nephew on the throne.

"The priests present had their Bibles in hand and were preparing to recite passages from it, but before they had a chance to do so, a howl filled the palace and all of the icons fell to the ground and the pillars of the golden throne quivered and the throne fell to the ground also, throwing the king's brother's son to the floor, where he lost consciousness.

"At this point, the faces of the priests lost their color and the bodies of those present began to tremble and shiver from freight. Then the senior priest told my grandfather, 'O King! Forgive us for this evil omen that has occurred, as the portent of this occurrence is that the Christian religion will soon wither away.'

"My grandfather took what happened as a bad omen and anger appeared on his countenance. But he commanded the theologians and priests to set the throne right again and to return the icons and sacred statuary and crosses to their original positions and to bring order back to the proceedings. He then ordered the son of another brother of his to be brought to the palace chamber and that I be married to him instead, so that this brother's good fortune might drive away the omen from the other ill-fated brother.

"The ceremony was resumed according to the King's order, and the second brother's son was seated atop the throne and the priests started to recite passages from the Bible. Only a few moments had passed from their recitations when the howl was heard again and the icons and statuary and crosses and throne tumbled to the ground all over again and the ill omen of this brother conjoined with that of the other brother's.

The dignitaries and those present at the ceremony never became aware of the mysterious cause of these events, and did not realize that what occurred was not an ill omen and had nothing to do with the two brothers and their sons; but that rather, these events were a clarion call of justice [which emanated] from the domains of reality which are beyond the ken of ordinary human perception (*al-ghayb*) which gave the glad tidings of felicity for the brotherhood of man in the future that awaits humanity. With the occurrence of these two unusual and frightening events, the dignitaries and those present at the ceremony dispersed and my grandfather returned to his chambers in the palace in the depths of grief and distress.

"When nightfall arrived, I went to sleep and in the dream world I saw His Eminence Jesus ﷺ and Simeon and a few other Disciples gathered in my grandfather's palace where they had erected a pulpit of light whose grandeur and height was such that it seemed as if it stretched to the heavens themselves. They had placed this pulpit of light in the same place that my grandfather's throne had been positioned earlier.

"Then His Eminence the Prophet ﷺ Muhammad and his *wasī*[132] and son in law His Eminence Ali ibn Abī-Tālib ﷺ and a few other of the Imams ﷺ illuminated the palace with the light of their steps. Then His Eminence Jesus ﷺ hastened forth to welcome and honor His Eminence the Seal of Prophethood,[133] and the Messiah placed his hand around His Eminence's neck [in a show of respect and friendship].

"After a while His Eminence the Prophet ﷺ Muhammad said, "O Rūhallāh![134] I have come here to ask for the hand of Malīka, the daughter of your successor Simeon, for my son, who will succeed to the office of the imamate before too long [i.e. Imam Hasan al-Askari ﷺ].

"Then His Eminence Jesus ﷺ turned to Simeon and said, "O Simeon! True honor and dignity within this world have turned toward you. Accept the betrothal of the progeny of Muhammad to your daughter."

"Simeon said, 'I accept this betrothal'."

"And so, all present gathered around that rostrum and made a circle around it. Then the Apostle of God ﷺ gave a sermon followed by

---

[132] *Wasī*: ministerial inheritor, legatee, executor, and successor.
[133] This is one of the titles of the Prophet Muhammad ﷺ.
[134] *Rūhallāh*: Literally meaning "Spirit of God", it is one of the titles of the prophet Jesus ﷺ.

one delivered by His Eminence Jesus ﷺ and betrothed me to Imam Hasan al-Askari ﷺ. Then all of the progeny of His Eminence the Prophet ﷺ Muhammad, i.e. all of the Imams ﷺ and their people and the Disciples of His Eminence Jesus ﷺ gathered with those present and testified to this betrothal.

"When I awoke from this felicitous dream, I was amazed, and did not relate the contents of the dream to my father and grandfather for fear that they might put me to death, preferring instead to keep this valuable treasure secure in my breast. But every day and during each of my waking moments the passion and love for seeing that brilliant leader of the community of faith throbbed in my breast to the point that eating and drinking during day or night became difficult for me, and every moment that passed from the time of this dream turned my pallor more and more jaundiced and my body grew weaker, and the signs of my hidden passion gradually became manifest. [This state of affairs continued in this manner to the point that] there was no physician in the cities of Byzantium who my grandfather had not summoned in order to cure my illness. My grandfather had become restless and very depressed.

Things went on like this for a long time and no one was able to cure my illness, until one day, because my grandfather had given up hope of finding a cure for my illness, he told me out of the love he had for me, "O my daughter and the light of mine eyes! Is there anything in the world that you desire in your thoughts that you can give voice to so that I can grant you your wish?"

"I cast my eyes downward and remained silent for a moment, then said, "O honorable grandfather! I see the doors of relief as being closed to me. But if you cease the torment and torture of the Muslim prisoners of war which are holed up in dungeons and free them from their bondage, I hold hope that His Eminence Jesus ﷺ and his honorable mother Lady Mary ﷺ will look with kindness upon me and that the Lord will return me to health because of their prayer and intercession on my behalf."

"When I made this suggestion, my grandfather acted on it and ordered all of the prisoners of war be freed. Presently I took some food in and showed a slight improvement in my health, which made my father and family very happy. My father also allowed the condition of all of the prisoners within his prisons to be improved.

"A fortnight passed, after which one night I dreamt that Her Eminence Lady Fātima ﷺ came to me accompanied by a thousand heavenly angels. Her Eminence Lady Mary ﷺ then turned to me and said, "This queen regnant (*khātūn*) is one of the best women of this world. She is your [future] husband's [great grand-] mother and the honorable mother of the [Imams of the] Ahl al-Bayt ﷺ and the daughter of the Most Noble Prophet ﷺ and the most preeminent woman among all of the women of the world. She is the mother of the Hasanayn.[135]" I then stood up excitedly and placed my hands on the hem of her blessed gown and shed tears of woe and remorse and complained to her of the events of my life.

Then Her Eminence Lady Fātima ﷺ said, "O Malīka! How is my son supposed to be able to come to visit you whereas you assign partners to the one and only God ﷻ the Sublimely Exalted and live your life according to the religion of the Christians, whereas my sister Mary ﷺ the daughter of 'Imrān has anathemized and turned away from your religion and has turned to God ﷻ. If you now desire for Almighty God ﷻ and Jesus ﷺ and Mary ﷺ to be well pleased with you, and for my son to visit you, repeat the following formula after me:

I bear witness that there is no deity other than Allāh; And I bear witness that Muhammad is His Messenger.

"After I pronounced these blessed words, that dear mother took me into her arms with pleasure and kindness and consoled me and said, "O Malīka! Now you can await my son, for I will send him to you."

---

[135] *Hasanayn*: the title by which the two sons of Imam Ali b. Abī-Tālib ﷺ by Lady Fātima ﷺ Imam al-Hasan ﷺ and Imam al-Husain ﷺ are referred to.

"When I awoke from my dream, I repeated in my wakeful state that blessed formula which I had heard from the most preeminent lady of the world and awaited the arrival of her son.

"When the day was spent and nightfall arrived, I went to sleep again. I saw His Eminence Imam Hasan al-Askari ﷺ in my dream state. His countenance shone like the sun. I told him, "O Proof of God ﷲ (*hujjatullāh*)[136]! Why do you deprive me of seeing you and why do you keep your distance from me whereas my heart is in bond to your love?"

"His Eminence ﷺ said, 'The reason for my delay in coming to you was your idolatrous state [prior to your attesting to the unicity of God ﷲ and to the Messengerhood of the Prophet Muhammad ﷺ]. But now that you have entered into Islam, I shall come to you up until the time that God ﷲ the Sublimely Exalted brings us together in the material world also.'

"I awoke from my dream, and after that night, His Eminence ﷺ visited me in my dream state every night."

Bushr ibn Sulaymān asked Her Eminence Lady Narjis, "How were you able to hide among the prisoners and escape?"

Malīka (Narjis) said, "On one of these nights, His Eminence Jesus ﷺ said to me, 'Your grandfather shall send his army to fight the Muslims and will himself accompany his army. Disguise yourself as one of the court attendants and follow in the path of your grandfather.' So that is what I did, until the Muslim army reached us and took us as prisoners, and my fate was as you saw me. From the time I left until now, no one other than you knew what had become of me or that I am the daughter of the emperor of Byzantium. The old man whose property I became as his share of the spoils of war asked me my name and I said I was called Narjis. He said, "This is a name that is given to bondmaidens.""

Bushr said, "It is wondrous strange that you are a Byzantine but can speak Arabic so well."

---

[136] *Hujjat*: see footnotes #6 and #7 for an explanation of this key word.

Narjis said, "My grandfather loved me very much and strove diligently in my education and training and wanted me to be conversant in the best mode of social interaction; and so he selected a skilled translator who knew Arabic to work as my mentor, and it was she who taught me the Arabic tongue, but it was a process that took several years."

Bushr continues his report thus: We travelled on our path until we finally reached Sāmarrā. The first thing I did was to take Narjis to His Eminence Imam Ali an-Naqī ﷺ. His Eminence ﷺ said to her, "O Narjis! Do you see how God ﷻ the Sublimely Exalted showed you the dignity of the way of Muhammad and of his Ahl al-Bayt ﷺ and the religion of Islam, and demonstrated the ignominy and abjection of the Christian religion?"

Narjis replied, "O son of the Apostle of God! What can I say, when you are more knowledgeable than I?"

The Imam ﷺ then said, "I want to honor you and to hold you in high esteem. So tell me which of these two options that I will recount to you is your preference: that I should give you ten thousand Sovereigns (*ashrāfi*), or to give you glad tidings by means of which you shall attain to eternal honor and dignity?"

Narjis said, "O son of the Apostle of God! Give me the glad tidings of the honor which is to be my lot, as I have never been after the wealth of this world and have no desire for it."

The Imam ﷺ then turned to Narjis and said, "O Narjis! I give you the glad tidings that you will give birth to a son who will be the king of the East and the West, and he will fill the world with justice and equity with his sword of righteousness when it will have been filled with iniquity and oppression."

Narjis said, "Who will be the father of this son of mine?"

His Eminence ﷺ said, "The person for whom Muhammad asked for your hand in wedlock."

Imam Hādī then asked Narjis, "To whom did His Eminence Jesus and his *wasī*[137] betroth you?"

Narjis replied, "They betrothed me to your son [Imam Hasan al-Askarī]."

His Eminence the Imam asked, "Do you know him?"

Narjis replied, "Ever since I entered into Islam at the hands of the First Lady of the world, there has not been a single night where he has not come to visit me in my dreams."

The Imam then called for his attendant Kāfūr and said, "O Kāfūr! Go at once to the house of my sister Lady Hakīma and bring her here."

Kāfūr told Lady Hakīma of her brother's message and she came over to see him. When she was in their presence, the Imam turned to her and said, "This is Narjis, the lady who I had told you about before."

Then Lady Hakīma embraced Narjis and caressed her and treated her with tenderness, becoming very happy at having met her.

His Eminence the Imam then said, "O daughter of the Apostle of God! Now come and take Narjis back with you to your home and teach her the ways of our religion and how to perform her religious obligations."

7. The Reign of the Abbāsid Caliphs during the Time of the Imam

The short six-year tenure of the office of the imamate of Imam Hasan al-Askarī coincided with the reign of three Abbāsid caliphs, including the tyrant Muʿtazz, the caliph during whose reign Imam Hādī was martyred, as were a number of other prominent Ālids.

Muʿtazz was such a diabolical tyrant that he once imprisoned his brother Muʾayyad on some pretext and then subjected him to forty beatings of a cane and eventually divested him from his heir-apparency. After the

---

[137] *Wasī*: ministerial inheritor, legatee, executor, and successor.

passage of some time, he imprisoned him again; and when he heard that the Turks (among his army) were plotting to free his brother from his imprisonment, he ordered his brother's execution in the prison. It has been related that Mu'ayyad was rolled in a poisoned blanket which was then tied tightly at both ends, and left to die therein; and that Mu'tazz then summoned his senior courtiers and judges and showed them his brother's body and invited them to witness that Mu'ayyad's body was whole and that he had not been tortured to death in his prison, so that they could then testify in public that he had died a natural death.

During Mu'tazz's caliphate over seventy Ālids[138] and people from the house of Ja'far at-Tayyār and 'Aqīl ibn Abī-Tālib who had risen in insurrection in the Hijaz[139] were captured and taken to Sāmarrā. The loyal companions of Imam Hasan al-Askari were under extreme pressure during the reign of this same tyrannical caliph. When some of His Eminence's companions would write him letters informing him of what was happening and complaining of the caliph's oppression, in response to the last letter, the Imam stated, "O loyal companions of mine! And O sincere and steadfast Shī'a! There will be relief in three days' time."

The Imam's prophecy came true after the passage of three days, because the Turkish contingent within the Abbāsid court conspired against the caliph because they considered his reign to be against their interests. They thus bided their time and waited for an opportune moment and rose up in rebellion against him and forced him out of office. They then made a lesson of him for others by placing him in a locked cellar and keeping him there until he died.

Muhtadī succeeded al-Mu'tazz to the throne of the caliphate, and he too, like the rest of the Abbāsid clan, was a tyrant and a hypocrite. He pretended to be a pious man and avoided the pleasures of the world for the benefit of the public, driving out the court singers and dancers and jesters,

---

[138] A member of the House of Ali b. Abī-Tālib.

[139] The region where Mecca and Medina are located.

and banned all of the unseemly behavior that was par for the course in the previous Abbāsid courts; and attended to the needs of the disadvantaged out of a pretense of piety and presented his court in such a way that it was as if a window of hope had been opened unto the possibility of justice and equity, and that everyone could now rest assured that things have returned to the way they are supposed to be. But it did not take long before he too, like the tyrants and oppressors before him, showed his true colors.

This Abbāsid caliph imprisoned Imam Hasan al-Askari ﷺ for a period and even ordered his murder. But his own death did not allow him to carry out his evil intention.

A number of Ālids[140] rose up in insurrection against this tyrant during his ignominious reign so that perchance they could send him to his doom, but their efforts were unsuccessful and some of these men were rounded up and imprisoned, where they suffered grievous torture and eventually met their deaths.

Ahmad ibn Muhammad says: When the caliph al-Muhtadī began to raid the property and belongings of the *mawālī*,[141] I wrote a letter to His Eminence the Imam al-Askari ﷺ: "Praise be to God ﷻ the Sublimely Exalted who caused him [the caliph al-Muhtadī] to overlook us in his wrath. It [the news or rumor] has reached us that he has intimidated you and sworn to eradicate any traces of the Family of Muhammad from the face of the earth. [… Asking whether this was true.] [But] the Imam ﷺ wrote in reply in his blessed manuscript, "How short his life is to be. He shall be put to death in ignominy, humiliated and disgraced." And so it came to pass as the Imam ﷺ had prophesied, as al-Muhtadī was put to death by his Turkish guards and was succeeded by al-Mu'tamid.

The caliph al-Mu'tamid took the reins of the caliphate in hand and began his reign, and like his predecessors before him did nothing but live the life of revelry and debauchery and practice wickedness and oppress

---

[140] A member of the House of Ali b. Abī-Tālib ﷺ.
[141] *Mawālī*: Non-Arab freedman.

his people. He went to such extremes in his licentiousness and depravity that his brother al-Muwaffaq gradually took over the reins of governance from him and stripped him of his power and authority so that al-Mu'tamid was a caliph in nothing but his title. It was not long before al-Muwaffaq died and his son al- Mu'tamid ran the business of governance on his uncle al- Mu'tamid's behalf.

Eventually al- Mu'tamid died in the year 259 AH/ 873 CE and his nephew formally acceded to the caliphate. Imam Hasan al-Askari ﷺ was martyred during the reign of the tyrant al- Mu'tamid together with a number of other prominent Ālids who were put to death in the most egregious way, some of whose bodies were torn to pieces after their deaths.

There was much political turmoil and wars during al- Mu'tamid's reign, to the point that some historians have estimated that he killed something in the neighborhood of half a million people. In any event, during those times society took a special interest in the Immaculate Imams ﷺ as they had become aware of the Imams' refusal to accept the legitimacy of the tyrannical reign of the Abbāsid caliphs. The Abbāsids saw that the Imams ﷺ did not tread on any path other than the path of righteousness, and that they were continuously engaged in an ongoing struggle against the forces of oppression. The people had also started to become wise to the fact that these latter forces had nothing but rancor and hatred toward the House of the Prophet ﷺ and had obviated the intensity of their hatred and repression of this luminous series of Imams ﷺ.

During the reign of al-Muhtadī Imam Hasan al-Askari ﷺ was taken to the prison of Sālih ibn Wasīf. The caliph assigned two of the most wicked people among the guards of his court to watch over His Eminence the Imam ﷺ in order to make the conditions for the Imam ﷺ all the harder; but these two fell under the influence of the acts of devotion and worship of the Imam ﷺ (as mentioned earlier). On another occasion, His Eminence Imam Hasan al-Askari ﷺ was taken to Nahrīr's dungeon. There Nahrīr treated the Imam ﷺ very harshly. Nahrīr's wife told him, "O husband! Be afraid of Almighty God! Do you not know the personality and station of the person who is in your house?" His wife then talked about the piety and honor of that nobleman and then said, "I fear for your future for the wrong you are committing against His Eminence."

But Nahrīr's response was to swear an oath that he would cast the imam into the midst of wild beasts of prey."

Having obtained his superior's permission, Nahrīr let Imam Hasan al-Askari loose among wild beasts, having no doubt that they would kill the Imam. But when some time passed and he went to check on the Imam, he saw that he was in complete health and occupied in his devotions to his Maker, with the beasts of prey forming a circle around the Imam. After this, he ordered the Imam to be taken back to his home.

Al- Mu'tamid also imprisoned Imam Hasan al-Askari and his brother Ja'far during the tenure of his reign in Ali Jarīn's dungeon and constantly asked about His Eminence's condition. Ali Jarīn would invariably report back to the caliph that the Imam spent his days fasting and his nights engaged in ritual devotions to his Lord. Al- Mu'tamid asked Ali Jarīn one more time to be sure, and the latter gave him the same report. At that point, al- Mu'tamid instructed Ali Jarīn, "Go to him at once and give him my regards and tell him that you have come to take him back to his home."

Ali Jarīn reports: When I entered the chamber, I saw that the Imam had donned his [outside] garments and was ready to leave. When His Eminence saw me, he stood up and I gave him the caliph's message. The Imam then mounted his ride but paused. When I asked him the reason for his tarrying, the Imam said, "My brother Ja'far must also come with me."

I said, "The Emir has only instructed me to free you, and no mention has been made of Ja'far."

His Eminence told me, "So now go back to the Emir and tell him that my brother and I are of one family and have left our families back there together. If I return there without being accompanied by Ja'far, certain [familial] issues will arise which the Emir is not unfamiliar with." I went to the Emir and related what had taken place, and the Emir ordered Ja'far to be freed also.

From what was related in a summary fashion it is very clear that His Eminence Imam Hasan al-Askari ﷺ lived at a time when the political climate was extremely repressive and caused much difficulty for him. For this reason, the Imam's ﷺ friends and companions and partisans (*Shī'a*) could not come and go to see him as they pleased. Some of the Imam's ﷺ devotees and followers were able to see him by way of his family members who would help them gain access to the Imam ﷺ.

It is related that during the imamate of Imam Hasan al-Askari ﷺ a man from among the Ālids left Sāmarrā on some business and left for the territory known as Jabal, which is the mountainous region in western Iran west of the Zāgros Mountains up to Hamedān. During his journey he came across one of the Shī'a of the Imam ﷺ who was from Halwān. The Halwānite asked him where he was coming from.

Ali said, "From Sāmarrā."

The Halwānite asked, "Do you know such and such a district and such and such a street?"

Ali said, "Sure, I know them."

"Do you have any news of Hasan ibn Ali ﷺ?"

"No, I have no news of him."

"What business brings you to Jabal?"

"I have come here to earn a living."

Then the Halwānite said, "O man of the Ālids! I have fifty Dinars.[142] Take these coins from me, but I give them to you on condition that you come back with me to Sāmarrā and take me to the house of Hasan ibn Ali ﷺ and show him to me."

---

[142] Silver coins.

The Ālid accepted the condition and they set off and after a while entered Sāmarrā, whereupon the Ālid took the Halwānite to the Imam's ﷺ house.

8. Guidance

Ibn Sabbāgh, the Sunni scholar of the Māliki rite relates a hadīth report from Abū-Hashem al-Ja'farī who said: Sāmarrā was stricken with a severe drought. The Abbāsid caliph al-Mu'tamid ordered the people to gather in order to make the *istisqā* supplication or to pray for rain. So the people gathered in the congregational mosque for three consecutive days and prayed for rain and offered their devotions, but it did not rain.

On the fourth day Jāthlīq, the archbishop of the Christians, went out to the desert together with a group of his followers and priests where they proceeded to engage in acts of worship [and pray for rain]. Whenever one of the priests raised his hands heavenward, large drops of rain would rain down and it would start to rain.

Jāthlīq repeated these supplications on the next day and it rained so much that the people no longer supplicated the Lord for rain. This event caused consternation and bewilderment and doubt in the hearts of the Muslims, to the point that many Muslims inclined toward the Christian religion. In order to solve this problem, the caliph sent someone to seek the help of Imam Hasan al-Askari ﷺ.

These events took place at a time when the Imam ﷺ was imprisoned. They took the nobleman to the court of the caliph, where al-Mu'tamid told him: "Go and see to the community of your ancestor, for they have all lost their way."

The Imam ﷺ said, "Ask Jāthlīq and the rest of the priests and bishops to gather in the desert on the morrow and offer their devotions."

The caliph said, "Given the extent of the rain that we have had, the people are not desirous of any more rain. So what purpose can an outing to the desert serve?"

Imam Hasan ibn Ali al-Askari

The Imam said, "God willing, I want to remove any doubt that exists from the hearts of the community of my forefather."

So the caliph ordered Jāthlīq and the rest of the priests and bishops to gather in the desert the next day, which was a Tuesday.

Imam Hasan al-Askari also went to the desert on the following morning, accompanied with a large company of Muslims. When the two groups met, Jāthlīq and the priests proceeded to raise their hands heavenward, offer their devotions and pray for rain. Moments later clouds began to cover the sky and drops of rain began to rain down.

Presently the Imam instructed his attendants to take one of the priests by the hand and withdraw what he was holding between his fingers. When they did so, it turned out that he was holding onto a bone from a human skeleton. His Eminence took the bone and wrapped it in some cloth, then turned to the priest and said, "Now make your prayers for rain again."

The priest raised his hands heavenward, but the clouds parted to the point where the sun could be seen once again. All of the people were astonished at what had just happened, and the caliph asked His Eminence , "What is [the significance of] this bone?"

The Imam said, "This is the bone from the body of one of the apostles of God which these priests have removed from its burial place. And the bone of no Prophet will appear without rain also appearing with it."

The caliph and all of the Muslims praised the Imam , after which they tried out the bone. Having tested the bone, they saw that what the Imam had said was indeed true.

Ishāq al-Kindi was one of the materialist philosophers of Iraq. He was occupied with writing a book in which he claimed that the Quran

contained contradictions and had secluded himself from the people for a long time, staying at home and working on his book in earnest. One day one of Kindi's students came to Imam Hasan al-Askari ﷺ. The Imam ﷺ told him, "Is there not an intelligent man among you to dissuade your master from pursuing such a useless task?"

The student replied, "I am one of the master's students. How can I interfere in this matter or in anything else, for that matter?"

The Imam ﷺ replied, "Go to your master and offer your help out of friendship, and then say that you have a question, and ask whether the master will give you leave to ask it. Your master will certainly give you leave to put your question to him. And so, at that point, you can ask him, "If the narrator of the Quran comes to you, would you own to the possibility that the intended meaning of His words is different than that which you interpret, and that the intended meanings can be meanings of which you are not aware?" Your master will say, "Yes, it is possible." Because when Kindi pays heed to a matter, he understands it. So when you hear his response is in the affirmative, then say, "How did you attain to certainty in your belief that the intended meaning and purpose of the Quran is that which you think it is? Is it not possible that the narrator of the Quran has an intended meaning and purpose to His words which you have not yet understood, and that your interpretation of the words of the Quran are different than what their actual meanings are."

The student went to Isḥāq al-Kindi and followed the Imam's ﷺ instructions to the letter. He initially opened the conversation in friendship so that he could avail himself of the opportunity of putting the questions to his master, after which he posed the questions. Kindi asked his student to repeat his questions. When the master heard the questions a second time, he went deep into thought and considered [the implications of] the question to be within the realm of possibility based on linguistic and semiotic considerations.

Kindi then turned to his student and swore him to tell the truth and asked, "How did this question come to you?"

His student said, "It was just a thought that came into my mind, and so I thought I would ask you about it."

But Kindi said, "It is impossible for you and the likes of you to attain to such a question! Now tell me where you came across it!"

His student said, "O my master! Abū-Muhammad [Imam Hasan al-Askari ؑ] taught it to me and instructed me as to how to pose it."

Kindi said, "Now you have spoken the truth. Such a question cannot have emanated from any source other than that of that honorable household."

He then took everything that he had written and burned it in his fire.

Ya'qūb ibn Ishāq reports: I wrote a letter to Imam Hasan al-Askari ؑ asking how a creature and devotee of God ﷻ should worship his Maker when he does not and cannot see him.

In response, His Eminence ؑ wrote, "O Abā-Yūsuf! God ﷻ is so sublimely exalted above all of our possible imaginings of Him that His [infinite] horizons are greater than affording the possibility of even my forefather the Apostle of God ﷺ being able to see him."

I then asked His Eminence ؑ, "Has the Apostle of God ﷺ ever seen him?"

In reply to my letter, His Eminence ؑ wrote, "God ﷻ the Sublimely Exalted manifested His grandeur and magnificence to the heart of the Apostle of God ﷺ to the extent of the Apostle's [finite] capacity."

Abū-Hāshim al-Ja'farī reports: Someone asked Imam Hasan al-Askari ؑ, "Why is it that a destitute woman inherits only one share [of her father's inheritance], whereas men inherit two shares?"

His Eminence said, "Because in the field of battle, the responsibility for waging *jihād* does not fall on the shoulder of women, and they are likewise exempted from paying the expenses of the household, and for paying the just retribution price for an unintended death (manslaughter). It is for these [and other social] considerations that men's share of inheritance is twice that of women's."

Abū-Hāshim states: I thought to myself and said, "When Ibn Abī'l-'Awjā put this question to Imam Ja'far as-Sādiq, the answer was the same as that which His Eminence the Imam just said."

As I was busy in this thought, suddenly Imam Hasan al-Askari looked at me and said, "Indeed, O Abū-Hāshim! Ibn Abī'l-'Awjā put this same question to Imam Ja'far as-Sādiq. Know that when a question is posed to one of us [Imams], the answer of each [and every one] of us will be the same, and the Imams that follow [past Imams] will say the same thing, just as you heard the same answer today. The first and last of us are equal [to each other] in terms of their knowledge and station [of learning]; and the excellences of the virtues of the Apostle of God and the Commander of the Faithful (*amīr al-mu'minīn*)[143] [with respect to their knowledge] are [also] equal [to one another].

It is related that one day, Hasan ibn Zarīf wrote a letter to Imam Hasan al-Askari in which he asked the meaning of the words of the Apostle of God concerning the Commander of the Faithful Ali ibn Abī-Tālib. [The phrase in question was] *man kuntu mawlāʰᵘ fa hadha Alīᵃⁿ mawlā.* [i.e. "Of whomsoever I have [hitherto] been lord and master (*mawlā*), [so too] this [here] Ali shall [henceforth similarly] be his lord and master."]

---

[143] A title that the Shī'a reserve exclusively for Imam Ali, as it was during the time of the Prophet.

The Imam replied, "The Prophet's intended meaning was to designate Ali to his succession as God's viceregent and to appoint His Eminence Imam Ali to [the office of] the imamate of the community; so that if differences should arise in the community, the party of God, meaning those who follow God's will and commands, are [separated from those who do not and are thus] identified [and distinguished from one another]."

Hirawi reports: one day one of Isbāt's sons turned to me and said, "O Hirawi! I have written a letter to Imam Hasan al-Askari in which I informed him of the differences which have arisen between his followers and asked him to show a manifest sign in order to resolve these differences."

In response to the letter the Imam wrote: "Verily God the Almighty and the Magnificent does indeed communicate with rational human beings. No one is more capable of bringing manifest signs than the Seal of Prophethood and the Master of the Prophets, the Prophet Muhammad. Yet his nation accused him of being a magician and a sorcerer. And verily, those who were open to guidance were indeed guided by the Prophet, whose miracles were a cause of the reassurance of a great number of people. What this means is that we speak [and act] in accordance to that which God the Sublimely Exalted commands, and remain silent when He so wills. If God desired for the truth to remain veiled, he would not have commissioned the prophets to give warnings and glad tidings to humanity. The prophets of God manifested the truth irrespective of the weakness or strength of their position, and at times ministered to humanity in order to perfect Almighty God's will and in order to reinforce it and to drive it home (*tanfidh*)."

His Eminence the Imam ﷺ then turned to me and said, "O Hirawi! The people of the world are divided into several groups. There is a group which is on the Right Path (*sirāt al-mustaqīm*) and on the road to salvation, who have outstretched their hand of exigence toward the truth and toward God ﷻ the Sublimely Exalted, and are committed to the principles and creed of Islam and live their lives in accordance with its tenets and injunctions. The people of this group never allow any doubt to enter their hearts and [rely upon and] seek refuge only in Almighty God ﷻ."

"O Hirawi! The second group are those who do not take the truth from those who know the truth (*ahl al-haqq*; reference to the prophets and Imams ﷺ), and do not learn from them the lessons of how to befriend the truth. The people of this group are like those who travel the seas; and whenever the seas are calm, they are calm, but whenever the seas are turbulent, they become unsettled and agitated. And the third group are those over whom Satan has assumed mastery and control; the people of this group engage in contumacy with those who know the truth (*ahl al-haqq*) [and their respective ministries] out of envy (*hasad*) and are engaged in a struggle against truth and justice with their innermost beings (*bātin*)."

"O Hirawi! The person who has abandoned the truth and the Right Path and wanders to the left and to the right [of this Path], leave that person to his own volition and devices. The shepherd is capable of gathering his flock with the least effort whenever He so desires. You mentioned a difference that has arisen among our friends. If exaltedness and sublimity is to be the criterion, then there is no doubt that he who is appointed to the office of the governance and guardianship and viceregency of God ﷻ has been so appointed advisedly and with due and careful consideration [by God]. This means that the Immaculate Imam ﷺ is more worthy of making decisions [concerning matters pertaining to the community at large] and of issuing the orders to have those decisions implemented than anyone else."

"O Hirawi! Treat those who live within the province of your rule righteously, and refrain from revealing our mysteries and secrets, and shun the quest for power and authority; and know that these two acts – revealing our mysteries and secrets and seeking power – send people to their perdition."

"O Hirawi! You mentioned the journey to the land of the Persians in your letter. Travel to Persia, for God ﷻ the Sublimely Exalted desires that which is good for you [to result from this journey]. God ﷻ willing, you will return to Egypt in safety and security under God's protection. Remember me to our devotees and trusted friends and enjoin them to righteousness and the pious fear of Almighty God and govern in accordance with the terms of the trust [of the office which has been entrusted to you] and let them know that [the status of] those who reveal our mysteries and secrets is equivalent to [the status of] those who are at war with us."

Hirawi continues: When I read the part of His Eminence's ﷺ letter which stated "God ﷻ willing, you will return to Egypt in safety and security…", I did not understand what it meant, until I went to Baghdad and decided to go to Persian from there, but obstacles arose so that I was not able to go on this journey, and I had no choice but to return to Egypt. And this is when I realized why His Eminence ﷺ had said I would return to Egypt.

Muhammad ibn al-Hasan ibn Maymūn reports: I once wrote a letter to Imam Hasan al-Askari ﷺ complaining of my indigence. But then I came to my senses and thought to myself, "Did not Imam Sādiq ﷺ say, '[The value given to] indigence by us is higher than [the value given to] satiety and wealth by others, and [the world that unfolds after] our dying shall be better than [the value given to] staying alive [in this world] by our enemies'."

Not long had passed from my having written the letter when His Eminence ﷺ wrote in reply to my letter that, "When the [burden of] sin of our devotees becomes great Almighty God ﷻ frees them of this burden by means of poverty and indigence, thereby forgiving them of much of their sins. Whenever you are with us and are afflicted by indigence, this is better [for you] than being with the enemy and being free of need and want. O Muhammad! We are a sanctuary to those who seek refuge in us, and a [guiding beacon of] light for those who seek our guidance to the Right Path, and a sentinel for those who seek the protection [of our guardianship]; and one who is devoted to us is positioned at the lofty peak of proximity to us. And know that he who veers from us and from our Path is heading for the Fire of perdition."

9. From the Letters and Will of Imam Hasan al-Askari

Hadith report compilations and books of history have recorded many of the Imam's ﷺ wills and testaments which His Eminence ﷺ has written to some of his companions. In these letters the Imam ﷺ gives advice to his companions concerning how best to lead one's life, and beautifully explains various Islamic thoughts and themes to his devotees, as well as discussing some of the ordinances of the sacred law of Islam and that which has been made licit and illicit by the Lawgiver. Included among these letters is one addressed to the great early Shī'a scholar Ali ibn Husayn ibn Bābūya al-Qomi.[144] The letter begins as follows:

"In the name of Allāh, the Most Compassionate, the Most Merciful. Endless praise be to God, the Cherisher and Sustainer of the world and of all who dwell within it. Heaven and [all that

---

[144] Known as Sheikh Sadūq and compiler of one of the four "canonical" books (*kutub al-'arba'a*) of hadīth scripture of Shī'a Islam, *man lā yahdhuru'l-faqīh*.

is] good shall be the ultimate end for those who harbor the pious fear of God ﷻ [in their hearts] and for those who only follow and obey and worship the one and only true God; and Hellfire shall be the ultimate end for the unbelievers. Enmity and the transgression [of the bounds of the natural order] is the lot of the wicked, and there shall be no God ﷻ other than Allāh. It is He who is the greatest Creator. And [may His] endless [blessings of] peace and mercy be [showered] upon His greatest devotee, Muhammad and his Purified Family ﷺ.

"O Ali! O great man, and O he who is a scholar of the Quranic sciences and who is the beneficiary of the trust of my followers. After devotion to and worshipping God, I enjoin you to [harbor] the pious fear of God ﷻ [in your heart], to offering your ritual devotions to the Almighty, and to be sure to pay the poor due (*zakāt*). There is [certainly] the hope that God ﷻ the Sublimely Exalted will help you to succeed in attain to that [mode of conduct] which is pleasing to Him, and to grant you worthy progeny from your seed."

"O Ali! The ritual devotions of one who does not pay the poor due shall not be accepted [by God ﷻ on Judgment Day]; and I counsel you to pass by the sins of others and to temper your anger [against those who transgress your rights], and to maintain relations with and abide by your duties to your kith and kin (*silat-al rahim*); and to be a brother to your brothers in faith and to strive to see to their needs in their times of hardship and to give them peace of mind; and to be patient and have forbearance with the ignorant; and to always dwell deeply on God's religion and to become [even more] familiar with the Quran; to be steadfast in your work, and to make righteousness and good cheer your boon companions and to enjoin the doing of that which is right, and forbid the doing of that which is wrong (*amr bi ma'rūf wa nahy min al-munkar*), for God ﷻ the Sublimely Exalted has stated that

لَّا خَيْرَ فِي كَثِيرٍ مِّن نَّجْوَاهُمْ إِلَّا مَنْ أَمَرَ بِصَدَقَةٍ أَوْ مَعْرُوفٍ أَوْ إِصْلَاحٍ بَيْنَ النَّاسِ ۚ وَمَن يَفْعَلْ ذَٰلِكَ ابْتِغَاءَ مَرْضَاتِ اللَّهِ فَسَوْفَ نُؤْتِيهِ أَجْرًا عَظِيمًا ﴿١١٤﴾

[4:114] No good comes, as a rule, out of secret confabulations - saving such as are devoted to enjoining charity, or equitable dealings, or setting things to rights between people: and unto him who does this out of a longing for God's goodly acceptance We shall in time grant a mighty reward."

"O Ali! Refrain from all that is indecent and obscene. It is enjoined on you [to offer] night prayers [and devotions to the Lord frequently]. Verily the Apostle of God ﷺ enjoined the following to our master Ali ibn Abī-Tālib ؏: "O Abul-Hasan ؏! [Offering] the night prayers [and devotions to the Lord] is enjoined on you. [And he repeated the formula twice more:] Night prayers! Night prayers! Any who take the night prayers lightly are not [a part] of us."

"Thus, act on what I have advised; and order my followers [similarly] to act on what I have enjoined you to do. And it is enjoined on you to be humble and act with humility and wait for the Opening (*al faraj*; reference to the advent of the Lord of the Age ؏ or universal savior); for, verily, the Prophet ﷺ of God ﷺ has stated, "The most excellent of the acts of my community is waiting for the Opening."

"O Ali! Our Shī'a will continually be in a state of sorrow and grief until my son the Qā'im's¹⁴⁵ advent. Verily the Prophet of God has given glad tidings that he will fill the world with equity and justice, just as it will have become filled with injustice and oppression prior to his advent and insurrection."

"O great man! And O he who is the beneficiary of my trust! Have patience and forbearance in the face of the harsh injustices [that you face] and enjoin my Shī'a to do the same. Verily the Earth belongs to God Who shall make His bondsmen inherit it, and a felicitous conclusion awaits the righteous and those who harbor the pious fear of God in their breasts."

"And may God's peace and serenity and mercy and bounty and grace be showered upon our Shī'a."

"And Almighty God is sufficient unto us, for He is the best Trustee (*wakīl*), Guardian and Helper.

In another one of his wills to his followers (*Shī'a*), Imam Hasan al-Askari has stated: I enjoin you to the pious fear of God; and to piety in your religion; to struggling [earnestly] in the way of God; to truthfulness in your speech; to returning trusts to those who have entrusted them to you; to prolonging the duration of your prostrations [during your prescribed ritual devotions]; and to [establishing and maintaining] goodly relations with your neighbors; as all of these were the Way of the Apostle of God. O those who harbor the pious fear of God in their hearts! Be kind to the members of your family and to your next of kin, and perform praiseworthy

---

¹⁴⁵ *Qā'im*: the One Who will successfully rise up [in insurrection against the tyranny and oppression of illegitimate rule for the cause of the House of the Prophet Muhammad].

acts in their favor, and participate in their funeral processions, and inquire about the health of those who are ill and visit them on their sick beds. Give your kith and kin their due. And know that if any one of you is pious in the practice of his or her religion, and is truthful in his or her words, and is true to his or her trusts and is kind and of good cheer, it will be said that this person is a Shī'a, and this will please me. [Be sure always to remember to] fear God ﷻ the Sublimely Exalted. [Act in such a way as to] become the ornaments that adorn us, and not to be the occasion of our shame. Draw kindness toward us and repel all that is indecent and obscene away from us. For whatever good is spoken of in reference to us, that is what we are about and we are free of [the taint of] and disassociate ourselves from [any and all] error and sin. There are rights that have been determined for us in the Book of God; and we have [an additional right which belongs to us on account of our] kinship with the Prophet ﷺ, the Apostle of God; and God ﷻ has purified[146] us, which is a distinction which no one else can lay claim to without making a liar of himself."

> "O human beings! Give much thought to death and to the remembrance of Almighty God ﷻ. Recite the Quran frequently and send blessings of peace unto the Prophet ﷺ of God ﷻ and

---

[146] The Imams are the "*Ahl al-Bayt*" ﷺ of the Prophet, meaning the members of his household, who have been purified of all defilement and sin in accordance with Sura 33:33 (the *Āyat at-Tathīr* or the Verse of Purification), who defer perfectly to the way and paradigmatic example of the Prophet and continue in his path, expounding his teachings by their words as well as by embodying them by way of example. [33:33] *and be constant in prayer, and render the purifying dues, and pay heed unto God ﷻ and His Apostle: for God ﷻ only wants to remove from you all that might be loathsome, O you members of the [Prophet's] Household, and to purify you to utmost purity.*

unto his Purified and Immaculate Household, for each instance of such supplications to God ﷻ is the equivalent of ten goodly acts.

"And lastly, be sure constantly to bear in mind my counsel to you, for I entrust you, my Shī'a, to God ﷻ the Sublimely Exalted; may His peace and blessings be unto you all."

10. Some of the Miracles of Imam Hasan al-Askari

Like his father and forefathers before him, His Eminence Imam Hasan al-Askari ؉ had a special connection to Almighty God ﷻ and to the angels and to the domains of reality which are beyond the ken of ordinary human perception (*al-ghayb*), and was privy to the supernatural knowledge [and powers] which are part and parcel of the tenure of the office of the imamate. Many hadīth reports have been reported concerning His Eminence's ؉ miracles and supernatural knowledge and powers. Here we shall content ourselves with citing only a few examples of such reports.

This hadīth report has been related by Abū-Hāshim al-Ja'farī, who states: I was at the service of Imam Hasan al-Askari ؉ once, and I wanted to obtain a piece of silver from His Eminence ؉ in order to make a ring out of it for myself so that it would bring me blessings (*tabarruk*).[147] But when I sat down next to His Eminence ؉, I forgot all about this intention. When the time came and I rose to leave the Imam's ؉ presence, the Imam ؉ gave me a ring and said, "O Abū-Hāshim! You asked us for some silver, but we gave you a ring instead. You [thus] profited by the addition of the gemstone and the cost of the labor of making the ring. May this ring bring you [the] blessings and grace [of Almighty God]!"

---

[147] *Tabarruk*: the property of a relic or some mundane object which has been blessed or charged in some other way with sacral properties.

I turned to the Imām and said, "I bear witness that you are the *walī* [148] of God and that you are my Imam, and that I consider obedience to you as nothing less than my religious duty (literally, 'as my religion')."

His Eminence said, "May Almighty God bless you and have mercy on your eternal soul."

There is another report from Abū-Hāshim al-Ja'farī in the book *Nūr al-Absār* (The Light of the Eyes) wherein he relates the following: Four others and I were holed up in Sālih ibn Wasīf's dungeon when Imam Hasan al-Askari and his brother Ja'far were brought into our cell. My companions and I gathered in a circle around the Imam in order to see what we could do for him. In this same prison, there was a man from the tribe of Banī Jamh who claimed to be an Ālid.[149] One day His Eminence told us, "If there weren't among you a person who is a stranger, I would tell you about [the conditions of] the time when humanity's salvation will occur. His Eminence then pointed to the Jahmite, indicating to him that he should leave; When the Jahmite had left, His Eminence turned to us and said, "This man is not your friend; keep your distance from him, for he has prepared a report of all that you have said, and this missive is presently on his person hidden in his clothes."

A couple of us proceed to search the man's clothing and found the report that he had secreted away there; and we found that he had written some important and dangerous things about us to the caliph.

---

[148] *Walī*: regent, sovereign, lord and master; patron, guardian, protector, custodian.

[149] A member of the House of Ali b. Abī-Tālib.

Imam Hasan ibn Ali al-Askari

Muhammad ibn Rabi' ash-Shaybāni reports: I had engaged a Dualist[150] in discussion and debate in the city of Ahvāz, after which I left for Sāmarrā. Some of the words of the Dualist had left their impressions in my heart and soul.

Some time passed and I was in Ahmad ibn Khasīb's house where we proceeded to engage in discussions and debate. At the same time, Imam Hasan al-Askari ﷺ was returning from a public event, and I came across him on his way back. His Eminence ﷺ looked at me for a while, and then pointed at me with his blessed finger and said, "O Muhammad! God ﷻ is singular and unique! He is only One! Believe in His unicity!!"

When I heard what he said, I fainted.

Ismāīl ibn Muhammad reports: One day I was seated at the door of Imam Hasan al-Askari's ﷺ house and was waiting for him to return home. When I saw the Imam ﷺ approaching from afar, I went to greet him and complained to him about my indigence, swearing an oath that I did not have even a single Dirham to my name.

The Imam ﷺ said, "O Ismāīl! You swear [such] an oath while you have two hundred Dirhams buried under the ground?!"

The Imam ﷺ then turned to me and said, "O Ismāīl! By mentioning this I did not mean to imply that I would not give you something!" The Imam ﷺ then made an indication to his attendant, saying, "Give him whatever you have on you."

At hearing this, the Imam's ﷺ attendant gave me one hundred Dinars. I gave thanks to God the Sublimely Exalted and wanted to leave

---

[150] One who believes that there are two deities who are ontically co-equal (and thus equally powerful).

The Unknown Imams

when His Eminence ﷺ turned to me and said, "O Ismāīl! I fear that you will lose those two hundred Dinars for which you have a great need."

I went to check up on the buried Dinars and found them all where they should be. I changed their hiding place and hid them in a place where no one would ever find them. Much time went by, and a day came when I became in need of those Dinars. I went to fetch them, but however hard I searched, I could not find them. This came as a hard blow to me. After a while I realized that my son had found the hiding place and taken the gold coins, and not a single coin was left for me. Indeed, things came to pass just as His Eminence ﷺ had foretold.

Muhammad ibn Abbās reports: Once a group of my friends and I had gathered round and were discussing the miracles of Imam Hasan al-Askari ﷺ when a *nāsibī*[151] who was among us said, "I will write a scroll without using any ink. If Abū-Muhammad ﷺ is able to answer it, [it will be proved to me that] he is with the truth."

All of us wrote what questions we had in our respective letters, and the *nāsibī* man wrote his words on a scroll without using any ink, and we sent his scroll together with ours to the Imam ﷺ.

After a while we received the answers to all of our questions from the Imam ﷺ who had written the name of the *nāsibī* man and the names of his mother and father on the blank scroll which he had submitted. When the man saw the Imam's ﷺ response, he grew faint and passed out. When he came to, he attained to faith in the rightfulness of the Imam ﷺ and became one of his devout followers.

---

[151] See *footnote* #90.

Imam Hasan ibn Ali al-Askari

Omar ibn Abī-Muslim reports: Samīʻ Musmaʻī was my next-door neighbor. He harassed me inordinately. One day I wrote a letter to the Imam ﷺ asking him to pray for me so that God the Sublimely Exalted might make an opening [in this knot] for me. In reply the Imam ﷺ wrote: "I write to give you glad tidings of a swift resolution to your problem. You will soon become the owner of your neighbor's house!"

My neighbor died within a month of my receipt of this reply, and thanks to the bounty of the Imam ﷺ I bought his house and made it an annex to my own.

Abū-Hamza reports: I had seen, on numerous occasions, Imam Hasan al-Askari ﷺ talking to his bondsmen, friends and companions who were of different nationalities (from Turks to Byzantines to Daylamites and Russians) in their own tongues. I was astonished and could not figure out how the Imam ﷺ had mastered so many languages while he was born and raised in Medina [where no other languages were spoken, other than Hebrew, and Arabic, of course].

[As I was thinking this] His Eminence ﷺ glanced in my direction and said, "Verily God ﷻ the Sublime and Magnificent has distinguished his *hujjat*[152] from other bondsmen of His, and has endowed him with knowledge of everything." After a pause, he addressed me again, saying, "O Abū-Hamza! The Imam is well aware of the various bounties [which God ﷻ has in store for His creatures], as well as of the events and trials and calamities which are ahead and how things relate to each other. And if this were not the case, there would be no difference between the Imam ﷺ and the people [he has been commissioned to lead]."

---

[152] *Hujjat*: see footnotes #6 and #7 for an explanation of this key word.

11. Some of the Companions of the Imam

Although the close companions of the Imam ﷺ are relatively few in number on account of the severe restrictions placed on the access to and egress from the Imam's house by the Abbāsid authorities and because of the general climate of political repression; but nevertheless, those who were able to gain access to him notwithstanding these restrictions were able to benefit greatly from his wisdom and from keeping his company.

Here we will provide a few brief biographies of these special companions of the Imam ﷺ.

Ahmad ibn Ishāq al-Ash'arī al-Qomī

Ahmad ibn Ishāq was a close companion of Imam Hasan al-Askari ﷺ who was his representative in Qom. He acted as an intermediary for the people of that town, taking their problems to the Imam ﷺ and returning with the Imam's ﷺ solutions.

This great man also lived during the imamates of Imam Jawād ﷺ and Imam Hādī ﷺ and had benefitted from the wisdom of their words and deeds, relating hadīth reports from both of these blessed Imams ﷺ.

Sa'd ibn Abdullāh states with respect to Ahmad ibn Ishāq's passing: Ahmad was stricken by a severe fever within three *parasangs*[153] of the Dhahāb (or Halwān) bridge and became severely ill, such that we had lost hope of his recovery. When we reached Halwān, we decamped in a caravanserai in order to rest. At some point Ahmad said, "Friends! Let me be alone here in this place and let all of you gather your belongings and decamp somewhere else."

After this, each of us went to a different place. It was close to daybreak when I got to thinking, and suddenly I saw Kāfūr, Imam Hasan

---

[153] *Parasang*: any of various Persian units of distance; especially an ancient unit of about four miles (six kilometers).

al-Askari's ﷺ attendant, appear and say, "I give you condolences, and may God ﷻ grant you patience and make up your hardship with a worthy reward." He then pointed and said, "The ritual washing (*ghusl*)¹⁵⁴ and enshrouding of your righteous companion has been performed, so arise and see to his burial. Verily, Ahmad was held in more esteem by my lord and master Imam Hasan al-Askari ﷺ and was dearer to him on account of his spiritual proximity to God, the Mighty and Majestic." Having delivered this oratory, Kāfūr disappeared from everyone's sight.

Abū-Hāshim Dāwūd ibn Qāsim al-Jaʿfarī

Dāwūd ibn Qāsim al-Jaʿfarī was a progeny of Jaʿfar at-Tayyār who was the chieftain of his clan. He resided in Baghdad and was held in high esteem by the Imams ﷺ and knew the Imams al-Hādī ﷺ and al-Askari ﷺ very well, a knowledge which was manifested through his exemplary behavior. During the lesser occultation,¹⁵⁵ this great man was a deputy (*nāʾib*, pl.

---

[154] *Ghusl*: a form of ritual ablution of the entire body in accordance with directions provided by the revealed law.
[155] Lesser Occultation: *ghaybat as-sughrā*, the period of about 69 years (between 260/872 and 329/939).

nawwāb)¹⁵⁶ of the Lord of the Age¹⁵⁷ (may God ﷻ hasten the advent of his noble person). He has also written some books, some of which have been referred to by the great scholars within Shī'a Islam.

Abū-Hāshim was a valiant and chivalrous defender of freedom. When the head of Yahyā ibn Omar the Zaydite was brought to Muhammad ibn Abdullāh at-Tāhir, the governor of Baghdad, some people congratulated the governor for this "victory". But Abū-Hāshim went to the governor and courageously told him: "O Emir! I have come to you to congratulate you on the killing of someone whom, had the Prophet ﷺ been alive, he would undoubtedly have been mourning the death of." The governor fell silent as he had nothing to say in response to Abū-Hāshim's words.

---

¹⁵⁶ Deputies (*nā'ib*, pl. *nawwāb*). The Imām al-Mahdī ﷺ remained in hiding during the early years of his Imāmate, during which time he communicated with his followers through a series of four deputies (*nā'ib*, pl. *nawwāb*). The period where the Imām was in communication with the community of the faithful came to be known as the Lesser Occultation (257 AH/ 869 CE) and lasted about seventy-two years, and during this time, the Shī'a maintained their contact with their Imām by way of the four Deputies. During the interim period of 69 years known as the minor occultation, the august and blessed presence of the Imām communicated with his community through a series of four successive deputies (*nāib*, plural *nawwāb*). During this time, as well as prior to it (during the time of the previous Imāms), the Imāms designated specific individuals to act on their behalf in all matters having to do with the community of their faithful followers who were in cities and towns far from Medina or other cities such as Kufa and Samara where the Imāms were domiciled.

¹⁵⁷ *Sāhib az-Zamān* or Lord of the Age ﷺ: the promised universal savior of Islam, the Imam al-Mahdi, who is the son of Imam Hasan al-Askari ﷺ and whose advent is awaited by all Muslims. (The Sunnites do not identify the Lord of the Age ﷺ as the son of Imam Hasan al-Askari ﷺ, not believing him to have been born as yet.)

Abdullāh ibn Ja'far al-Hamyarī

Abdullāh ibn Ja'far al-Hamyarī was a great Shī'a dignitary who lived in Qom and was a pious companion of Imam Hasan al-Askari ﷺ. He has left a large number of books behind, including the book *Qurb ul-Asnād* which has continually been a source of reference for Shī'a scholarship through the ages. Abdullāh ibn Ja'far went to Kufa in the decade of the 290's AH (902 – 912 CE), whereat he shared his knowledge of hadīth reports with the people of that town and educated them in this specialized field.

Abū-'Amr 'Uthmān ibn Sa'īd al-'Amri

'Uthmān ibn Sa'īd was a devotee of and the first of the four deputies[158] of the Lord of the Age (may God ﷻ hasten the advent of his noble person) during the Lesser Occultation.[159] He was an honorable and trustworthy devotee who acted as a representative of Imam Hādī ﷺ, Imam Hasan al-Askari ﷺ, and of the Imam al-Mahdī or the Lord of the Age ﷺ. He saw his training from age eleven onwards at the hands of Imam Hādī ﷺ. It is even reported that this nobleman was occasionally the beneficiary of *karāmāt*.[160] Imam Hādī ﷺ and Imam Hasan al-Askari ﷺ referred the

---

[158] During the Lesser Occultation, the Imāms designated specific individuals to act on their behalf in all matters having to do with the community of their faithful followers who were in cities and towns far from Medina or other cities such as Kufa and Samara where the Imāms were domiciled. These four deputies were:
  1. 'Uthmān b. Sa'īd al-'Amri (260/ 874 – 875)
  2. Muhammad b. 'Uthmān al-'Amri (d. 304/ 916 – 917)
  3. Al-Husayn b. Rūh an-Nawbakhtī (d. 326/ 937 – 938)
  4. Ali b. Muhammad as-Sāmarrī (d. 329/ 940 – 941)

[159] See footnotes 156, 157 & 158, above.

[160] *Karāmāt*; singular, *karāmat*: impossible wonders. God's munificence in His granting of supernatural knowledge or powers to those who have proximity to Him other than prophets and Imams ﷺ. These are so called in order to

people to 'Uthmān ibn Sa'īd for resolving their creedal and legal questions. These two Immaculate Imams 🕮 have said concerning this noble man: "Abū-Amr is our Trustee and is to be trusted. Whatever he says is [= can be taken to be equivalent to being] from us, and whatever instructions he gives to the community at large will be from us."

12. Martyrdom

Shaykh Sadūq reports Abū'l-Adyān as having related: I was at the service of Imam Hasan al-Askari 🕮 and was tasked with delivering the Imam's 🕮 letters to various towns and villages. One day, His Eminence 🕮 asked for me while he was bedridden with illness. He gave me some letters that had to do with business relating to the city of Madāin, and then told me, "O Abū'l-Adyān! You shall return from your journey back to Sāmarrā in fifteen days at which point you will hear the sound of wailing and moaning coming from my house. They will be performing the ritual washing (*ghusl*)[161] of my body and enshrouding it and preparing it for burial at that time."

I said, "O my Imam! If this event takes place, God 🕮 forbid, who will the office of the imamate belong to?"

His Eminence turned to me and said, "The person who seeks the response to my letter, he will be my successor and the Imam after me."

I repeated my question: "O my Imam! Is it possible for you to provide another indication?"

His Eminence said, "Whoever says my funeral prayers shall be my successor and the Imam after me."

I said, "O Proof of God 🕮 (*hujjatallāh*)[162]! Say something else [= something more specific]!"

---

distinguish them from miracles which, strictly speaking, belong exclusively to prophets and Imams 🕮.

[161] See footnote #155.

[162] *Hujjat*: see footnotes #6 and #7 for an explanation of this key word.

His Eminence indicated a sack and said, "Whoever says what is in the sack shall be my successor and your Imam after me."

The awe in which I held His Eminence the Imam ﷺ and my tears of remorse and sorrow [at his impending loss] prevented me from asking about the sack. I thus asked permission to leave and left town and delivered the letters to the people of Madāin. After a few days had passed from the beginning of my journey, I gathered the responses to the letters and made my way back. When I reached Sāmarrā, I witnessed what the Imam ﷺ had foretold: the sound of wailing and moaning could be heard coming from the Imam's ﷺ house. Ja'far[163] was seated at the door to the house of the Imam ﷺ and the people paid their respects and offered him their condolences for the Imam's ﷺ martyrdom. And then Ja'far and a number of the Imam's followers (*Shī'a*) began to get ready to offer the ritual prayers. Ja'far was standing in the position of the prayer leader, and as he was getting ready to pronounce the *takbīr*[164] and commence the prayer, when a beautiful small child with a russet pallor and curly hair entered into the chamber where the prayers were to be performed, pulled at Ja'far's robe and said, "It is more appropriate for me to say the prayers over my father's body than for you to do so." At that point, Ja'far stood back and the noble child said the funeral prayers for his father, and having seen to the burial of that dear Imam and of his honorable father, he pointed at me and said, "O Abū'l-Adyān! Return to me the replies of the letters that have been entrusted to you." After this, that honorable child mentioned each of the other signs one by one.

---

[163] The Imam's ﷺ brother.
[164] *Takbīr*: The chanting of the words *allāhu akbar* (God ﷻ is great or God ﷻ is greater) [than any other power]; the proclamation of the greatness and utter transcendence of God.

The Abbāsid caliphs had heard[165] that the Imams ﷺ of the community would be twelve in number, and that the last of them would rise up in insurrection after a period of occultation and uproot the apparatus of tyranny and oppression and put an end to the reign of illegitimate rule and fill the world with equity and justice. And their consciousness of this widely circulated prophecy of the Apostle of God ﷺ caused them considerable distress and anxiety. For this reason, they monitored and controlled the movements of Imam Hasan al-Askari ﷺ intensely and did everything they could to prevent the Imam ﷺ from having a son. Their efforts even went so far as imprisoning the Imam ﷺ on several occasions, and they eventually poisoned and martyred him.

The Imam's influence within the community, and the Abbāsid's concern for a Shi'ite or Ālid insurrection in particular, put fear in the heart of the Abbāsid caliph al-Mu'tamid, who was also very concerned that the Imam's ﷺ poisoning would become public knowledge and backfire.

The Abbāsid caliph used any and all means to try to keep the martyrdom of the Imam ﷺ hidden and to veil this great treachery from the public. The Sunnite scholar Ibn Sabbāq al-Mālikī relates the following from Abdullāh ibn Khāqān, one of the senior courtiers of the Abbāsid court: When Imam Hasan al-Askari ﷺ was martyred, the caliph al-Mu'tamid was in such a state of disarray that we were all shocked and none of us expected such behavior to emanate from a powerful caliph. But when His Eminence ﷺ was suffering from [the] pain [induced by the poison], al-Mu'tamid sent five elect courtiers – all of whom were court magisters (i.e. theologians cum doctors of the sacred law) – to the house of the Imam ﷺ, ordering them to remain in the Imam's ﷺ home and to report back everything that took place there. He also sent a number of nurses to see to the medical needs of the Imam ﷺ and to care for him. Additionally, the caliph instructed the Qāḍī Ibn Bakhtiār (a confidant of the caliph) to

---

[165] There are hadīth reports to this effect from the Prophet in numerous Sunnite sources and well as Shī'a ones.

round up ten more men that he trusted and to send them to the Imam's ﷺ house with the instruction to remain there day and night and to monitor the Imam's ﷺ condition. Two or three days later the caliph was informed that the Imam's condition had deteriorated substantially and that it was doubtful that he would recover. The caliph again ordered them to monitor the Imam's condition very closely, and they complied.

A few days passed in this way until the day of the Imam's ﷺ martyrdom arrived. When the news of the great Imam's martyrdom reached the people, the city of Sāmarrā erupted in commotion, with wails and cries of lament being heard in every quarter and up to the heavens. All of the shops and the great bazaar closed, and everyone attended the funeral procession, from the Banī-Hāshim, to the courtiers, to the senior officers and commanders of the armed forces, to the judges, poets, and the common folk.

The tumult in the city of Sāmarrā that day made it seem as if it was the Day of Resurrection. His Eminence's body was ritually washed (*ghusl*)[166] and enshrouded and prepared for burial, and when the Imam's corpse was ready to be buried, the caliph sent his brother Isā ibn Mutawakkil to say the funeral prayer for the Imam ﷺ in order to continue the pretense of the court's sadness at the loss of the Imam ﷺ. When they placed the bier on the ground in order to say the funeral prayer, Īsā approached the enshrouded corpse and unveiled His Eminence's ﷺ blessed face and displayed it to all present, including the Ālids, Abbāsids, the judges and scholars, saying, "This is the corpse of Abū-Muhammad al-Askari ﷺ and he has died a natural death. So and so, and so and so, who are the caliph's attendants, were witness to this fact." He then covered the corpse and ordered that it be taken to the grave and buried. After the prayers were completed as described, they took Imam Hasan al-Askari's

---

[166] *Ghusl*: a form of ritual ablution of the entire body in accordance with directions provided by revealed law.

body to a room in which his father was buried and buried him next to his father.

Given the above, the Imam's stature and the position of high esteem he enjoyed in society and among the people is quite clear; and it is equally clear, therefore, why the Abbāsids were so concerned for the stability of their order, and so concerned that their poisoning of the Imam not be exposed, and why they went to such lengths to portray his death as one brought about by natural causes.

After the martyrdom of Imam Hasan al-Askari, al- Mu'tamid put on the pretense that the Imam did not have any male issue by making a show of distributing his wealth and property between the Imam's mother and his brother Ja'far, so that the Shī'a of the Imam would lose hope of their being a twelfth Imam that succeeded the Imam al-Askari. At the same time, al- Mu'tamid assigned secret search parties to seek out and apprehend the Imam's son. Thus, a lot of pressure was brought to bear by al- Mu'tamid's agent against the family and close companions of the Imam, but they were not able to get their hands on the *Qā'im*[167] Imam (may God hasten the advent of his noble person). This is because Almighty God, the Sublimely Exalted, keeps him safe under His own protection, away from the dangers posed by the wicked.

Imam Hasan al-Askari was martyred on the eighth of Rabi' al-Awwal in the year 260 AH/ 874 CE.

13. A Sampling of the Words of the Imam

Someone saw Imam Hasan al-Askari when he was a child, while he was crying among a group of other children who were busy at play. This person thought to himself that the reason for the Imam's tears was that, unlike

---

[167] *Qā'im*: the One Who will successfully rise up [in insurrection against the tyranny and oppression of illegitimate rule for the cause of the House of the Prophet Muhammad].

the other children, he did not have any toys to play with. So he turned to the Imam ؑ and asked, "Would you like me to get you some toys?"

The Imam ؑ said, "Simpleton! We were not created for playing games."

The man asked, "Then for what purpose were we created?"

The Imam ؑ replied, "Almighty God ﷻ created us so that we might acquire knowledge and so that we would worship [Him]."

The man then asked, "For what reason and on what basis do you say this?"

The Imam ؑ said, "On the basis of the words of God ﷻ the Sublimely Exalted who has stated in the Quran: [23:115] *Did you, then, think that We created you in mere idle play, and that you would not have to return to Us [for account]?*"

- ❖ Moderation and the avoidance of extremes is enjoined on you.
- ❖ There are two characteristics in man that tower above all of his other virtues: faith in God ﷻ and helping his brothers [in faith; or his brothers in the brotherhood of man].
- ❖ Beware not to let the [surety of your receiving your] daily subsistence which is your [assured] lot [from your Lord and Sustainer] prevent you from performing your religiously mandated duties [to God].
- ❖ How unattractive is the sight of a true believer (*mu'min*) who is attracted to something which causes his ignominy and abasement.
- ❖ Do not quarrel and argue as this brings about a loss in your honor and esteem, and do not jest as this will embolden others against you.
- ❖ Anyone who attains to a familiarity with God ﷻ will become appalled at mankind.
- ❖ Verily, a measure has been fixed [as the appropriate amount to give] in charity, such that giving anything more would be profligate; and a measure has been determined for precaution, such that anything more would amount to fear; and a measure has been determined for frugality, such that anything more would amount to miserliness; and

a measure has been determined for courage, such that anything more would amount to recklessness.
- Offering your salaams[168] when greeting others and sitting at the foot of a gathering are indications of one's humbleness.
- When people's hearts are sprightly and keen, place knowledge and wisdom into them, but leave people to themselves when they are dejected.
- Showing good cheer and exuberance before one who is dejected or depressed is contrary to the norms of courteous comportment (*adab*).
- Humility is a blessing that does not foster envy.
- Being quick to laugh at anything is a sure sign of ignorance.
- Anger is a key that opens the door to every wickedness.
- He who gives moral counsel to his brother in private has adorned his character; but he who does so openly and in front of others damages his reputation.
- In order to entrain the proper mode of spiritual comportment and courtesy (*adab*) in yourself, it suffices you to refrain from doing what you would not have others do.
- The excellence of one's countenance is his or her outer beauty, but the excellence of one's mind is his or her inner beauty.
- He who is content at sitting in a gathering at a lower position than is worthy of his station will be sent blessings by God ۞ and His angels continuously up to the time that he arises from his position.
- Do not honor anyone by means of anything that is disagreeable or unpleasant to him.
- The movement and pilgrimage toward God ۞ is a journey that cannot be undertaken without spending one's nights in devotion and worship.
- Moral filth and abominations are housed in an arena the key to which is lying and deceit.

---

[168] A prayer for serenity offered in greeting.

www.ingramcontent.com/pod-product-compliance
Lightning Source LLC
Chambersburg PA
CBHW021430080526
44588CB00009B/480